NEW INTERNATIONAL
BIBLICAL COMMENTARY

Old Testament Editors,
Robert L. Hubbard Jr.
Robert K. Johnston

1 AND 2 SAMUEL

Old Testament Series

NEW INTERNATIONAL BIBLICAL COMMENTARY

1 AND 2 SAMUEL

MARY J. EVANS

Based on the New International Version

© 2000 by Hendrickson Publishers, Inc.
P. O. Box 3473
Peabody, Massachusetts 01961–3473

First published jointly, 2000, in the United States by
Hendrickson Publishers and in the United Kingdom by the
Paternoster Press, P. O. Box 300, Carlisle, Cumbria CA3 0QS.

Printed in the United States of America

First printing — May 2000

Library of Congress Cataloging-in-Publication Data

Evans, Mary J.
    1 and 2 Samuel / Mary J. Evans.
        p. cm. — (New International biblical commentary. Old
Testament series; 6)
    Includes bibliographical references and indexes.
    ISBN 1–56563–215–X (paper)
    1. Bible. O.T. Samuel—Commentaries. I. Title: First
and second Samuel. II. Title. III. Series.
    BS1325.3 E83   2000
    222′.4077—dc21   00–023014
                                               CIP

ISBN 1–56563–215–X (U.S. softcover)
ISBN 1–56563–579–5 (U.S. hardcover)

British Library Cataloguing in Publication Data
A catalogue record for this book is available
from the British Library.

ISBN 0–85364–727–5 (U.K. softcover)

For Ashley and Margaret, Joy and Robert,

representing many other fellow church members from Sale and Croxley Green who have over many years provided support, encouragement, love, and tolerance.

Table of Contents

Foreword... ix

Preface.. xi

Abbreviations xiii

Introduction 1

§1   Hannah's Child (1 Sam. 1:1–28)........................ 15
§2   Hannah's Song (1 Sam. 2:1–11) 20
§3   Eli's Successor (1 Sam. 2:12–36) 23
§4   Samuel's Calling (1 Sam. 3:1–4:1a) 28
§5   The Ark—Lost and Regained (1 Sam. 4:1b–7:1) 31
§6   Samuel's Ministry (1 Sam. 7:2–17)..................... 38
§7   The Request for a King (1 Sam. 8:1–22) 41
§8   The Anointing of Saul (1 Sam. 9:1–10:8)............... 44
§9   The Coronation and Confirmation of Saul
     (1 Sam. 10:9–11:15) 49
§10 Samuel Addresses the People (1 Sam. 12:1–25).......... 55
§11 Saul's Initial Problems (1 Sam. 13:1–22) 60
§12 Jonathan's Success (1 Sam. 13:23–14:23) 65
§13 A Foolish Curse (1 Sam. 14:24–52)..................... 69
§14 Saul Is Rejected (1 Sam. 15:1–25).................... 73
§15 Introducing David (1 Sam. 16:1–23) 78
§16 David's Growing Fame (1 Sam. 17:1–18:5)............... 83
§17 Saul's Resentful Fear of David (1 Sam. 18:6–19:24) ... 87
§18 Jonathan Is Faithful to His Covenant with David
     (1 Sam. 20:1–42)..................................... 93
§19 David's Flight—The Priests at Nob (1 Sam. 21:1–22:23) 97
§20 Saul Seeks Out David (1 Sam. 23:1–29) 102
§21 Saul's First Escape (1 Sam. 24:1–22)................. 107
§22 David and Abigail (1 Sam. 25:1–44) 112
§23 Saul's Second Escape (1 Sam. 26:1–25)................ 117
§24 The Philistine Campaign (1 Sam. 27–29) 122

§25   Victory and Defeat (1 Sam. 30:1–31:13) 130
§26   The Report of Saul's Death (2 Sam. 1:1–16). 138
§27   David's Lament (2 Sam. 1:17–27)....................... 142
§28   David's Rise to Power Begins (2 Sam. 2:1–3:5) 145
§29   The Murders of Abner and Ish-Bosheth (2 Sam. 3:6–4:12). . 150
§30   Confirmation and Consolidation (2 Sam. 5:1–25) 157
§31   The Ark Comes to Jerusalem (2 Sam. 6:1–23) 161
§32   God's Covenant with David (2 Sam. 7:1–29). 167
§33   War and Peace—Enemies and Friends (2 Sam. 8:1–9:13) ... 172
§34   The Ammonites Are Defeated (2 Sam. 10:1–19) 178
§35   David and Bathsheba (2 Sam. 11:1–12:31) 182
§36   Amnon, Tamar, and Absalom (2 Sam. 13:1–39) 192
§37   Absalom—In Geshur and Jerusalem (2 Sam. 14:1–15:9). ... 196
§38   Absalom's Rebellion Begins (2 Sam. 15:10–16:14) 202
§39   Plans for Civil War (2 Sam. 16:15–17:29) 209
§40   Absalom's Defeat (2 Sam. 18:1–19:8a).................... 214
§41   Return to Jerusalem (2 Sam. 19:8b–43)................... 219
§42   Sheba's Rebellion (2 Sam. 20:1–26) 223
Additional Information (2 Sam. 21:1–24:25) 228
§43   The Famine, Its Cause, and Its Remedy (2 Sam. 21:1–14)... 229
§44   War Stories (2 Sam. 21:15–22).......................... 232
§45   A Psalm of Thanksgiving (2 Sam. 22:1–51) 234
§46   A Final Statement (2 Sam. 23:1–7) 238
§47   The Honors List (2 Sam. 23:8–39) 241
§48   The Census and Its Aftermath (2 Sam. 24:1–25).......... 245

For Further Reading 251

Subject Index 257

Scripture Index... 263

Foreword
New International Biblical Commentary

As an ancient document, the Old Testament often seems
something quite foreign to modern men and women. Opening
its pages may feel, to the modern reader, like traversing a kind of
literary time warp into a whole other world. In that world sisters
and brothers marry, long hair mysteriously makes men super-
human, and temple altars daily smell of savory burning flesh
and sweet incense. There, desert bushes burn but leave no ashes,
water gushes from rocks, and cities fall because people march
around them. A different world, indeed!

Even God, the Old Testament's main character, seems a
stranger compared to his more familiar New Testament counter-
part. Sometimes the divine is portrayed as a loving father and
faithful friend, someone who rescues people from their greatest
dangers or generously rewards them for heroic deeds. At other
times, however, God resembles more a cruel despot, one furious
at human failures, raving against enemies, and bloodthirsty for
revenge. Thus, skittish about the Old Testament's diverse portrayal of God, some readers carefully select which portions of the
text to study, or they avoid the Old Testament altogether.

The purpose of this commentary series is to help readers
navigate this strange and sometimes forbidding literary and
spiritual terrain. Its goal is to break down the barriers between
the ancient and modern worlds so that the power and meaning
of these biblical texts become transparent to contemporary readers. How is this to be done? And what sets this series apart from
others currently on the market?

This commentary series will bypass several popular approaches to biblical interpretation. It will not follow a *precritical*
approach that interprets the text without reference to recent
scholarly conversations. Such a commentary contents itself with
offering little more than a paraphrase of the text with occasional
supplements from archaeology, word studies, and classical theology. It mistakenly believes that there have been few insights

into the Bible since Calvin or Luther. Nor will this series pursue an *anticritical* approach whose preoccupation is to defend the Bible against its detractors, especially scholarly ones. Such a commentary has little space left to move beyond showing why the Bible's critics are wrong to explaining what the biblical text means. The result is a paucity of vibrant biblical theology. Again, this series finds inadequate a *critical* approach that seeks to understand the text apart from belief in the meaning it conveys. Though modern readers have been taught to be discerning, they do not want to live in the "desert of criticism" either.

Instead, as its editors, we have sought to align this series with what has been labeled *believing criticism*. This approach marries probing, reflective interpretation of the text to loyal biblical devotion and warm Christian affection. Our contributors tackle the task of interpretation using the full range of critical methodologies and practices. Yet they do so as people of faith who hold the text in the highest regard. The commentators in this series use criticism to bring the message of the biblical texts vividly to life so the minds of modern readers may be illumined and their faith deepened.

The authors in this series combine a firm commitment to modern scholarship with a similar commitment to the Bible's full authority for Christians. They bring to the task the highest technical skills, warm theological commitment, and rich insight from their various communities. In so doing, they hope to enrich the life of the academy as well as the life of the church.

Part of the richness of this commentary series derives from its authors' breadth of experience and ecclesial background. As editors, we have consciously brought together a diverse group of scholars in terms of age, gender, denominational affiliation, and race. We make no claim that they represent the full expression of the people of God, but they do bring fresh, broad perspectives to the interpretive task. But though this series has sought out diversity among its contributors, they also reflect a commitment to a common center. These commentators write as "believing critics"—scholars who desire to speak for church and academy, for academy and church. As editors, we offer this series in devotion to God and for the enrichment of God's people.

ROBERT L. HUBBARD JR.
ROBERT K. JOHNSTON
Editors

Preface

The opportunity to share in a commentary series that takes seriously both the complexities of the text and the interests of the reader is a rare privilege and one that I have greatly appreciated. Immersing oneself in the books of Samuel inevitably means facing the challenge to one's own life and faith that arises from the incisive and uncompromising observations of people and events with which the books confront us. That challenge is not always an easy one to face. The sharp light that illuminates the struggles, failures, and personality defects of the characters as well as their strengths and achievements shines also onto our own faces. Reading Samuel (and writing about it) brings fascination and frustration, fear, anger, and despair, joy, laughter, and determination as different elements come into focus within the stories the text presents. My hope is that this commentary will help readers appreciate and respond to the dynamism and the challenge of these texts. The focus is usually on the characters, but the backdrop is the involvement of God in his world and with his people. God's activity is not always immediately perceived, understood, or appreciated by the characters described, but the writers convey a conviction that it is there. The fact of God's involvement brings hope both to these characters and to readers of the text.

The additional notes and the further reading lists only partially indicate the great debt I owe to many, many scholars. In general, only those who have been specifically referred to or cited are listed, but I am grateful to all those whose work I have read, appreciated, and benefited from even when their names do not appear within this work.

I would also like to take this opportunity to express my debt and my gratitude to my students, who over many years have provided stimulation and often brought or provoked new insights; to London Bible College, for the provision of the sabbatical leave within which the bulk of this commentary was written and for the ongoing support and stimulation provided by my colleagues; to Sylvia, Gavin, and Kitty Collinson, for providing a congenial place to write; to Doug Flint, Edna Sansom, and Richard Judd for their help in preparing the manuscript; and finally to my friends, my family, and my church family, to some of whom this book is dedicated, because they are part of the backdrop of God's involvement in my own life.

Abbreviations

AB	Anchor Bible
Bib	*Biblica*
BAR	*Biblical Archaeology Review*
CBQ	*Catholic Biblical Quarterly*
ch(s).	chapter(s)
ExpTim	*Expository Times*
GNB	Good News Bible
Gk.	Greek
Hb.	Hebrew
Int	*Interpretation*
IB	*The Interpreter's Bible*
JB	Jerusalem Bible
JBL	*Journal of Biblical Literature*
JETS	*Journal of the Evangelical Theological Society*
JSOT	*Journal for the Study of the Old Testament*
JSOTSup	Journal for the Study of the Old Testament: Supplement Series
LXX	Septuagint
MT	Masoretic Text
NCB	New Century Bible
NIV	New International Version
NT	New Testament
NIBCOT	New International Biblical Commentary on the Old Testament
OT	Old Testament
OTL	Old Testament Library
RSV	Revised Standard Version
SJT	*Scottish Journal of Theology*
SBLDS	Society for Biblical Literature Dissertation Series
TynBul	*Tyndale Bulletin*
TOTC	Tyndale Old Testament Commentaries

VT	*Vetus Testamentum*
VE	*Vox Evangelica*
WBC	Word Biblical Commentary
ZAW	*Zeitschrift für die alttestamentliche Wissenschaft*

Introduction

Biblical commentaries by their nature tend to concentrate on the meaning and significance of individual sections. However, it is important that we also see what are essentially close-up or limited-range pictures in their wider context. In order to understand and appreciate the details of the individual stories we need to know something of the nature and structure of the book as a whole as well as its place in the canon of Scripture.

There is no doubt that 1 and 2 Samuel should be seen as one book. Although the old Greek translation of the Hebrew text (the Septuagint, usually abbreviated LXX) is in two parts, the division seems arbitrary, and the split did not occur in the Hebrew text until the advent of the printing press in the fifteenth century. This original unity makes sense of the tradition of using Samuel's name to describe the whole book even though Samuel makes no appearance in 2 Samuel. But the two books of Samuel are also closely linked with other material. The break at the end of 2 Samuel 24 is ancient, but it does not mask the close connections with the books of Kings. The material in 1 Kings 1–2 follows directly from the account in 2 Samuel 20. Moreover, the LXX links Samuel and Kings and describes them as the four books of Reigns or Kingdoms.

Pulling back even further we see connections with Joshua and Judges. All these historical books are known in Hebrew tradition as the Former Prophets. This title indicates some kind of unity and makes the point that all these books, including 1 and 2 Samuel, are more than mere records of events. They contain teaching that could be described as prophetic. In recent years the close relationship between the historical books and the book of Deuteronomy has come into focus; connections identified include common concerns for the development of the community, a common understanding of required ritual, and sometimes common phraseology (cf. 1 Sam. 1:3–4 // Deut. 12:5–7, 17–18; 1 Sam. 8:1, 5, 11 // Deut. 16:18–19; 17:14–20; 1 Sam. 17:32 // Deut. 20:1–4; 2 Sam. 14:11, 16 // Deut. 19:4–10; 32:9). Although these links with Deuteronomy are stronger in 1 and 2 Kings than they are in 1 and 2 Samuel, it is now very widely accepted that those who were responsible for the final compilation of Samuel and Kings had a close awareness of the content and purposes of Deuteronomy. Hence the common description of these historical books as the Deuteronomic History.[1] We must also note links with Chronicles, which covers much of the same ground. Finally, the widest focus takes in the prophetic books, the later history of David's kingdom, and the accounts in the New Testament arising from the coming of another of David's descendants, Jesus Christ.

Authorship

Any investigation of the authorship of the books of Samuel is fraught with difficulty. Samuel, whose death is recorded before the end of 1 Samuel, cannot be the author of the complete book of 1 and 2 Samuel. However, it is possible that he left some records[2] that later writers or editors used in compiling 1 Samuel. The main difficulty is in deciding what in this instance we mean by "author."

The books of Samuel cover events taking place over two full lifetimes. On a number of occasions throughout the books, there is so much incidental detail that it is hard to avoid the conclusion that participants or eyewitnesses have played a major part in formulating the account. However, a strong sense of common purpose also underlies the whole. How is it possible to take seriously both the vivid contemporary nature of the accounts and the clear underlying unity? The same witnesses cannot be involved in the different time periods. If we take Samuel and Kings together, then there is about five hundred years between the birth of Samuel and the exile of Jehoiachin (1 Sam. 1 and 2 Kgs. 25). The answer to this question must lie in editorial hands guiding the whole but making comprehensive use of earlier source material that would have been written or strongly influenced by different eyewitnesses. This basic understanding is virtually unquestioned, even though there is extensive disagreement among scholars as to the number and extent of the underlying sources and the way in which the editing has taken place.[3] If this view is correct, then more than one person has been involved with each section of the text as we have it, and it is impossible to be clear where the input of one ends and another begins. Thus, in the light of this and in an attempt to indicate both the unity and the diversity within the books, I have followed the convention suggested by Iain Provan[4] and used the plural forms "authors" and "writers" rather than the singular when referring to "the human forces responsible for the book's creation."[5]

Together these writers have produced a work of significant literary and theological merit. The product of their work brings together an in-depth awareness of the complexities of human character and relationship, a remarkable political insight, and an enviable facility in handling literary devices and techniques. All this combines to convey a message from and about God. Stories of the complications, hurts, and joys of human life are told with wit, acumen, and deep perception to encourage the reader to think about what it means to live as God's people in the light of the covenant that is set out in Deuteronomy. Baldwin helpfully describes Samuel as "the product of highly developed literary art, purposively selective, often restrained, sometimes repetitive, sometimes silent, but by whatever means intending to engage the reader in an active relationship with the text."[6]

The Text

Although these should not be overstated, there are a number of problems with the Hebrew text of Samuel.[7] The Masoretic Text[8] (MT) seems to have suffered from transmission problems in a number of instances. In a few places this means that the Hebrew is unintelligible. Because of this, many scholars have preferred the reading from the LXX where these problems are not found. Although there are some variations, the Hebrew fragments from the books of Samuel that have been found within the Qumran scrolls reflect the text of the LXX rather than the MT. It is also true that the text of parallel passages in Chronicles is, in general, in agreement with the LXX rather than with the MT.

Sources

We have already noted the difficulty in ascertaining the precise limits of the different documents that were used in formulating the final text of Samuel. No evidence external to the text proves that any of these suggested documents ever existed independently, although in some instances the internal textual evidence is strong. The main outline is clear, however, and is defined by the historical events described within the book and by the key characters. The first section (1 Sam. 1–15) focuses first on Samuel (chs. 1–7) and then on Saul (chs. 8–15). It may be that official accounts from Shiloh, or even Samuel's own records, were used here. From this point on the central character is David (although the focus occasionally settles on others, such as Joab and Absalom for short periods of time). It is suggested that within this general focus on the life of David there are two main source documents. One, sometimes known as the History of David's Rise,[9] covers 1 Samuel 16 to 2 Samuel 5, and the other, often referred to as the Succession Narrative or more recently as The Court History of David,[10] includes 2 Samuel 9–20 and 1 Kings 1–2.[11] An Ark Narrative has been identified that has been made use of in 1 Samuel 4–6 and 2 Samuel 6.[12] It is also possible that the poetic elements of the text, as in the songs attributed to Hannah and David, came from a separate source and were added at a later stage. However, the evidence for this is less clear, and all the poetic elements within the text sit comfortably within their own contexts.

Within 1 and 2 Samuel as a whole, and within its individual sections, we can identify three major areas of interest and concern. W. Brueggemann[13] identifies these as "socio-historical, personal and theological," but this can be more simply expressed as politics, people, and preaching. These three streams come together into the unity of the books of Samuel that can be described as art, as history, as propaganda, or even as theology. Which of these descriptions would best describe 1 and 2 Samuel is a question that would probably not have concerned the original writers at any of the stages of the book's formation. Within the limits allowed by the restraints of a brief introduction I wish to examine some of the aspects of these three streams and to introduce the possibility that there is a theme that unites them.

Politics

The books of Samuel cover a time of significant political change. Before the arrival of the prophet Samuel, Israel consisted of a group of related tribes bound together by ethnic origin and religious beliefs but with no recognized centralized structure. Leadership was intermittent, often local, and dependent on the character and gifting of those called by God to lead his people. Religious observance was also intermittent. There were recognized shrines; some, like Shiloh, had significance beyond one tribe, but there was no political or religious center acknowledged by all. By the time Solomon took the throne at the beginning of the books of Kings, Israel was a full-scale monarchy with an integrated national government and a widely recognized capital city. Not long after that, religious worship was centralized in the new temple. Leadership, although still acknowledged as being appointed according to God's choice, had become more institutional than charismatic, with the leader's authority stemming as much from the office he held as from his own character and gifting. The explanation for, and perhaps defense of, these dramatic changes is found within the books of Samuel.

One of the reasons for the unification of the tribes under a single monarch was the need to provide an effective, unified defense against encroachment by other tribal groups, notably the Philistines. At this time there was no major world power, just a number of diverse groups. Some, like the Philistines (from Crete) and the Israelites, traced their origins from outside the area in which they now lived. There was little stability and constant vying for territory. Sociological pressures like the growing tendency toward urbanization, moves away from subsistence farming, and the increase in trade groupings also played a part in the changing patterns of government. In Samuel we have the record of events presented with a clear awareness that attitudes toward these changes varied. For example, there were those who strongly supported the idea of a monarchy and those who did not.

There is also an awareness that some of the changes, for example the change from tribal diversity to national unity, may not have been as well-founded as might at first be assumed. The accounts constantly evidence intertribal rivalries that quickly led to the division of the young monarchy into two kingdoms. As J. W. Flanagan puts it, "The history of David's court was a history of strife and struggle. The underlying tensions that would eventually separate the kingdoms of Judah and Israel after Solomon's reign posed a threat to the dual monarchy even in the time of David. The king sought security in acts of benevolence toward the houses of Saul and Nahash but he could not prevent hostilities from arising."[14]

The way in which the writers make it clear that political factions existed within Israel and the sympathetic consideration that is given to different positions could be seen as indicating an objective perspective. However, it could also be argued that Samuel was written with specific political ends in mind. Leonhard Rost's view that at least the latter part of Samuel was primarily intended to show that Solomon was a legitimate and in fact the most appropriate heir to David (cf. n. 9) may not be too easy to substantiate. However, the writers do seem to stress elements that indicate the legitimacy of the line of David, and it is likely that this stress was deliberate. The history shows that David has good title to the throne in both the north and the south and conveys an underlying sense that God is with David and his house and has ceased to be with Saul and his house. Alongside this, the text emphasizes David's innocence of charges that, although they have not actually been brought against him, are likely to have been to the forefront of the minds of his opponents. The writers have no qualms about speaking of David's guilt in some areas, but they want to show that he is not guilty of treason. He is defended against implied charges of usurping Saul's position and of being involved in the killing of Saul, of Ish-Bosheth, and of Abner.[15] Political concerns are not the only interests of the writers of Samuel, but they do form part of those interests.

People

The second major interest of the writers of Samuel is in the personalities, attitudes, and behavior of the characters described. This interest goes far beyond what would have been needed to make political points. Minor incidents with no obvious political or national significance are recorded in detail. Word portraits of a whole range of people enable the reader to know and understand the individuals, their motivations, and their personality traits. With the possible exception of Nabal, the anti-hero, characters are not portrayed in monochrome colors. These are real people with faults and failings as well as gifts and virtues. The sympathy of the reader is moved from one character to another and back again. The traitorous Ahithophel (2 Sam. 16) emerges as a tragic character rather than an evil one. Joab's fierce loyalty and great diplomatic and military skills are portrayed alongside his relentless ambition and pitiless determination. Eli's blundering is pictured alongside his careful mentoring of the young Samuel. The depiction of Saul's gradually increasing paranoia does not blot out the brave, shy warrior he had once been.

The most effective character portrayals are perhaps to be found in the latter half of 2 Samuel within what is called the Succession Narrative. However, the same interest in psychology and emotional reactions can be seen throughout the books. The inner character of the individuals is recorded with the same brilliance as are their political and military actions. In the snapshots of the minor characters like Jonathan and Michal, the focus remains remarkably sharp. In the more extensive video portrayals of Samuel, Saul, and David, the detail and acumen are striking.

As Brueggemann points out,[16] no exploration into Samuel would be complete if it did not recognize the prominent emphasis on the extraordinary character of David. Perhaps K. R. R. Gros Louis is right in seeing a deliberate contrast in the consideration of national leaders between the public and the private areas of life.[17] The private Saul sees the private David as a son. The public Saul cannot cope with the threat to his power, or more particularly to his dynasty. In clear public roles, with Samuel or Nabal, Achish or Abner, Nathan or Shimei, David is seen as making good decisions. Where his private emotions come in, with Bathsheba, Amnon, or Absalom, it is a different story. Perhaps David never fully realized the extent to which public responsibilities inevitably set limits on private life. Another way of looking at this material would be to suggest that whereas Saul and David were both potentially great leaders, neither was able to cope with power; they are most praised for their characters and behavior *before* they were recognized national leaders.

Other motifs that help to bring out the personalities of characters in general, and of David in particular, are those of deception,[18] of giving, and of grasping.[19] David is constantly both deceiving (for example, Uriah) and being deceived (as by Nathan, or Joab, or the woman of Tekoa). David refuses to seize the throne, but he has no qualms about seizing another man's wife. The remarkable fact about David's characterization is that he emerges as a likeable, even engaging, character. In spite of his major faults, which appear at times to be just as bad if not worse than those of Saul, one is not surprised that David continued to be known as a "man after [God's] own heart."[20] The writers' conclusion seems to be that David's willingness to recognize and accept his own failings and David's ongoing trust in God outweighed his deficiencies. When presented with the evidence, the reader, including Luke (Acts 13:22), is inclined to agree.

Preaching

The third underlying interest in the books of Samuel, alongside a concern for social and political structures and a fascination with human character and behavior, is the need to present an adequate theology. There is only a small amount of explicit theological analysis, although what there is has been seen as significant. However, God's involvement with his people and the importance of their reactions to him, his word, and his will, lie behind all of the accounts. The writers apparently wanted to explore what it meant for Israel to live, or to fail to live, in the light of the covenant principles that are set out within the book of Deuteronomy. Questions as to whether the covenant could be broken and whether once it was broken it was possible to be restored were significant at a number of stages in Israel's history. This is particularly true during the time of exile, which was probably when the books of Samuel and Kings came together in their finalized form. First and 2 Samuel, as much as Kings, deal with the relationship between God's sovereign purposes for Israel and the failure of the people to live in obedience to God's will.[21] The monarchy was not, at least from this Deuteronomistic perspective, a replacement for the theocracy of the judges; rather, it was an alternative, and potentially more effective, way in which that theocracy could be worked out. The sadness conveyed throughout most of Samuel and Kings was that the potential dangers of the monarchy, recognized from the start by Samuel in 1 Samuel 8, proved stronger than the potential benefits. But the overall perspective sees God as being at work in spite of all the human failures.

The five most explicitly theological passages are 1 Samuel 2, where Hannah's song sets out the doctrine of God's sovereignty; 1 Samuel 7, where Samuel speaks of the victory that God would bring in response to Israel's repentance and ongoing commitment; 1 Samuel 12, where in his farewell speech Samuel again speaks of God's ongoing commitment to a faithful people; 2 Samuel 7, which details the covenant that God was initiating with David and his descendants; and 2 Samuel 22, which records David's hymn of praise.[22]

Power: An Integrating Perspective

We cannot view the political, personal, and theological or apologetic interests of Samuel in isolation from each other. They interact and influence one another at the deepest level. Brueg-gemann points out that both overspiritualization and overratio-nalization will lead to an inadequate understanding of the book as a whole.[23] To interpret the material in an entirely religious or overly pious way is to ignore the down-to-earth presentation of everyday affairs. To interpret the accounts without taking seri-ously the religious and theological considerations of the writers is to change Israel's view of itself and its development. Neither option is satisfactory.

The question remains as to whether there is a way of tak-ing seriously both the realism and the spirituality and also bring-ing together the three streams of concern detailed above. I would suggest that there is, and that the solution is to be found in the concept of power. The book of Samuel examines and reflects on the nature, accession, use, and abuse of *power*. The book begins with a powerless woman, who, because of her childlessness, lacks hope. The narrative breaks off before the death of David so that 1 Kings also begins with weakness. It takes up the story at the point where the formerly powerful David has become inef-fective, incompetent, and possibly incontinent, unable even to keep himself warm (1 Kgs. 1). And yet there is a sense of God em-powering Hannah and empowering David even at the point of weakness. These bookends of weakness set the rest into context: the search for adequate leadership; the question of the rightness or wrongness of the monarchy; the issue of the succession; the descriptions of the way in which individuals cope with or re-spond to power; the relationship between God's sovereignty and human power.

An underlying questioning is of the obsession with author-ity that has plagued human beings throughout their history. Even though on the surface the narrative seems to be interested in those who are powerful, I would suggest that the writers im-ply that true power, which belongs only to God, lies outside of that human obsession. Human power is presented, in general, as a corrupting influence. We see this with Saul, with Joab, and even with David, all of whom are presented as men of great po-tential who are entrusted with great responsibilities but who, in different ways, are unable to cope with the trust laid upon them. It seems inconceivable that the writers were not aware of this emphasis in the material that they were producing. There is here a foretaste of the New Testament teaching that God's power is made perfect in weakness (2 Cor. 12:9). One of the characters

who comes across most positively within the book of Samuel is
Jonathan, who did not consider the power of his father something to be grasped (cf. Phil. 2:6) but instead willingly supported
David. It seems that, like David, Jonathan can in some senses be
pictured as a forerunner of Christ.

Thus, within the text there is both a description of the
power struggles within Israel and a critique of the attitudes that
view power as so important. Samuel provides a reflection on the
nature of power, both human and divine. The writers introduce
serious questions about the validity of the view of power in Israel
at the time. The narratives indicate God's desire to lead the
people on to a greater understanding of God's purposes and values, which are different from theirs. However, the narratives also
recognize that human obsession is always within human power
and that God deals with his people where they are. Thus the
story and the reflection on the story are both important. There is
value in the ongoing process of history as well as in the underlying critique of that history, and the book of Samuel provides
both.

Notes

1. M. Noth (*The Deuteronomistic History* [JSOTSup 15; Sheffield:
University of Sheffield Press, 1981]) sets out the arguments for this theory in detail. He concludes that all the books from Deut. through 2 Kgs.
have a single editor. This explains any underlying unity that is found in
all the diverse material compiled from a range of different sources. More
recent approaches are discussed by D. A. Knight, "Deuteronomy and
the Deuteronomists," in *Old Testament Interpretation: Past, Present and Future* (ed. J. L. Mays, D. L. Petersen, and K. H. Richards; Edinburgh: T&T
Clark, 1995); cf. B. Peckham, *History and Prophecy: The Development of
Late Judean Literary Traditions* (Garden City, N.Y.: Doubleday, 1993), pp.
518–655.

2. 1 Chron. 29:29 speaks of "records left by Samuel the seer, . . . Nathan the prophet and . . . Gad the seer." The writers of different sections
within Samuel or any overall editors may have made use of such records.

3. B. Peckham, for example ("The Deuteronomistic History of
Saul and David," *ZAW* 97 [1985], pp. 190–209), argues for two Deuteronomic editions, DTR1 and DTR2. The first brings together the basic
narrative, and the second, which is much more interested in theological

arguments and the meaning of events, relates to the first as a commentary relates to a text. In Peckham's view, the second edition depends on the first, corrects it, and incorporates it into a different system of interpretation. P. K. McCarter (*I Samuel* [AB 8; Garden City, N.Y.: Doubleday, 1980], p. 18) asserts that the prophetic influence has been underestimated and that Deuteronomistic editing only overlies an existing prophetic history. I. W. Provan (*Hezekiah and the Book of Kings* [Berlin/New York: de Gruyter, 1988]) provides detailed arguments for his thesis that a well-developed edition of the Deuteronomic History covering the material up to Hezekiah was available long before the exile.

   4. I. W. Provan, *1 and 2 Kings* (NIBCOT; Peabody: Hendrickson, 1995), pp. 2–5. To accept the existence of several participants in the production of the text that we possess does not mean that either the text or the events it describes should thus be seen as incoherent, unreliable, or contradictory. In relation to Kings, Provan argues cogently and persuasively that "the book of Kings can indeed be seen as a carefully crafted and coherent entity" (p. 5). In past years it was common for literary-critical scholars to view the text of Scripture as merely the end product of the sources that underlay it and to view only these often hypothetical sources as worthy of serious study. It can only be a matter for rejoicing that the inadequacies of this tendency have now been so widely recognized. Editorial hands may have added or brought out specific perspectives, but we cannot assume that they have done so in a way that treats their original material with contempt. Rather, they have done an efficient and effective job so that the insights of the original sources are not lost and the text as we have it reads smoothly. It makes sense.

   5. Ibid., p. 4.

   6. J. Baldwin, *1 and 2 Samuel: An Introduction and Commentary* (TOTC; Downers Grove: InterVarsity, 1988), p. 16.

   7. A more detailed study of the textual difficulties within the books of Samuel may be found in R. W. Klein's commentary (*1 Samuel* [WBC; Waco: Word, 1983], pp.xxvi–xxviii), or in J. Mauchline's commentary (*1 and 2 Samuel* [NCB; London: Oliphants, 1971], pp. 33–34). Comments on specific problems will be found within the additional notes (e.g., at 2 Sam. 1:17–27; 4:6–7).

   8. The Masoretic Text (MT) is the standardized Hb. text that was produced in the early years of the Christian era. At this point, to avoid confusion, all other known Hb. versions were destroyed. Many copies were made of this standardized text, but most of these that are extant date from several centuries after the original production. Thus the opportunities for errors in transmission were many. The Septuagint (LXX) was a translation from the Hb. into Gk. produced in the early second century B.C. and became widely used. The Dead Sea Scrolls discovered at Qumran include three portions of Samuel that date from the first to the third centuries B.C. and are much older than any known

Hb. manuscript. They are therefore invaluable in resolving textual difficulties.

9. The document that looks at the history of David's rise is perhaps less cohesive than the later Succession Narrative, but P. K. McCarter nevertheless views it as having an identifiable purpose and point of view ("The Apology of David," *JBL* 99 [1980], pp. 489–504).

10. There is wide acceptance of a single, highly gifted author for the material known, since Leonhard Rost's book (*The Succession to the Throne of David* [trans. M. Rutter and D. Gunn; Sheffield: Almond Press, 1982]), as the Succession Narrative or the Succession Document. Some scholars, such as R. C. Bailey (*David in Love and War: The Pursuit of Power in 2 Samuel 10–12* [JSOTSup 75; Sheffield: JSOT Press, 1990]), query the unity of the document, but their perspective has not been generally taken up. In recent years there has been less agreement about the narrative's theme. Although the question of succession is present, it is not obvious that it should be seen as the main focus of the authors. Solomon does not appear until the end, and the interest in the Absalom narratives is more on how David will deal with this threat to his own survival than on whether or not Absalom will be the one to succeed him.

11. The History of David's Rise could begin at 1 Sam. 15:1; 16:1; or 16:14 and could end at 2 Sam. 5:10; 5:25, or even include parts of chs. 6 and 7. However, D. Gunn (*The Story of King David: Genre and Interpretation* [JSOTSup 6; Sheffield: University of Sheffield, 1978]) argues that 2 Sam. 2–4 should be included within the Succession Document. R. P. Gordon (*1 and 2 Samuel: A Commentary* [Exeter: Paternoster, 1986], pp. 22–45) provides more detailed information about the various source theories.

12. Cf. A. F. Campbell, *The Ark Narrative, 1 Sam 4–6, 2 Sam 6: A Form-Critical and Traditio-Historical Study* (SBLDS 16; Missoula, Mont.: Society of Biblical Literature, 1975); P. D. Miller and J. J. M. Roberts, *The Hand of the Lord: A Reassessment of the "Ark Narrative" of 1 Samuel* (Baltimore: Johns Hopkins University Press, 1977).

13. W. Brueggemann, *First and Second Samuel* (Interpretation; Louisville, Ky.: John Knox, 1990), p. 2.

14. J. W. Flanagan, "Court History or Succession Document: A Study of 2 Samuel 9–20, 1 Kings 1–2," *JBL* 91 (1972), p. 181. See also F. H. Polak, "David's Kingship—A Precarious Equilibrium," in *Politics and Theopolitics in the Bible and Postbiblical Literature* (ed. H. Graf Reventlow, et al.; [JSOTSup 171; Sheffield: JSOT Press, 1994]), pp. 119–47.

15. Further discussion of these issues can be found in McCarter, "The Apology of David," pp. 489–504, and in D. F. Payne, "Apologetic Motifs in the Books of Samuel," *VE* 23 (1993), pp. 57–66. Payne argues that apologetic concerns in Samuel go beyond a defense of David. It could also be argued that the text is concerned to show that neither Samuel, Saul, David, nor Solomon came to power in a way that might be

seen as illegitimate or usurping. "The purposes of the individual sources may have varied considerably, but the compiler has selected materials time and time again which have the effect of protecting the reputations of all his chief characters" (pp. 63–64).

16. Brueggemann, *First and Second Samuel*, pp. 2–5.

17. K. R. R. Gros Louis, "The Difficulty of Ruling Well: King David of Israel," *Semeia* 8 (1977), pp. 15–33. In this article, Gros Louis helpfully compares David with Shakespeare's young Prince Hal. As Hal could learn from his father's guilt and paranoia, so David could learn from Saul. But Hal, when he became king, recognized that change necessarily accompanied his new responsibilities and therefore banished his former life, in the person of Falstaff. David was not able to set aside his private desires in quite the same way.

18. Cf. H. Hagan, "Deception as Motif and Theme in 2 Samuel 9–20, 1 Kings 1–2" *Bib* 60 (1979), pp. 301–26. Hagan identifies eighteen instances of deception within these narratives. He concludes (p. 324) that "in every case, deception is the decisive weapon of the weak against the equally deceitful enemy."

19. D. Gunn, "David and the Gift of the Kingdom (2 Sam 2–4, 9–20, 1 Kgs 1–2)," *Semeia* 3 (1975), pp. 14–45. The portrayal of David's sons indicates that they inherited the grasping side of his nature but not the giving, his compulsion to possess but not his ability to wait for what is desired.

20. 1 Sam. 13:14; Acts 13:22. The original reference was in a speech to Saul stating that he would be replaced by a "man after God's own heart." It could be inferred that this description also applied to Saul before his enthronement and does not necessarily indicate a permanent application to David that would survive all future faults and failings. However, Luke, presumably reflecting popular tradition and belief, seems to have understood it in that way.

21. W. J. Dumbrell, "The Content and Significance of the Books of Samuel: Their Place and Purpose Within the Former Prophets," *JETS* 33 (1990), pp. 49–62, sees 1 and 2 Sam. as providing "a theological endorsement of the kingship of Yahweh." He argues that these books "thus concern the clear conduct by Yahweh of Israel's affairs and inform us of how difficult and indeed impossible it proved for Israel to understand this" (p. 50). Cf. J. S. Ackerman, "Knowing Good and Evil: A Literary Analysis of the Court History in 2 Samuel 9–20 and 1 Kings 1–2," *JBL* 109 (1990), pp. 41–60.

22. J. Baldwin (*1 and 2 Samuel*, pp. 32–37) sees 1 Sam. 7 and 12 and 2 Sam. 7 as theological markers that focus the change in leadership from Samuel to Saul to David. However, the two poems, which come at the beginning and end of Samuel, set the rest within a context of the sovereignty of God, his care for the people, and the demands that he would make of them. B. S. Childs (*Introduction to the Old Testament as Scripture*

[Philadelphia: Fortress, 1979], pp. 272–75) notes the way that 1 Sam. 2 and 2 Sam. 22 form an *inclusio* of theological reflection indicating the theocentric emphasis of the writers, although Childs does not perhaps go far enough in bringing out the specific concentration on the powerlessness of humans as well as on the power and empowering of God.

23. Brueggemann, *First and Second Samuel*, pp. 2–3.

§1 Hannah's Child (1 Sam. 1:1–28)

1:1–2 / That the writers of the books of Samuel are interested in people is apparent from the beginning. The reader is plunged, without introductory analysis of the purpose of writing or preliminary theologizing, into an encounter with real people who are in a real situation, involved in real relationships, and encountering real problems. These first two verses present us with three characters. **Elkanah,** the husband of **Hannah** and **Peninnah,** is introduced in detail, which usually indicates significance. We learn of his place of birth, **Ramathaim** Zuphim, his tribe, **Ephraim,** and his ancestry. Elkanah was likely a notable citizen from his area. Although polygamy was probably not widespread among ordinary people, it is not surprising that such a citizen would have two wives. As elsewhere in Samuel and Kings, there is no criticism or comment on this fact. It may be that here, as on other occasions when polygamous marriages are mentioned, the tension described between wives or children is intended to lead readers to reach conclusions about the consequences of polygamy. However, the text does not explicitly draw those conclusions. The only indication that the writers' real interest here is in Hannah is the inclusion of her name both first and last in verse 2: Hannah, Peninnah, Peninnah, Hannah.

Since Peninnah had many children, including several sons, Hannah's childlessness was to Elkanah little more than a minor inconvenience, one easily overcome by their mutual affection (v. 8). But to Hannah it was a personal tragedy. The reader's mind is inevitably drawn to the situation of Sarah or Rachel, and the question is implicitly raised as to whether in this case, too, the agony of barrenness will eventually be taken away. It is striking that the authors choose to begin this narrative—which deals so often with power struggles between the leading men of the country—with a powerless, barren woman.

1:3–8 / Having introduced the characters, the writers skillfully draw a picture of their lives together. This is a family concerned to follow the ways of the Lord; they go year after year to offer sacrifices at **Shiloh,** his wives and children fully involved by Elkanah in the procedure. But it is not a happy family. The rivalry seen between Sarah and Hagar (Gen. 16) and particularly between Rachel and Leah (Gen. 29–30) is again brought to mind. There is an implication that Elkanah **loved** Hannah in a special way and that Peninnah's reaction was to taunt Hannah about her childlessness. At least in that area Peninnah's supremacy could not be questioned. It is not surprising that the taunting should be particularly pronounced at the annual trip to Shiloh. The **portions of the meat** given to the different family members may have been for each one to offer but are more likely to have been the part of the fellowship offering (Lev. 7:11–18) that was assigned to them to eat. It is all the more poignant that Hannah's sorrow prevented her from eating any of her special portion. At the place where everyone's thoughts were on the blessing of the Lord, both Hannah's negative status as the one whom the Lord had chosen not to bless with children and her positive position as the loved wife were emphasized. Elkanah's love for Hannah is undoubted; his understanding of her position is not. Her childlessness did not matter to him because he had other children, so he could not comprehend why it should matter to her. But the text, describing Hannah as weeping and unable to eat, shows the extent to which it did matter. Elkanah's love for her is undoubted, but particularly in this polygamous situation, it was not enough to replace one child, let alone the ten he suggests it might.

1:9–16 / The writers clearly and sensitively portray the deep distress of Hannah's prayer at the door of the sanctuary. Prayer is the natural response to Hannah's situation: it is God, the giver of life, who has closed her womb, and it is only God who can open it. Hannah's prayer is not meant to be a bribe to God: "give me a son and I promise I'll give him back." Hannah's longing for a son may have been inherently selfish, but it was not exclusively so. Rather, Hannah is communicating her personal longing for a son and her genuine desire to dedicate to the Lord all that he gives her, including her son (she assumes that **a son** is necessary for her to do this). The prayer expresses no doubt that God will understand her position and will listen as she pours out her heart. The sensitivity of the writers contrasts with that of both Elkanah and **Eli.** Eli fails to spot the woman's distress and presumes she must be **drunk**—not an unreasonable assumption at this stage in the feasting—and his pastoral failures are made up for when he grasps the situation and responds to it.

1:17–20 / Eli gives Hannah his blessing and she receives this as God's blessing, apparently taking it for granted that her prayer has been heard. There is no evidence in the OT that the prayers of religious professionals are to be seen as more effective than those of any sincere believer. Nevertheless, it is possible that Hannah believed that Eli had exceptional powers. It is also possible that the peace she felt was a result of having expressed herself to God. She was comforted as much by her conviction that she was understood and accepted by God as she was by any conviction that a child had been promised. In either case, she felt comfortable taking part in the final worship sessions of their visit before returning to Ramah. Before their next scheduled visit to Shiloh, God **remembered** Hannah. Hannah conceived and eventually bore **a son,** called **Samuel,** which means something like "name of God," or as in the NIV margin "heard of God." This previously despised woman is now in the good company of Noah and the patriarchs, who were also remembered by God in times of particular need (Gen. 8:1; 19:29; Exod. 2:24).

1:21–28 / For the next few years Hannah opts out of the annual pilgrimage to Shiloh. Elkanah took whatever vow he had made seriously, and there was no question of Hannah's absence preventing him from going up for the sacrifice. Hannah also took her vow seriously. Her next visit to Shiloh would mean the beginning of Samuel's dedicated service of God, and that was not appropriate until he had been **weaned.** As soon as it was appropriate, however, sacrifices and gifts were brought to Shiloh, and the young Samuel was handed over into sanctuary service. Hannah took the lead in these ceremonies. Elkanah may have been included and was not opposed to the action she took, but it was her vow and the initiative in fulfilling it was hers. The final sentence of the chapter may simply be stating that Samuel was now at Shiloh, but it may be emphasizing that this was not something that had been forced on the little boy. He seems to have absorbed his call to worship God with his mother's milk.

Additional Notes §1

1:1 / It is impossible to be precise about the location of El-kanah's home. There were several Ramahs in Israel (the name is specified as Ramah in 1:19 and 2:11), and the longer name may be used here to specify a particular Ephraimite one. Whether **Zuph** refers to the town or the family is also not clear, although in 1 Sam. 9:5 Saul seeks out Samuel in the area of Zuph. It is explicit in this verse that Elkanah, and therefore Samuel, was an Ephraimite. This appears to contradict 1 Chron. 6:33–47, which presents them both as Levites belonging to the clan of Kohath. Perhaps the Chronicler could not envisage a non-Levite taking the role that Samuel took in Israel and therefore assumed that they must have been Levites. It is also possible that "Levite" became used as a general term for any dedicated person (cf. G. B. Caird, "The First and Second Books of Samuel," *IB* 2:877).

1:2 / Brueggemann suggests that Elkanah and Hannah's seemingly vain wait for the birth of a child, which will ensure their future, parallels Israel's difficult wait for God to give them David as king, through whom their future can be assured (*First and Second Samuel,* pp. 12–13). However, if the writers intend to bring out this parallel, it would have to mean that the emphasis is on Hannah, for we are told that Elkanah was not childless.

1:3 / Although before the temple was built there was no single center for worship and sacrifices took place at many sites, Shiloh appears to have been a significant shrine at that time. It was a fairly substantial structure, served by appointed priests and housing the central religious object of the Yahwistic faith, the ark of God.

As so often in OT narratives, characters who will later play an important role are introduced almost in passing. So we are informed here that Hophni and Phinehas served as priests alongside their father, Eli.

It is not clear, and it does not affect the point of the story, whether the visits of Elkanah's family were at the time of one of the regular feasts or were a private arrangement, perhaps associated with a vow (cf. v. 21).

1:4–5 / It would be possible to translate the Hb. as "one portion," but the "only one portion" of some versions is misleading. The NIV's **double portion** conveys the sense. The actual phrase is "portion of the face or nose" (Hb. ʾappāyim), perhaps originating from the custom of bowing down before those who deserved special respect (H. W. Hertzberg, *I and II Samuel,* [OTL; London: SCM, 1964], p. 24).

1:11 / Hannah's vow that if she is given a son he will be a Nazirite (Num. 6) dedicated to the Lord recalls the promise made to and the demands made of another barren woman before the birth of Samson (Judg. 13).

1:20 / The etymology of the name *Samuel* does not tie in with the explanation given by Hannah. In fact the word *Sh'l* ("to ask") ties in with the name *Saul* more than with Samuel. However, etymological explanations for names are never meant to be exact, and the suggestion that there has been an insertion here from a passage originally about Saul could be sustained only by destroying the cogency of the text.

The detailed description of preliminary events, followed by a brief statement that the child was born, parallels the birth accounts of Isaac and Samson (Gen. 21:2; Judg. 13:24).

1:23 / Weaning in ancient Near Eastern societies took place at a much later date than it does in today's world, particularly in the West. It would have been rare for a child to be weaned before the age of three, and a child could be five or even older before being fully weaned. Samuel was very young but had probably grown beyond the stage of being a toddler.

§2 *Hannah's Song (1 Sam. 2:1–11)*

In bringing her son to the Lord, Hannah also brings her own worship in a prayer-song. It was not unusual to come to the shrine, or later the temple, with particular praise at times of new birth or special celebration. Neither was it unusual for a woman to bring theological reflection in song; the songs of Miriam and Deborah immediately come to mind. Centuries later, Mary picks up Hannah's song as she rejoices at the thought of her own son. Whether this song was Hannah's own composition or a known psalm that she chose to use on this occasion is somewhat irrelevant. It is probably not irrelevant, however, that the beginning of the book's main theologizing statement comes from the lips of a woman. We have here a reflection on power and powerlessness—in particular the power of God and the powerlessness of human beings—spoken by one who was powerless but who had been, at least in her mind, empowered by God. It provides an appropriate introit for the history of Israel. This history moves from the kingless, oppressed, and usually powerless nation seen in Judges to the liberated and unified nation provided through David and (if Samuel and Kings are seen as a whole) on to the powerful nation found in the reign of Solomon, before moving back to the oppressed and powerless nation of the siege and exile. Hannah's psalm is not found elsewhere in the OT, but it reflects the language of other psalms, perhaps particularly Psalm 113. It is appropriate in this situation, but it would fit equally well into any situation where questions of power and powerlessness arise. It could be used when any person or family or nation becomes aware of the security found in God's strength rather than in their own.

2:1–2 / The subject of the first verse is Hannah, who is exulting with every part of her being in her new situation, but the focus in verse 2 is on **the LORD** who has brought **deliverance.** The **horn,** symbolizing strength, is spoken of here and in verse

10. This repeating of a phrase is a common literary technique known as *inclusio,* and it serves to emphasize the completion and completeness of the section. The uniqueness, the holiness, and the strong security of Israel's (and Hannah's) God are the basis of faith and understanding. This is the backdrop against which the sometimes sorry history of human power struggles is told.

2:3–5 / These power struggles are clearly pictured in the arrogant posturing described in verse 3 and the reversed fortunes of warrior and weak, satiated and hungry, barren and fruitful in verses 4 and 5. God does weigh actions, and the result of God's judgment might mean that positions in society are turned upside down.

2:6–10 / It is clear that human posturing is a waste of time. The Lord **brings death and makes alive,** the Lord **humbles and . . . exalts.** The Lord's actions do not follow human expectations. Those who are desperately poor and powerless, seated in the ash heap, can be transformed by God into powerful princes. The Lord, who had against expectations brought new life to Hannah in the person of Samuel, could also bring new life to the people of Israel. The earth belongs to God, and God alone is in control. What counts is obedience to and trust in God. **It is not by strength that one prevails,** at least not by human strength, and opposition to God will lead to shattering disaster. But the one who is appointed by God—God's **king**—will receive God's **strength.**

God's ultimate control had transformed Hannah's position, turned her bitter tears into strong rejoicing, and resulted in her horn being lifted high. Similarly, God's ultimate control would also lead to **the horn of his anointed** being exalted.

2:11 / That being so, we return to the narrative: Elkanah and Hannah return home, and Samuel remains with Eli at Shiloh, **minister**[ing] **before the** LORD—this unique, holy, and powerful God.

Additional Notes §2

It is often assumed that the writers put a later psalm into the mouth of Hannah because the song is separate from the rest of the text, it interrupts the narrative, and, although it mentions barrenness, it is seen as more appropriate to a discussion of kingship than to the birth of a child. The psalm does form an appropriate introduction to the national history, but its exuberant tone of praise together with the reflection on power are appropriate as an expression of Hannah's feelings.

2:1 / Those versions that use a more modern metaphor to translate "horn" sometimes miss out on the *inclusio*. It is always difficult for translators to represent the extra stylistic touches that help to bring out the meaning of a text.

2:5 / We are told that Hannah eventually had a total of six children (1 Sam. 2:21), but **seven** represents the perfect situation, and that is how Hannah felt after the birth of just one child! Compare this with Ruth 4:15, where Ruth is being seen as more help to Naomi than the ideal "seven sons."

2:6 / Even life is under God's control. The picture of the Lord causing people to enter and leave Sheol, the place of the dead, is a powerful one. Sheol was not a place of life after death but a place of death from which in general there was no return (Isa. 14; Job 3).

2:8 / The very poor would be consigned to living near the garbage dump outside of the town. Covering oneself with **dust** or **ash** came to be a symbol of utter despair and degradation (Job 2:8).

The foundations of the earth, literally "pillars"; the ancient world pictured the earth as being built on pillars, "which permit the world not to sink into chaos" (Brueggemann, *First and Second Samuel,* p. 19).

§3 Eli's Successor (1 Sam. 2:12–36)

2:12–17 / Eli's sons come back into the picture in verses 12 and 17, another *inclusio* emphasizing that they misused their position and, in contrast to Hannah, had no regard for either the power or the judgment of God. The sons showed contempt for God, his offerings, the people who brought those offerings, and their own calling. As priests, they had power and misused it.

Priests had a right to a portion of certain offerings. Leviticus 7:28–36, for example, speaks about the share of the fellowship offering that belonged to the priest who carried out the sacrifice. The priest's share was part of the offerer's gift to God and was to be separated out after the blood was removed and the **fat was burned.** Fat, like blood, was seen as representative of life, and life belonged to God alone. Offerings could be made in various ways, and meat could be cooked by boiling or roasting, usually at the offerer's discretion. The practice of separating out the priest's portion with the use of a **three-pronged fork** is not known elsewhere and could be seen as inconsistent with the Levitical regulations that specified the priest's portion as the breast and the right thigh.

However, the problem was not with this method of separating out a random portion as the priest's share but with the way in which Eli's sons saw that share as being the main point of the sacrifice. They set aside the people's preferences in favor of their liking for meat cooked in their own way, and they ignored God's requirement that the fat be burned. The underlying assumption was that the authority of the priest was real, and the power of God was irrelevant and could be ignored, and their receiving their portion before God's portion was separated out further emphasized this sin.

2:18–21 / In contrast with the grasping materialism of Hophni and Phinehas is the thankful service offered by Samuel and his mother. **Samuel was ministering before the LORD,**

presumably as his age allowed and under Eli's direction. The on-going contribution of Hannah—giving Samuel to God and giv-ing clothes to Samuel—is mentioned, alongside Eli's blessing. It appears that Eli did not participate in his sons' irreverent greed, and his cooperation with those coming to offer sacrifices con-trasts with the bullying of his sons and their servants. God's gra-cious response to this obedient service, giving Hannah five more children, provides a further contrast with God's condemnation of Eli's sons (vv. 27–36).

2:22–26 / Not only did Eli not participate in his sons' ac-tivities, but also he recognized and opposed them. Perhaps there is a criticism of him in that although he gave them a **rebuke** and tried to persuade them, he took no direct action; however, it may be that for a **very old** man, direct action would have been impos-sible. The general sinfulness of the sons included sexual immo-rality, possibly involving misuse of power, but their sins were primarily **sins against the LORD**. The sons **did not listen** because they had no regard for and probably no belief in God's power. However, the text portrays their not listening as an expression of God's power, preventing any repentance that could lead to for-giveness because **it was the LORD's will to put them to death.** Verse 26 serves the same purpose as verses 18–21, contrasting and emphasizing Samuel's rightness as opposed to the sons' wrongness to succeed to Eli's position. Whereas the sons of-fended both people and God and their sin was very great (v. 17), Samuel was becoming great in a different way, **in favor with the LORD and with men.** By emphasizing the sons' not listening to their father, the writers may be preparing us for the account of the way in which the boy Samuel did listen to God (ch. 3).

2:27–36 / The result of the behavior of Eli's family is set out in the long prophecy given by this unknown man of God. First, the calling of Eli's family is outlined. God had selected their ancestor out of all the tribes of Israel to be his priest and to carry out all the priestly functions, providing them with the necessary means to do so. But they, and Eli is included alongside his sons, had shown scorn for God's regulations. Maybe Eli had been un-able to resist eating the delicacies prepared from the meat his sons had provided. By eating the portion assigned to God, Eli had aligned himself with his sons' sin, and the ongoing proph-ecy, although involving the sons, is directed primarily to Eli.

There had been a promise of ministry **forever** for Eli's family, but the nature of that ministry was dependent on the family members' ongoing commitment. Dishonoring God had brought into play the conditional nature of that promise, and although Eli was ninety-eight (4:15), he would be the last of his line to live to be an **old man.** This section raises questions about the extent to which a promise that appears to be eternal can be dependent on the behavior of those receiving the promise, and about how families, and by extension members of a nation, are interdependent. The debate about corporate and individual responsibility found in Ezekiel 18 shows that questions like this continued to trouble Israel.

The relationship between Eli's family and the Aaronic priesthood is not clearly defined. The promise mentioned is made to the clan of Aaron (Exod. 29:9; Num. 25:13) but the **father's house** whose **strength** will be **cut short** is that of Eli. This leaves room for other groups of Aaron's descendants to take over an ongoing ministry.

Eli receives some reassurance that **good will be done to Israel.** The condemnation of his family will not mean the end for Israel, an important point for one who had been appointed as a spiritual leader for the nation. But the disaster awaiting his own family will be confirmed shortly by the deaths of **Hophni and Phinehas,** named for the first time in this chapter.

The **faithful priest** who will replace Eli's line is not named, but the reader and presumably Eli might assume from the context that Samuel is being referred to. However, the reference to this priest acting as **minister before my anointed one** has led most scholars to conclude that the priest is Zadok, who was priest to David and who was apparently promoted by Solomon (1 Kgs. 2:35). This does not alter the fact that the immediate replacement of Eli's family was Samuel. Similarly, it points to the Christian understanding that sees both the most "faithful priest" and the true "anointed one" as Jesus Christ. The replacement of one chosen line by another after a failure to fulfill the demands of a calling prepares us for the parallel situation in later chapters, when Saul's line is replaced by David's.

Additional Notes §3

2:18 / The **linen ephod** was a garment worn by priests (cf. 22:18; 2 Sam. 6:14). We do not know its precise nature, but it could have been an undergarment, perhaps a form of loincloth. It is to be differentiated from the ephod carried by the priests as a means of divination. Samuel's wearing the priestly garment may indicate that the custom of Levitical service being taken up only at the age of twenty-five (Num. 8:24–26) was not known or not applied at this time, or it could indicate that Samuel was a special case.

Perhaps the authors deliberately continue the reflection on powerlessness by providing in vv. 18–26 this clear contrast between the lack of spirituality on the part of the adult priests and the service given by the child and the very old man.

2:22 / The **women who served at the Tent of Meeting** probably carried out the same kind of tasks as did Levitical servers. The phrase is the same one seen in Exod. 38:8. It was common in ancient Near Eastern religions to have religious prostitutes surrounding important shrines, but the practice was always unacceptable in Yahwism, the religion of those who followed the God of Israel, *YHWH*. Hophni's and Phinehas's treatment of the female servers showed again their contempt for people and for God's will.

Shiloh was a more substantial structure than the original Tent of Meeting (1:9; 3:3, 15), and for some scholars the description here therefore becomes a problem: if the sanctuary was not a tent, this reference must indicate an editorial mistake. However, it is not unusual for traditional terms to remain even after the form has changed, and Shiloh never had the permanence of the temple built at Jerusalem (cf. Baldwin, *1 and 2 Samuel*, pp. 65–68, Gordon, *1 and 2 Samuel: A Commentary*, pp. 74–75, 83).

2:25 / God's will as the controlling factor in all that happens is usually taken for granted in OT writings. However, this does not mean that human accountability is set aside. The young men's actions caused the problem, just as Pharaoh in Exod. 5:2 made the decision to oppose the God of Israel that led to his being incapable of changing his mind after God hardened his heart.

2:27 / **Man of God** is often synonymous with "prophet" in the OT, as in 2 Kgs. 1:9. This man behaves in a prophetic manner and uses the standard prophetic introduction, **This is what the LORD says.**

2:30 / Many prophetic pronouncements were assumed to be conditional even if conditions were not specified, a point that is brought out in the story of Jonah. Jonah's unwillingness to pronounce judgment on Nineveh is based on the fact that he knew that if they were to repent the situation would change and God might forgive them (Jonah 4:2).

2:35 / On the **faithful priest** referring to Zadok see Gordon, *1 and 2 Samuel: A Commentary,* p. 88; Caird, "1 and 2 Samuel," 2:891.

2:36 / The priests and Levites who had no appointed tribal areas depended on their priestly service for the income on which their families lived. To forfeit their appointment as priests meant to forfeit their livelihood. Their only recourse in these circumstances was to beg for food and for work.

§4 Samuel's Calling (1 Sam. 3:1–4:1a)

The calling of Samuel follows the revoking of the calling of Eli's family. This reinforces the impression that whatever other successors there may be (Zadok, Jesus Christ), the writers intend Samuel to be viewed as in some sense a replacement for Eli's sons. Eli is pictured in this chapter and earlier (2:18–21) as graciously mentoring the gifted young Samuel, grooming him for a task that he must have wished could have been carried on by his own family. It seems probable that the writers intended to provide a contrast to the later picture of Saul as he, with ungracious resentment, sought to prevent the gifted young David from replacing his own family.

3:1 / An editorial comment precedes the next part of the story. The lack of **visions** and the mention of the fact that **in those days the word of the LORD was rare** emphasize the unexpected nature of what happened to Samuel. This was not a young boy, having reached a certain age, automatically beginning to function within the kind of spiritual experience known to his elders. Samuel carried out his service willingly and naturally, but without as yet a conviction that it involved a personal connection between himself and his God or a direct responsibility toward the people. He served God through serving Eli in the temple.

3:2–18 / The story continues with the young Samuel asleep in the area where **the ark of God** was kept, a fact that shows how fully he had been integrated into priestly service. He hears a voice and immediately goes to Eli—maybe it was a regular occurrence for the almost blind Eli to need help. Samuel's willingness to get up three times in the night, apparently without complaint, to attend to the ailing old man speaks well for the character of the young priest and draws attention to his worthiness to receive the prophetic word. Eli, equally patient at being disturbed, realizes that something unusual is happening and that God is involved in it.

The choice of the child to hear God's word picks up the earlier emphasis on the power and control of God and his ability to empower the powerless, whether to give a child to a barren woman or to speak through an inexperienced child. Samuel seems unsure that Eli has it right, and although he obediently responds to the fourth call, he does not use the traditional formula that Eli had given him, **Speak, LORD.** Instead he omits the name of the Lord. In quoting direct speech the writers draw attention to that fact. When Eli asks for a report of the message he too is wary, asking **what was it he** (as opposed to the Lord) **said to you,** needing to hear the report before he concludes that **He is the LORD.**

Samuel's youth does not prevent him from being given the responsibility of hearing an adult message of fierce judgment, made more difficult because it was directed at Eli. The modern tendency to protect children from hard truths is not reflected here. Samuel's reaction was to get back to his normal duties: he **opened the doors of the house of the LORD.** This note of everyday reality puts his experience in perspective. But Eli insists on hearing what has been said to Samuel. The message confirms what he knows; he confirms that the message is from the Lord and accepts it. If he had been less compliant with his sons at an earlier stage, then the situation might have been different, but Eli's character is presented consistently throughout the narratives.

3:19–4:1a / Having once heard the word of God, Samuel's priestly duties become supplemented with prophetic responsibilities, and he becomes a mature man of God, a **prophet** widely recognized throughout **all Israel.** The contrast between 3:21 and 3:1 is marked. The **word** of **the LORD** was no longer rare but, through Samuel, available to all.

Additional Notes §4

3:3 / Exod. 27:20–21 tells us that the lamp in the temple was to be kept burning every night from evening till morning. The reference to the light **not yet** having **gone out** indicates that the voice came to Samuel sometime before dawn.

It is sometimes assumed that mention of the ark means the voice came to Samuel from there (Caird, "1 and 2 Samuel," 2:893), but the text

(v. 10) states that the LORD came and stood there. It is more likely that the specific reference is in preparation for the next series of stories centered around the ark.

3:15 / J. G. Janzen ("Samuel Opened the Doors of the House of Yahweh," [*JSOT* 26] 1983, pp. 89–96) suggests that this phrase about opening the doors has symbolic significance, that the doors are being opened on to a new era of hearing God's word. However, Samuel's fear of telling Eli of the vision, reported in the second half of the verse, does not support this theory.

3:19 / **He let none of his words fall to the ground:** The words given to Samuel by God proved to be reliable. This reliability, perhaps including accurate predictive prophecies, enabled the people to recognize him as a true prophet.

3:20 / **From Dan to Beersheba:** This expression refers to two towns in the north and south of the country. They are not quite on the borders of the land but near enough for this to have become a common way of stressing that **all Israel** means the whole nation (2 Sam. 17:11). Samuel's reputation had reached as far as Saul's father's servant (1 Sam. 9:6).

§5 The Ark—Lost and Regained
(1 Sam. 4:1b–7:1)

Having introduced the problems of leadership in Israel, only partially resolved by Samuel's new role, the narrative moves on to prepare the reader to hear the story of Israel's kingship. The underlying theme of the nature of power continues: can God's power be manipulated by manipulation of the sacred ark, which represents God's presence in Israel? The answer to this question is clear, but it is not explicitly stated. It is likely that the writers make use of a source detailing the history of the ark (cf. p. 4 above).

4:1b–11 / Attention so far has been focused on a fairly small group of people. Now the picture widens to give a view of the situation in the nation. The constant tension between the Israelites and the Philistines, seen in Judges, continues. A battle is described, and not unusually, the Israelites are defeated. The theological understanding is the Israelites' conviction about the power of God. Their defeat was not to be ascribed to the superior strength of the Philistine gods but to a decision on the part of the all-powerful Yahweh.

However, their conviction that God could control even the Philistines to bring about his purposes did not prevent them from asking questions about their own attitudes and behavior or from assuming that the physical presence of the ark would make a difference to their campaign. Theological development is rarely uniform, and it was not here. The OT writers were well aware that it was possible for Israel to grasp some profound and difficult concepts relating to God and his work in the world and yet misunderstand or ignore some simple and obvious truths.

The ark was fetched, Hophni and Phinehas accompanying it. Both the Israelite and the Philistine camps were impressed by the advent of such an important sacred symbol onto the battlefield. But the battle recommenced, the Israelites perhaps complacent, the Philistines desperate. In spite of the presence of the ark or perhaps because of their misunderstanding of the implications of that presence, Israel was comprehensively defeated. Thousands of Israelites, including Eli's sons, were killed, and the ark that was intended to protect them was captured.

4:12–22 / News of the defeat was brought to Shiloh. The reader is drawn into the situation and can see and feel the tension in Eli as he waits for news and the breathlessness of the messenger who announces himself to the sightless old priest. Eli's fear for the ark of God maybe indicated that he did not share the Israelites' misunderstanding and that he knew their attempt to manipulate God was a mistake. Nevertheless, the news of the loss of the ark was too much of a shock for Eli, who fell off his chair. Perhaps the mention of his weight being a factor in his death relates to 2:29, when his desire for choice food involved him in his sons' contempt for God's offering.

The shock sends Eli's daughter-in-law into premature labor, and the tragedy, heightened by her death, is recorded in the name of her son, **Ichabod, . . . the glory has departed.** She is almost certainly not alone in thinking that Israel's **glory**, normally associated with the Lord, has left them. Baldwin's suggestion that the "glory has departed" refers to God leaving the ark rather than leaving Israel (*1 and 2 Samuel*, p. 72) does not fit with the text. Both Israel and Philistia thought that Israel's God had been captured. Both began to doubt the power of which Israel had been so confident and the Philistines so afraid.

This was the end of an era. Eli's family did not die out (1 Sam. 14:3), but they no longer played a significant part in the nation's leadership. The ark never returned to Shiloh, and Shiloh no longer had any significance as a theological or political center. Indeed, Jeremiah uses Shiloh as an example of the deliberate setting aside by God of something that he had previously blessed and used (Jer. 7:12–15).

5:1–12 / A note of humor creeps into the narrative as the ark's encounter with Philistine cities is described. Both Israel and Philistia had to realize that Israel's God had not lost control. The importance of outsiders understanding the nature and power of Yahweh is a theme that recurs throughout the OT. One of the reasons for the exile, for example, was that the nations should not think that the Lord did not care about Israel's idolatry and immorality, whereas the return from exile was so that the nations might not think that the Lord is powerless (cf. Ezek. 6; 36). The same pattern is found here. Israel must not think that they can manipulate God by moving the ark, but Philistia must not think that the capture of the ark means the powerlessness of God. Hannah's conviction that the Lord is in control (2:6–10) is reinforced.

The monotheistic emphasis in this chapter is unavoidable. The Philistine god, Dagon, is pictured as powerless even in the heart of his own territory, whereas the Lord is powerful everywhere. The irony is clear—the ark of God had been placed beside Dagon, as if to indicate worship, but Dagon is found first **fallen on his face** before Israel's God in the prototypical worship position and then **broken**.

R. P. Gordon (*1 and 2 Samuel: A Commentary*, p. 92) picks up the humorous element in the text when he pictures Dagon as "turned into Humpty Dumpty," but the outbreak of painful tumorous boils would have been far from funny to the Philistines. The capture of the ark had brought them a great deal of pride, but now its presence brought danger.

6:1–12 / It was apparent to the Philistines that the disasters befalling them were related to their possession of the ark, but it took **seven months** before they decided the way to handle this crisis was to send the ark back. To do that could be seen as a politically significant admission of weakness and could be interpreted by the Israelites as an invitation to attack; the Philistines' reluctance is unsurprising.

It was vital to conduct the transaction in the least damaging way possible. The Philistines wanted to pacify Israel's God in order to prevent further devastation, but they needed to do this without inciting Israel to battle at a time when Philistia was recovering from epidemic disease. Their solution was masterly and shows why they were such a formidable enemy. The **new cart** indicated that they took the holiness of God seriously, and the inclusion of **gold rats** and **tumors** demonstrated their recognition of God as the cause of their disease, which was carried by rats and resulted in tumors. The gold from these items provided tribute from each of the five cities, and it symbolically removed the disease from their territory.

However, sending the cart without human attendants avoided the necessity of a humiliating personal encounter and allowed for the possibility that Yahweh was not the cause of their problems, without causing further offense if their suspicions were correct. Their scheme involved a real test for Yahweh, and the Philistines weighted the odds against the cows' traveling back to Israel by choosing cows not broken to the yoke and by penning up their calves. In normal circumstances the mother cows would stay close to their calves; their distressed lowing indicates a desire to do just that. When the cart was taken **straight** back into Israel's territory any remaining doubts as to whether or not Yahweh was in control were removed. The Philistine leaders had remained watching at a safe distance to make sure that they had a correct understanding of what had gone on.

6:13–7:1 / **Beth Shemesh** was on the border of Israelite and Philistine territory. Recognizing the significance of the arrival of the ark, the local people stopped their harvesting (the wheat harvest normally took place around May/June) and immediately sacrificed the cart and the cows. Because both had been used only for sacred purposes, their use in sacrifice was appropriate. The mention of **Levites,** rare in Samuel and Kings, seems to relate to Beth Shemesh as one of the towns populated by Levites (Josh. 21:16) rather than these being Levites brought from outside to carry out ark-related duties. The rock on which the ark was placed was probably a significant landmark that allowed the ark to be set before the people and presumably in the sight of Philistia almost as a victory trophy.

The sacrifices having been carried out, new blessing might have been expected for Israel, but it was not to be. The sin of the local folk, as with Uzzah (2 Sam. 6), involved not treating the ark with proper respect. The ark was not to be touched or opened by ordinary people, and the treatment of the ark as a victory trophy could have been part of the problem. It was important that the Israelites see the recovery of the ark not as a transfer of control from Philistia back to Israel but as it was—an expression of God's sovereignty over both Philistia and Israel.

Apparently that change in attitude had not yet taken place. The failure to understand the awesome nature of God's sovereignty and to respect the ark as a symbol of God's presence led to further tragedy. Seventy people died because of their irreverent actions. Joshua had warned the ordinary Israelites to keep as much as a thousand yards away from the ark (Josh. 3:4; cf. Num.

1:51), but these seventy had the temerity to look into the holy ark of God.

Why the people of **Kiriath Jearim** should be more confident of their ability to look after the ark is also not clear. The alternative name for Kiriath Jearim is Baalah (2 Sam. 6:2), which may indicate that a previous Canaanite shrine had been situated there, as was probably also true for Shiloh, and thus the population might be seen as used to handling sacred things. The dedication of **Eleazar** does not specify that he was a priest, although the name occurs in priestly genealogies (Num. 3:2), but he was set aside for this particular task. In any event, the ark remained in the care of his family for many years, until David decided that it could serve other purposes. Perhaps the safety resulted from a genuine change of attitude on the part of the people (7:2).

Additional Notes §5

Within these Ark Narratives, Samuel is notable by his absence. This has sometimes been seen as indicating that chs. 4–6 originated separately from chs. 1–3, with the original writer of chs. 4–6 being unaware of Samuel's existence. However, apart from Samuel there are several connections between the two sections and the point being made here is not related to Samuel's growing up. It could be that the writers want to make it clear that Samuel did not have a part in the way in which the Israelites attempted to use the ark.

4:1 / The LXX presents the Philistines as the aggressors in this fight.

Aphek is probably well north of the main Philistine area around the five cities of Gath, Ashdod, Ashkelon, Ekron, and Gaza. It may be that Shiloh was being threatened. The reason for the battle is not stressed; the two groups were constantly fighting, and the reasons for their antagonism is not the issue here.

Ebenezer may or may not be the place that is mentioned as receiving its name as a result of the victory there (7:12). In either case, the name of the Israelite camp ("stone of help") may be ironic.

4:3–5 / The stress on the **ark's** relationship to **the covenant** (Hb. *bᵉrît*) draws the reader's attention to the requirement on the people to keep the covenant and provides a background to the apparent failure of the ark to protect Israel. However, the LXX omits the word *covenant*, so it is probably not wise to lay too much significance on this stress. "Covenant" describes the special relationship between Israel and their God *YHWH*, a relationship within which both parties have responsibilities. God will guide, protect, and love Israel, and Israel must obey, serve, and love God. This covenant has many parallels with ancient Near Eastern suzerainty treaties made between conquering powers and vassal states, but the element of loving relationship makes it unique. Throughout the OT this covenant between God and Israel is an important concept, but it is given particular focus within Deut. and the books related to Deut. In these books the primary concern is how Israel functions as a covenant community.

4:5 / Contrast the **shout** of confidence and hope (v. 6) with the **cry** of desolation and defeat (v. 13).

4:9 / The Israelites did not use the term **Hebrews** among themselves. It is used by or to outsiders. The significance of this is not clear—it may be a matter of local usage.

4:10 / The number of deaths seems exceptionally large. The term **thousand,** here and in v. 2, could refer to a military grouping whose numbers were considerably less than a thousand. But this interpretation would not deny the comprehensive nature of the defeat.

4:13 / See additional note on 4:5.

4:18 / F. A. Spina ("Eli's Seat: The Transition from Priest to Prophet in 1 Samuel 1–4," *JSOT* 62 [1994], pp. 67–75) sees the three references to Eli's chair (1:9; 4:13, 18) as symbolic of his office, and the word used for chair *(kissē')* often refers to a throne of office. When Eli fell from his chair it signified also his falling from office. Samuel is never spoken of as seated on a *kisse'*, perhaps because his "role was to insure that whoever next occupied the *kisse'* in Israel was appropriate" (p. 73).

5:5 / The custom of avoiding treading on the threshold of a shrine is fairly common in tribal religions, and the comment here is sometimes seen as aetiological—providing an explanation for a known custom. In this instance the Philistines sought to avoid putting their feet—a sacrilegious insult—on the place where their god's hands and head had lain.

6:3–4 / Guilt offerings involved reparation, a payment made to cover any damages caused by the offerer (Lev. 5:14–6:7; 7:1–10). In this case the emphasis is on the payment to satisfy the supposed vengeance of God, rather than a recognition of any moral guilt.

The mention of **gold rats** and the fact that the LXX mentions rats in 5:6 indicates that the death that filled the city (5:11) was some kind of infectious plague carried by rats.

6:6 / The story of Israel's escape from Egypt seems to have been well known to the Philistines. The reference in 4:8 (where the story is somewhat confused, the plagues being thought of as occurring in the wilderness) makes it less likely that this is a later insertion put into their mouths.

6:19 / The Hebrew includes the figure of 50,070, but the grammar is unusual (the 50,000 is placed alongside the 70 without the normal conjunction), and the NIV's 70 is almost certainly correct. The loss of **seventy** men would be significant in a small town like Beth Shemesh (cf. D. M. Fouts, "Added Support for Reading '70 Men' in 1 Samuel VI:19," *VT* 42 [1992]: p. 394).

§6 Samuel's Ministry (1 Sam. 7:2–17)

In some senses this chapter is interim, signifying the passing of time until the writers come to the next main focus, the beginning of kingship. In chapter 7 we have Samuel's ministry and his credentials as an appropriate kingmaker established, but we also have the power of God presented in such a way as to indicate the writers' view that human kingship was unnecessary.

7:2–13a / **Twenty years** pass from the ark's lodging at Kiriath Jearim to the events at Mizpah, which result from the nation's turning to the Lord. Even at this stage, Samuel seeks evidence of the sincerity of their repentance. Was it **with all your hearts**? The people provide evidence in their wholesale setting aside of local deities.

Throughout the OT, God's help is tied to the recognition of his uniqueness—his help cannot be looked for as a supplement to that of other gods. When and only when it was clear that Israel's worship was of God alone, it was appropriate for them to come together and reaffirm their covenant with Yahweh, the Lord, and seek his help. The main reason for their mourning is their failure to deal with ongoing Philistine incursions into their territory, and this perhaps explains Samuel's wariness. But they had at last come to accept that the only way forward was through the power of God.

Samuel, acting as priest and as national leader, brings a **burnt offering** on behalf of the whole nation. How the Lord answered Samuel's crying out is not made explicit, though perhaps the thundering **with loud thunder** should be seen as the Lord crying out in response to Samuel and to the people.

The Philistine forces sought to take advantage of the Israelites' preoccupation with religious ceremonies, a strategy that was to prove their downfall. Although the men of Israel finished off the fleeing troops, the victory was brought about without

their assistance. In this final defeat of the Philistines the power of
God is demonstrated and affirmed once more. Only God ensured their defeat.

Samuel set up a memorial stone on the site of the massacre,
named **Ebenezer,** "stone of help," to remind Israel that where
human strength had not succeeded, the Lord's help had. Perhaps this reminder would help to remove the trauma of the earlier defeat at the same site (4:1–11). Large rocks and stones were
often used to mark significant religious events, and there may be
a link in the writers' minds with the stone of Beth Shemesh
(ch. 6).

Although the Philistines were not finally deafeated until
the early part of David's reign, their dominance had been broken. The writers probably want to emphasize that in the context
of the nation having been successfully helped by God alone, they
ask for a king.

7:13b–17 / The rest of the chapter tidies up loose ends.
It describes the final throes of Philistine influence and the loss of
the small towns between Ekron and Gath that they had taken
from the Israelites. Peace with the Amorites, the native Canaanites still inhabiting parts of the land, would be a side effect of the
diminution of Philistine power and the resulting increase in Israel's power. Then, Samuel's role has clearly developed from that
of Eli. He has a base at his family home in Ramah, but although
he built an altar there, this is not pictured as a central shrine in
the way that Shiloh was, nor does Samuel's role appear to be primarily that of a priest. He acted as circuit judge, traveling around
the area, exercising leadership, and directing the people toward
the Lord.

Additional Notes §6

7:2 / The timing is difficult. Some scholars, including Baldwin
and Caird, assume that **twenty years** refers to the whole time before
David took the ark to Jerusalem. However, this seems to be too short a
time to allow for all that happened throughout Samuel's ministry,
Saul's reign, and David's early years. It seems better, as Klein and
Gordon do, to take it as the time prior to the battle at Mizpah.

7:4 / The religious system in Canaan was complex. The term **Baals and Ashtoreths** summarizes the range of male and female deities that were worshiped in Canaan and had been taken up by many of the Israelite people.

7:6 / The ceremony of pouring water on the ground does not form part of the normal official rituals of Israel. It may signify that part of their fasting was the giving up of water, or it may indicate cleansing from pollution caused by worshiping other gods.

7:10 / Sin offerings and guilt offerings would seem to be more appropriate in this situation than the burnt offering, which was usually associated with praise and worship rather than with repentance. However, it is hard to know how the sacrificial system was applied at this early stage in Israel's history, and Lev. 1:4 makes it clear that the burnt offering, as much as the rest of the system, could effect atonement.

7:12 / Significant stones are mentioned, as either memorial sites or meeting places, in 14:33; 20:19, 41; 23:25; 2 Sam. 20:8; 21:10.

7:13 / The emphasis on **throughout Samuel's lifetime** may picture a resurgence of Philistine power after his death, during the final days of Saul's reign and beyond until their final defeat by David. The point is that Israel did not need a king to bring about military victories.

7:16 / The three places named on Samuel's circuit cover a fairly small area within a few miles' radius in the region north of Jerusalem. This may indicate that Samuel's influence was not as widespread as 4:1a suggests. However, Samuel appointed his sons to act as judges in Beersheba. The best known Beersheba is in the far south, well outside the range of Samuel's own circuit. Perhaps Samuel traveled more widely than the towns mentioned, or this may be another Beersheba not now identifiable.

§7 The Request for a King (1 Sam. 8:1–22)

8:1–5 / The parallels between the behavior of Samuel's sons and that of Eli's sons are unmistakable. The misuse of power may not have followed the exact pattern, but the contempt for God's law, God's people, and thus God was the same. The strong, competent Samuel had no more success in controlling his sons than had the ineffectual, food-loving Eli. The text gives no indication that Samuel tacitly concurred in his sons' misdoings as Eli did, but he appointed them, and he did not prevent their **dishonest gain** from **accept**[ing] **bribes and pervert**[ing] **justice.** Leadership from Samuel's family was no more a long-term solution to Israel's need for effective rulers than leadership from the priestly line of Eli had been.

These verses both explain the perceived need for a different style of leadership and raise the question as to whether inherited authority and status will always involve the abuse of power. This question often comes to the fore in the Kingship Narratives that follow, but the tribal elders see kingship as a way forward—maybe the only way forward. They believe that it will solve their need for a consistent and organized response to the continuing Philistine threat, as well as to ongoing internal injustices (v. 3).

The elders' motivation may also include a spiritual aspect, a belief that they need the kind of spiritual direction that helps rather than hinders their worship of the Lord. The fact that they come to Samuel with their request and that the corruption of **Joel** and **Abijah** is seen as a problem indicates that their request was not, at least in their own minds, a turning away from God.

Looking to **all the other nations** as a model, however, could hint that they saw following contemporary cultural patterns rather than seeking God's will as the way forward. The unreconciled ambiguity found in the attitude toward kingship throughout its somewhat questionable history is reflected. On the one hand, kingship could be seen as a rejection of God's own kingship, an unnecessary intrusion into the relationship between God and his chosen nation. On the other hand, it was a gift from God, a model and a channel through which God's relationship with Israel could be illustrated and strengthened.

8:6–20 / Samuel's displeasure stemmed primarily from his feeling of rejection. Unlike Eli, he seemed to have found it hard to accept that the people did not endorse his choice of his sons to follow him. This, along with God's sympathy for Samuel's position, is brought out in the injunction to Samuel to listen to what the people were saying. They had **rejected as their king** not Samuel but God.

In spite of the Philistine defeat (ch. 7), Israel had not fully accepted that God's power was sufficient. They felt that if they were to take their place as the equal of surrounding nations they needed a recognized military leader. The repetition in verse 20 of **like all the other nations** emphasizes the significance they placed on the status that other nations had and by implication their lack of awareness of God's power. The writers make it clear that God, after asking Samuel to make sure that the people understood what they were letting themselves in for, gave permission for the monarchy to proceed. When in spite of Samuel's clear warnings the desire for a king remained, the request was duly authorized. The monarchy then was seen as a gift from God.

8:21–22 / It is usually taken for granted that Samuel continued to view kingship in a negative light, but this chapter, after recording his initial displeasure, gives no indication of his personal feelings. He puts forward all the negative arguments in obedience to God's will and then with equal obedience acquiesces to God's command to **give them a king.** The implication of the final injunction, **Everyone go back to his town,** is that such a request might take time, but Samuel had it under control. Whether Samuel was happy with that situation or not remains a matter for conjecture, although 10:19 and 12:17 confirm that he was not. The picture of God not overruling human choices, even when those choices can be shown to be detrimental to his purposes for them, is consistent with the portrayal of God in different parts of the OT. God starts from where people are and then provides new choices that could lead them forward within his plans.

Additional Notes §7

It is often taken for granted that the ambiguous attitude toward kingship in 8:4–22 reflects two sources, one anti-monarchy and one pro-monarchy. If this is so, then the writers wished to present the reader with both points of view, and the two positions are allowed to remain in tension. The reader is left to draw conclusions as to how the potential was fulfilled.

8:11–18 / The picture of the authoritarian, oppressive ruler making severe demands on the children, land, servants, and property of ordinary Israelites is often assumed to come from a late document describing what happened in Israel under later kings. However, even if one does not wish to accept Samuel's words as a God-given prophecy, it is conceivable that similar patterns of behavior were observable in nations surrounding Israel before the Israelite monarchy had been instituted. Given the previous descriptions of the depravity of both Eli's sons and Samuel's sons, the reader might consider the possibility that all power is intrinsically corrupting. If this is so, then to increase the power of an individual to the extent that a monarchy **like** that of **other nations** would do is bound to lead to increasing corruption. The king's rights are seen as rights—oppressive, maybe, but not automatically corrupt. However, there is a sharp contrast between the picture of kingship presented by Samuel and the instructions about the conduct of kings in Deut. 17. Given the close links between these narratives and Deut. it is interesting that the negative picture presented here is allowed to stand. Samuel tries to dissuade the people from the idea of kingship. For a fuller discussion of the literary and historical questions relating to the structure of ch. 8 see Klein, *1 Samuel*, pp. 73–79.

§8 The Anointing of Saul (1 Sam. 9:1–10:8)

9:1–10 / With chapter 9 the focus moves from Samuel, although he still has a significant role to play, to Saul. In verse 3 Saul, in spite of his imposing physical presence and his good family background, enters the picture as a rather insignificant young man looking for lost **donkeys.** God's concern for and use of the powerless can be seen again here. It may be, therefore, that the grandiose introduction in verse 2 is inserted into an earlier account to serve as an introduction to Saul the king at the point when he is first mentioned. The presentation both of the significance of Saul's tribe and lineage and of his impressive character seems at odds with the picture that initially emerges of an indecisive and unconfident young man with what he sees as an insignificant background (v. 21).

It is hard to explain why the writers devote so much space to the apparently trivial matter of lost donkeys if it is not to draw the attention of later readers to the fact that kings are ordinary people from ordinary backgrounds with ordinary concerns. The stress on David's early life as a rural sheep herder probably serves the same purpose. The historical writers as much as the prophets resist the tendency to introduce the concept of a natural aristocracy into the mindset of a nation that was founded on the basis of a covenant brotherhood.

In this instance, Saul and his father's servant pursue an extended and fruitless search for the donkeys. It is not clear why they follow the path they do or travel so far, but they eventually find themselves in the area occupied by the Zuphites, Samuel's clan (1:1). Throughout this journey the servant takes the initiative. Saul suggests that they return, but the servant proposes that they seek out the **man of God** who lived in this area and had a reputation for unearthing truth. The servant's willingness to pay his own money as a fee for the seer signifies that his relationship with the family was unusually close.

It is unlikely that Samuel's main function as judge was to act as a fortune teller answering queries of this nature. However, common people somewhat removed from his sphere conceivably understood his reputation in that way, and the editorial comment in verse 9 explaining the relationship between **seer** and **prophet** may be intended to clarify this point. Samuel is not to be dismissed as nothing more than clairvoyant.

9:11–13 / The incident in which the two men asked the way of **girls** collecting **water** also brings out the down-to-earth reality of what was going on. Area sacrifices being presented as well as the personal sacrifices brought by the likes of Elkanah tie in with what we know of worship before the temple was built. It appears that a fellowship offering, possibly in conjunction with Samuel's periodic visits on his judging circuit, was made. It is not clear whether this was Samuel's home town of Ramah and he had just returned home, or whether he was briefly visiting a nearby town.

9:14–17 / The time lapsed between the decision to appoint a king and Samuel's meeting with Saul is unknown. Samuel's arrangement of this sacrificial feast was originally unconnected, but in some way God had made it clear to Samuel that the chosen king was about to emerge. The feast served as an opportunity for Samuel to get to know Saul and also, symbolically and unknown to Saul, as a precoronation celebration. The writers emphasize that although Samuel was to appoint the king, the choice of Saul was God's. Though the message instructs Samuel to **anoint** a **leader** who will **deliver my people** and also **govern,** the word for king is not used. Perhaps, other than the more formalized appointment structure, there was little difference originally between Saul's role as king and that of previous judges, maybe including Samuel.

9:18–27 / Samuel's reputation as a seer is confirmed by his immediate recognition of Saul and his reference to the **donkeys,** which are now **found.** Saul's lack of recognition of Samuel highlights Samuel's own insight. The initial message to Saul is ambiguous, though Samuel is concerned with something more than donkeys. His promise to tell Saul **all that is in your heart** may indicate recognition of an unstated ambition on Saul's part, perhaps to rid Israel of the Philistine problem. The statement that **all the desire of Israel** is turned to Saul and his family is obscure. Samuel perhaps wanted to be certain that this was God's way forward before he committed himself. However, Saul's response indicates that he has understood Samuel to be assigning him a significant task within Israel. His response may reflect a genuine humility and lack of self-confidence, but it may also be a normal part of Eastern good manners requiring self-effacement. The double mention of his tribe (v. 21) may have confirmed to Samuel that this was the Benjamite of whom God had spoken.

The significance of Samuel's words was confirmed to Saul by his being given the pride of place at the feast and being assigned the special portion of meat. The way in which Samuel singled out these unknown visitors must have caused comment, but no public action is taken at this stage. Samuel may merely have placed Saul where he could observe him and talk with him. Verse 25 indicates that the writers emphasized the extent to which Samuel took time to get to know Saul. He apparently felt satisfied with the results of his investigation.

10:1–8 / The anointing that took place the next morning was private, but the text does not indicate that Samuel had any remaining doubts that Saul was God's choice. If the appointment of a king was a public matter and if Saul was to be accepted by the people, it was important that his appointment was ratified by the whole people in a public meeting.

The brief ceremony of anointing is accompanied by detailed predictions designed to confirm to Saul that Samuel's actions were, as he had said, on behalf of **the LORD**. Saul will meet two men who will corroborate the finding of the donkeys, three men who will provide food for him, and a band of ecstatic prophets. Saul will be given spiritual power to join these prophets, and the experience will be life-transforming. Verse 6 explains how this youth could be transformed into a mature leader. The servant, who in 9:27 is told with clear symbolism to **go on ahead of us,** disappears from the account at this point, although he is mentioned briefly in verse 14. His role as mentor is over, and he can leave the scene. Saul can now, in the light of his awareness of God's power, make his own decisions. This is probably what is meant by Samuel's instructions that once all this happens Saul is to **do whatever** his **hand finds to do, for God is with** him. Samuel's detailed instructions about where and when to meet him thus seem incongruous, although later events show that the transformed Saul takes a little while to emerge. However, Samuel may be suggesting that if Saul needs Samuel's help, he can go to Gilgal and Samuel will meet him there within seven days.

Additional Notes §8

W. L. Humphreys suggests that 1 Sam. 9–31, usually seen as focusing on Samuel with Saul and then on David with Saul, should be seen as having Saul himself at the heart of the narrative ("The Tragedy of King Saul: A Study of the Structure of 1 Samuel 9–31," *JSOT* 6 [1978], pp. 18–27). The rise and fall in Saul's fortunes is an interest in the text, but R. P. Gordon is probably right to argue that to see the attention of the narrative as centered on Saul distorts the natural focus on David ("David's Rise and Saul's Demise: Narrative Analogy in 1 Samuel 24–26," *TynBul* 31 [1980], p. 39).

9:1–2 / The genealogy is unusually extensive for this kind of introduction but is provided to explain the significance of **Kish.** There is a slight discrepancy with the genealogy in 1 Chron. 9:36, 39, where Kish appears as the son of Ner. However, if Abiel is the same as Jeiel, Ner's father in Chronicles, it means that one generation has been omitted, a practice not unknown in genealogies. 1 Sam. 14:51 describes Ner as Kish's brother and Saul's uncle.

The word translated **young man** in v. 2 does not necessarily imply extreme youth. There is no problem with the description of Saul as having his own possibly teenage son by the time he takes up his position as king (13:1–2).

9:13 / The sacrifice is likely to be the fellowship offering, in which a portion of the animal is burned "before the LORD" and the rest is eaten by the worshipers in a celebratory meal. The mention of invited guests tells us that this feast had a particular purpose, but we are not made aware of it. It was normal practice to honor special guests by giving them choice portions.

The later Deuteronomic history is scathing about worship at the **high place** (e.g., 1 Kgs. 14:23; 2 Kgs. 17:32; 23:5, 8), but before the centralization of worship that came with the temple these were the accepted centers of worship. There are no connotations of pagan worship in this context.

9:27 / It is sometimes suggested that the contrast between the private anointing of Saul by Samuel and the public appointment at Mizpah (10:17–25) indicates two different sources. This is possible, but the distinction between calling and appointment is widely recognized in the OT, and there is no inconsistency here. There is a parallel with Elisha's private anointing of Jehu (2 Kgs. 9:1–13).

10:1 / As in 9:16 Saul is described not as Hb. *melek* ("king"), but as *nāgîd*, **leader,** or possibly prince, and his anointing is as *nāgîd*. This term has military associations, and the concentration may be on the task of leading the Israelites against the Philistines and other aggressors. The use of the term again makes it clear that the human king acts as God's agent, ruling on his behalf.

10:3–4 / If the three men are carrying sacrificial offerings, their handing over part of these to Saul could indicate that Saul's appointment is in some way sacral.

10:5–6 / Groups of **prophets,** sometimes associated with particular shrines, who were noted for ecstatic experiences often accompanied by music, were as well known in Israel as they were in Canaan. Samuel appears usually to have worked alone, but in 1 Sam. 19:20 he is associated with a group like this.

Gibeah, where this group was to be found, is Saul's home (10:26), which explains why those who knew Saul were able to observe his behavior. Mention of a **Philistine outpost** nearby would substantiate the view that Saul had ambitions to get rid of the Philistines.

§9 The Coronation and Confirmation of Saul (1 Sam. 10:9–11:15)

10:9–16 / The exact significance of the change in **Saul's heart** is not clear. The mention of the fulfillment of the signs may indicate that he was now convinced about his commission, although verse 16 could cast doubt on this. Only the third of Samuel's three signs is described in detail. Saul did meet the prophets and did temporarily **join in their prophesying,** an experience as unexpected to those who saw as it was to Saul. It gained proverbial significance as Saul became well known and possibly acted as a confirmation when Saul emerged as the finalist in the coronation lottery (10:20–21). Saul's reaction when this spiritual encounter was over was to go to the **high place,** presumably the shrine nearest to his home. Whether this was to worship or to come to terms with whatever change he felt in himself is not clear, but Saul was aware of God's involvement in all that was happening to him.

The encounter with Saul's uncle is refreshingly normal. The uncle's request that Saul should expand on Samuel's words may reflect a natural desire to hear more of an encounter with a famous leader; Samuel is well known to Saul's uncle. However, his uncle's question may indicate an apparent change in Saul that implied something more had occurred than a discussion about donkeys. In either case Saul's refusal to elaborate is a sign that he has not yet come to terms with his potential new status of **kingship.** The Hebrew word *melek* ("king") has not so far been used in the discussions between Saul and Samuel (cf. comments on **prophets** under additional note for 10:5–6). Perhaps Saul's encounter with the prophets had given him new insight into what lay ahead.

10:17–25 / The original request for a king had come from the tribal leaders, but it was appropriate that the whole of Israel be involved now that the decision was to be carried out. A national assembly was called at **Mizpah.** It is not clear how much of what Samuel says to the people is part of **what the LORD, the God of Israel, says.** It includes verse 18, but verse 19 could be from God or it could be the addition of Samuel's perspective. It is implied that Israel's rejection of God as the one **who saves,** in favor of a king who may or may not save (10:27), will have dire consequences. But the decision to allow a king had been made and had not been rescinded.

Under those circumstances it was important that the best man be found. Samuel could have announced the choice of Saul, but such a significant change in Israel's leadership structure had to be seen by all as being instituted by God. We cannot be sure of how the lottery took place; the selection of Saul when he was not present creates difficulties. But the indication of God's choice through the drawing of lots is fairly common throughout Scripture with various, sometimes now obscure, methods being used. In this instance the process begins with the possibility that any one of the Israelites could have been chosen and thus again argues against the concept of a natural aristocracy. The king is appointed from among the people and, whatever powers he might be assigned, he remains one of them.

Gradually, through the choice of tribe, then clan, then family, the lot fell on Saul. Then, with a touch of humor the writers tell us that Saul had **hidden himself among the baggage.** Saul's changed character had not yet increased his self-confidence. Saul's experience of Samuel's clairvoyant skills might have led him to realize that hiding was useless, but the point is that God's choice, once made, could not be set aside by running away. Saul is brought out, and his exceptional height is seen as a confirmation of God's choice. Deliberate irony may be intended, given the later account when, in the choice of David, God makes clear that he is not influenced by outward appearances.

The people now officially recognize Saul as king. Samuel knew that if this was to become more than the recognition of another charismatic judge, then some kind of written affirmation was needed. He explained to the people what was entailed, wrote down the regulations, and placed this royal protocol **before the LORD**—that is, presumably, at the shrine where the ark of God was kept. This follows what was known of procedure in royal appointments in surrounding nations.

10:26–27 / There was no precedent for what should happen next, and Saul, like everybody else, went back home.

The ceremony, as such ceremonies are apt to do, had greatly moved and challenged a number of people. Several **whose hearts God had touched** accompanied Saul, forming a unit of crack troops that could provide the basis for any military call-up. The main function of the king at this stage was viewed as military commander, a fact confirmed by the words of those who were not convinced: **How can this fellow save us?** Their refusal to bring gifts highlights the fact that most of the people had brought gifts. The first act of royal taxation, even if it was voluntary, had taken place.

11:1–11 / The first opportunity for Saul to exercise his new calling and confirm his role as military leader was provided by the Ammonites, a tribal group who lived on the eastern side of the Jordan and who were involved in skirmishes with Israel over many years, particularly in the eastern section. These Ammonites were so confident of their ability to defeat the citizens of **Jabesh Gilead** that they placed unacceptable and cruel conditions even on a negotiated surrender. The first thought was surrender; even with the terrible cost involved surrender remained an option. The response of the people of Gibeah was to weep, presumably because they assumed that surrender was inevitable, and their response shows how disheartened, despondent, and uncoordinated the Israelite community was. If Saul's kingship was widely known about, any relevance that it might have had not yet dawned on the people. Saul had not set up anything that could be seen as a court. He worked in the fields as he always had done.

Saul's anger and subsequent action when he did hear what had happened is attributed to the influence of the powerful **Spirit of God.** The significant part of Saul's action was finding a way of causing the Israelites to act in concert. He indicates that he and Samuel are working together, making sure that everyone understands that his action has spiritual backing. He also deliberately parallels the events of Judges 20 to frighten the people into coming together to help their fellow Israelites. The defeat of the Ammonites was an automatic corollary of the national cooperation that followed his action. Saul was able to assure the people of Jabesh Gilead that they would be delivered, his confidence presumably based on God but also on his now superior forces. That confidence was well-founded, and the Ammonites in that area were routed. Verse 11 indicates that Saul was beginning to think about tactics. This was a well-planned surprise attack, taking place at night with properly distributed forces.

11:12–13 / The ability to deal effectively with local guerrilla attacks was something that Israel had not experienced for some while. Thus their response in extolling Saul and castigating those who had refused to acknowledge Saul is unsurprising, if a little exaggerated given that this was a skirmish. Saul's refusal to respond to the invitation to get rid of those who had not recognized him illustrates his statesmanship. It was a time for graciousness, not revenge. He publicly ascribes the victory to God. Within this chapter the writers show Saul as the right man for the job, capable of acting as God's representative. There is no indication of Saul's later character problems.

11:14–15 / After he had proved himself in battle, it was appropriate that Saul's reign should be reaffirmed. This multistage appointment, beginning with a private anointing that was followed by public affirmation, then by proof that the appointee was capable of carrying out the task, and finally by ceremonial reaffirmation, is not out of line with other such appointments. For kings to be appointed in Israel, divine calling and public recognition were both important for the role to be effectively carried out. In this instance the reaffirmation took place with a great ceremonial when fellowship offerings were brought. This included the full recognition of God. The sacrifice was presented to him, part of it was burned, and in some sense God was seen as sharing in the fellowship meal. It also meant the full involvement of the people in eating that part of the sacrificial animal that was not burned. This ceremony uniting the nation under one leader took place at Gilgal, where Joshua first camped in the land.

Additional Notes §9

10:17 / Although we cannot be sure of the exact location, **Mizpah**, a few miles north of Jerusalem, was a common site for such assemblies (Judg. 20:1; 21:1, 5, 8; 1 Sam. 7:5). It was easily accessible from a range of areas and perhaps contained a large site with good acoustics.

10:20–21 / Josh. 7:14–18 and 1 Sam. 14:38–42 describe similar processes of choosing by lot. The priestly ephod, a metal object carried by priests and distinct from the garment of the same name, was sometimes used to discern God's views (Judg. 17:5; 1 Sam. 23:9; Hos. 3:4), as was the Urim and the Thummim (Exod. 28:30; 1 Sam. 28:6). The disciples drew lots to select a replacement for Judas within the Twelve (Acts 1:26).

Matri, the clan to which Saul belonged, is not mentioned among Saul's forebears in 9:1 and is unknown outside of this verse.

10:25 / The regulations concerning kingship are referred to in Deut. 17:14–20. Whether or not that section is written in response to the perceived failure of later kings, there is no reason to doubt the validity of the requirements.

10:27 / The opponents to Saul are not presented as a legitimate opposition group but as **troublemakers,** or sons of Belial (Hb. *benê bᵉlîyᶜal*). The writers indicate that although the monarchy may, as Samuel suggests (v. 19), be a rejection of God, opposition to the monarch is not automatically sanctioned. The king is God's choice, so to reject the king is to reject God. This could be further evidence for the combining of two sources with opposing views about kingship, but a deliberate ambiguity is still possible.

11:1–2 / Some kind of positive relationship developed later between Nahash and David (2 Sam. 10:2), but there is no alliance at this time.

Putting out the right eyes of those they conquered was a well-known tactic of the Ammonites (for details see Klein, *1 Samuel,* pp. 102–3). Nahash's motivation is the desire to shame, to **bring disgrace,** on the nation of Israel. This desire to shame appears to have been inherited by Nahash's son Hanun (2 Sam. 10).

11:8 / **Bezek** was probably a few miles from Jabesh Gilead, although on the other side of the Jordan. It was a well-chosen staging post for this kind of action, far enough away to avoid notice but near enough to use as a first base for attack.

11:12–13 / The Israelite army that was so soundly beaten by the Philistines when the ark was captured (ch. 4) appears to have been fairly large and united. The failure of that army may have led to the lack of coordination later. It may also be that the superstitious fear of attacking Israel arising out of the aftermath of the capture of the ark had led to a complacency on Israel's part, and thus any troops were unprepared for further fighting. By this time any fear would have faded, particularly among the less affected Ammonites.

11:14–15 / Like Saul's, David's appointment was multistaged. He was anointed (ch. 16) well before he became king. He was appointed king over Judah by the people (2 Sam. 2) seven years before the people of the northern tribes confirmed his appointment (2 Sam. 5). God's final reaffirmation of his appointment seems to come even later than that (2 Sam. 5:12; 7). The time elapsed between Samuel's command to Saul that he meet him at Gilgal (10:8) and the ceremony described here is not clear, nor can we be sure how this chapter fits with that request and its described fulfillment in 13:7–15. It is likely that various sources are combined into a single account.

§10 Samuel Addresses the People (1 Sam. 12:1–25)

Using speeches like this one of Samuel's to indicate important staging points, such as the end of the age of the judges, is common in the so-called Deuteronomic History. There are particular parallels here with the way in which Moses hands over power to Joshua and with Joshua's final speech (Deut. 31; Josh. 23).

This speech is included because it makes points of which the reader is expected to take note. Whether it records Samuel's words or is a later composition does not affect that fact. However, its combination of passion and ambiguity fits with Samuel's position.

12:1–2 / Samuel realized that the appointment of Saul meant a fundamental change in his own position. He had been acting as the primary national **leader,** carrying out a mixture of priestly and prophetic duties while functioning as a ruling judge. Now, although his priestly and prophetic roles will not cease and he can remain as a spiritual adviser, decisions about national policy are no longer his. The ceremony reaffirming Saul's position gives him a chance to clarify his own situation. As their leader, he had responded to their request and **set a king over** them. He now steps down, but in doing so he makes a final speech of justification, challenge, and encouragement. The mention of his age is possibly a little defensive, providing a reason why he can no longer carry out the task. The mention of his **sons** perhaps recalls the Israelites' problems with the behavior of his sons (8:4–5), but if this is intentional it is deliberately inexplicit.

12:3–5 / It was important to Samuel that the people publicly acknowledge his honesty and integrity. There must be no question that he had abused his office, no lingering doubt that his stepping down was punishment for misdoing. The memory of the hard message that he, as a child, had been given concerning

Eli must have remained with him. He had made certain that he had never taken advantage of his position and power. There had been no unjustified payments, no prophecies biased toward the wealthy, no hypocrisy, and no victimization.

The people concurred with this assessment. Samuel had in no way **cheated or oppressed.** Whatever doubts there might have been about the behavior of Samuel's sons, these did not impinge on the people's assessment of Samuel. The Israelites were willing to take an oath before God concerning Samuel's integrity. It may be that the writers deliberately show that Samuel had not been involved in the kind of oppressive behavior that he had warned them might result from the appointment of a king (8:11–18), a particularly significant point when Saul's reign proves to be unsuccessful. If Samuel is to be credible as the one who acts in the appointment of David, the reader must be sure of Samuel's integrity.

12:6–11 / Having clarified that point, Samuel moves on to a history lesson. The concept of historical continuity was important to all the OT writers, and it was common in this kind of speech to review previous events and actions. The purpose of this was to remind the current generation of the unchanging power of God and to challenge them to behavior that was appropriate to a people who followed this God. Their knowledge of what God had done in the past could inspire them to future faith and action.

The Lord, that is, Yahweh, their God, had **appointed Moses and Aaron** to lead them **out of Egypt.** We have seen (4:8; 6:6) that the knowledge of this had a significant impact on the Philistines, and part of the self-awareness of the Israelites was that they were a people whose God was a redeemer, powerful across the territory of other peoples and gods. Samuel wants to make sure that they understand what this God is like, that they remember what he has done for them. Samuel wants to **confront** them **with evidence before the LORD.** They ignore the content of this speech at their peril.

Verse 8 repeats the content of verse 6 and brings it up to date. They are **in this place** because of the Lord. Verses 9 and 10 summarize the story of Judges. This summary was announced as a description of God's **righteous acts,** but it emerges more as an analysis of the people's sin. Almost immediately on entering the land, they began to leave God out of the picture; therefore they were overrun by a series of enemies, including **Sisera, Hazor, the Philistines and the king of Moab.** They then turned to God, who sent a series of deliverers, including Gideon, described here by his alternative name of **Jerub-Baal, Barak,** who was the official military leader although Deborah took precedence at that time, **Jephthah and Samuel.** The point being made, both to the original listeners and to future readers, is that the system worked. Their failure to deal consistently with threats from outside was related to their constant turning away from God. The implication is that a change in leadership structures is not the answer to their problems.

The language in this section echoes Deuteronomy and the concerns for covenant loyalty that were so important to the Deuteronomist. The historical summary is a well-known element of covenant-treaty documents, as are the references to witnesses and to the keeping and failing to keep the requirements made within the treaty. All these provide further indications of covenant thinking.

12:12–15 / Samuel spells out the fact that kingship will provide no lasting solution. In the latest incident **Nahash** had been the aggressor, but rather than turning to God Israel turned to **a king.** Samuel's personal frustration is apparent. He hates the decision that has been made and is torn between the desire to express his criticism and yet to encourage the people to go on in the right way. They have a king; he is standing in front of them, given to them by **the LORD.** However, the key factor is, as it has always been, whether or not they **fear the LORD and serve and obey him and do not rebel against his commands.** This requirement applies equally to the people and to **the king who reigns over** them. Allegiance to God will bring security, rebellion will bring disaster in accordance with the benefits and punishments (blessings and curses) set out in the covenant documents. Differences in their own power structures (instituting a monarchy) do not change where the real power lies (with God).

12:16–19 / Samuel's frustration boils over. In order to convince the people that the power is God's and, although the text does not make this explicit, perhaps wanting people to remember that Samuel himself had had a significant part in the power play at a human level, he calls upon God to send a thunderstorm. Throughout history, dramatic weather conditions have had strong impact on people, and this was no exception. As a result of the storm, a particularly unusual occurrence at that time of year when the wheat was being harvested, the people were overawed. Presumably they recognized the storm as a sign of God's displeasure. Their **awe of the LORD and of Samuel** perhaps hints at mixed motives in Samuel. Their recognition that their request for a king had been influenced by a wrong understanding of God could have easily led to a revoking of the new system. But Samuel was well aware that, whatever fault there may have been in the original request, the way forward did now lie with kingship. In itself it did not conflict with and could, properly exercised, enhance the kingly rule of God. The ambiguity of Samuel's position is very well expressed within this speech.

12:20–25 / If verse 19 is meant to indicate that the Lord was viewed as particularly Samuel's God, then these verses speak strongly against that view. They all are chosen by God. Whatever **evil** they have done, the important thing is to wholeheartedly **serve the LORD** from this point on. They have not yet reached the situation where God is about to **reject his people**, and they are his people. The language again closely reflects that of Deuteronomy (e.g., Deut. 6:2, 5; 7:7; 10:12, 21; 11:16; 31:6). The point is that they must remember all that is implied in being God's people.

And Samuel, though opting out of the government of the nation and having made his displeasure with their decision clear, is not about to desert them. His roles of praying and teaching will remain. All the necessary information is there for them. If they or their king fail to follow up on that information they will be **swept away**, but it will not be Samuel's fault. He has done all in his power to point them to God and to inform them of God's truth.

Additional Notes §10

12:2 / Caird ("1 and 2 Samuel," 2:941) argues that the reference to the sons indicates that the writers were unaware of the earlier source relating their misdemeanors.

12:6–8 / It was commonly accepted throughout the ancient Near East that gods had power in their own territory that was weakened into nonexistence the farther their followers traveled from that territory. Thus groups who successfully invaded other territories were seen as having particularly powerful gods. This concept is recognized in the OT but is not seen as being relevant to the Lord, whose power is pictured as universal. However, it is probable that many ordinary people accepted the common worldview and were thus easily influenced to pay allegiance to local gods. Verse 6 clarifies that Samuel refers to the God of their ancestors; v. 8 begins the historical survey proper. The repetition may indicate two sources, but we need not assume that it does so.

12:9–10 / Several of the phrases used in this section are reminiscent of the language used in Judges and indicate an awareness of that written record. (e.g., **sold them into the hands of,** Judg. 3:8; 4:2; 10:7 and **cried out to the LORD,** Judg. 3:9; 4:3; 10:10).

12:11 / Several early sources have Samson, rather than **Samuel,** in this verse. Samson would fit comfortably in this list, and the names are similar enough for a mistake to be made. However, in this context it is feasible that Samuel would make a deliberate change from the expected list to emphasize that God still continued to intervene on behalf of the people, as the events at Mizpah showed (ch. 7). The Hb. has Bedan *(bᵉdān)*, a name unknown elsewhere, instead of **Barak.** However, the reference to Barak ties in with the mention of Sisera in v. 9. Bedan may therefore be an alternative name for the same person rather than an indication of a different tradition.

12:12 / Other aggressors than Nahash, primarily the Philistines, were in mind when the elders asked for a king, but the Ammonites, as the most recent problem, were at the forefront of everybody's mind. Klein concludes (*1 Samuel,* pp. 112–13) that this reference to the threat from Nahash led to a sinful request for a king, but his conclusion conflicts with the record in ch. 11 and seems unnecessary.

§11 Saul's Initial Problems (1 Sam. 13:1–22)

The relationship between chapters 10 and 11 and what is described in chapters 13 through 15 is obscure. First Samuel 13:8 appears to indicate that these events are related to Samuel's call to Saul to meet him at Gilgal (10:8). But if this is seen as an imminent appointment, it is hard to connect it with the events in the second half of chapter 10, the battle and further ceremony described in chapter 11, or the military activity found in 13:1–7a. The problem is solved if there was a second or a regular appointment to meet Samuel after waiting seven days.

Another solution is to see 10:8 as being misplaced at Samuel's first encounter with Saul and originally connected with a later meeting. It could also be that 10:8 was intended to imply that any time Saul sent to say he needed Samuel's help to discover God's will, Samuel would come to him at Gilgal within seven days. In any event, 13:1 is the start of a summarizing account of Saul's reign—far longer than, but nevertheless similar to, other such accounts found in 1 and 2 Kings.

13:1 / It is impossible to know what were the original figures. The textual evidence is mixed, with the Hebrew omitting both the "thirty" referring to Saul's age and the "forty," leaving Saul's reign at just two years, which is not correct. It may be that at some stage the verse was deliberately reformatted to match the introductions to other reigns (cf. 2 Kgs. 8:16; 12:1) and the original figures were lost or mixed up. It is possible that this verse originally indicated that it was two years between the reaffirmation ceremony at Gilgal and the events described in this chapter. This would allow enough time for the development of the standing army. What is clear is that this verse stands as an introduction to a section discussing the reign of Saul before David came into the picture.

13:2–4 / The situation has significantly progressed from that pictured in chapters 10 and 11. Saul's kingship gives him an accepted right to organize a military call-up. There is at least the beginnings of a standing army and perhaps of a court. The standing army was divided into two, and the young Jonathan accompanied and probably led the smaller unit. (Jonathan is mentioned without any introduction—not until verse 16 do we learn he is Saul's son.) Fortified by the success against the Ammonites, Jonathan took action against the Philistine outpost near Saul's family home at Gibeah. **The Philistines heard about it** understates the Philistine reaction of outraged hostility: that they would respond fiercely was inevitable. There is no explicit criticism of Jonathan's action, but his action contrasts with Saul's careful planning (ch. 11). The portrait of Jonathan as an activist rather than a strategist—somewhat hot-headed and naïve but good-hearted—ties in with what we see of him in later chapters.

The call-up message was sent throughout the land, either because Saul wanted to capitalize on Jonathan's victory or because there was no way of avoiding a major encounter with the Philistines and a united response was necessary. Saul's choice of **Gilgal** as the rallying point gave him the opportunity to send for Samuel to pray and bring sacrifices as he had promised (10:8). Gilgal was the place of his coronation and the place from which Joshua launched his campaign (Josh. 4:19) and was a good choice to boost Saul's and the people's morale.

13:5–7 / The extent of the Philistine resources is emphasized. This battle would involve something far bigger for the Israelites than the small-scale guerrilla attacks where they had had successful results. The Philistine decision to gather their army at Saul's base at Micmash (vv. 2, 5) displays arrogant confidence. Bringing their chariots is something of an irrelevance from a military perspective—chariots, like modern tanks, are not at their best in mountain country—but it could have given them an edge psychologically.

Some of Saul's makeshift army fled across the river Jordan and many others kept in safe places outside the camp, possibly intending to involve themselves in small side attacks. It is significant that some brave, if fearful, soldiers remained with Saul as he waited for Samuel. Saul is thus far depicted as doing everything that he should. He turns to the Lord before taking action, and he waits with what seems to be quiet confidence for Samuel's promised arrival within seven days.

13:8–12 / The text gives no reason for Samuel's failure to appear. But it was inevitable that Saul's growing confidence received a blow. He had held the troops together by his assurance that Samuel would arrive. He did not have the faith to depend on the promise of God's presence with him (10:7), confirmed by his encounter with the ecstatic prophets. He could not properly inspire his forces without further reassurance from Samuel. When this reassurance was not forthcoming and the troops began to disperse, he was faced with a dilemma. Apparently motivated by a desire to honor God before the battle, Saul **felt compelled** to offer the sacrifice himself and had no compunction, when Samuel arrived belatedly, about telling him what had happened. However, his decision was to prove disastrous for Saul.

13:13–14 / There is no question of the kingship being taken away from Saul at this stage. However, Samuel informs him that his behavior means that he will never be able to found a dynasty. Samuel's response may have had its root in his keen memories of the attempt of earlier military leaders to manipulate God by using the ark as a kind of good-luck charm. Saul's action could be seen as following a similar pattern and making the same theological error. God's presence and God's blessing could not be guaranteed simply by the use of cultic ritual, particularly not when it is wrongly applied by one who was not a priest. God remained the true king, and absolute obedience to him was essential for any lasting kingdom in Israel.

So far, apart from the brief reference to Saul's family in 9:20, there has been no indication that a dynasty was ever in view. It is possible, even probable, that Saul had pondered such a prospect. But Samuel's raising the possibility and then taking it away must have disturbed the king, who still had a job to do. The prospect of an appointed though unknown successor would have only added to Saul's problems. The tortured character that we see in later chapters perhaps owes something to this encounter with Samuel.

13:15–22 / The text does not specify whether Samuel made the proper offerings and gave his blessing to the Israelite forces. But the brief, bleak statement that **Samuel left Gilgal** symbolically expresses a turning point in the relationship between Samuel and Saul. There is no real closeness after this point.

What happened next sets the scene for the events of chapter 14. The dramatic encounter between two armies never took place, but Saul's small band of loyal troops took part in ongoing skirmishes with the larger and far better equipped Philistine forces. These forces were free to send **raiding parties** in every direction except that in which Saul's troops lay. The lack of an immediate surrender or a Philistine takeover speaks well for Saul's statesmanship and military prowess.

The insert explaining the dearth in Israel of blacksmiths capable of making metal tools and the exorbitant prices charged for supplying expertise is realistic. Only leaders could afford properly made metal weapons, a usual circumstance at this point in history. Some countries had, like Philistia, developed the technology to work well with iron. They were naturally reluctant to share their skills with potential enemies. However, the lack of blacksmiths had not been a barrier to Saul's earlier success, and therefore mention of this fact implies a weakening in Saul's divine empowerment.

Additional Notes §11

13:3 / As a Philistine outpost at Gibeah has already been mentioned (10:5), it is sometimes suggested that Geba is intended to represent Gibeah. Micmash was about 2 miles from Geba, which was 3 to 4 miles from Gibeah. However, the terrain around Geba and Micmash is rugged and includes steep ravines, making it likely that forces could see but not easily reach one another (cf. vv. 16–18). There would be plenty of hiding places among the rocks, and seeking out these hiding places does not imply desertion.

The call to **let the Hebrews hear** is unusual because Israelites did not generally refer to themselves as Hebrews. It may refer to a call made by the Philistines, or it may be that Saul encouraged non-Israelite troops to join in. If this is so, it is these outsiders who then flee back across the river (v. 7).

13:5–7 / The waiting before the fighting began would not be unusual. If the intention was a determinative encounter between armies, then within limits the starting point could often be delayed until both were ready.

Beth Aven is an alternative name for Bethel.

13:13–14 / David, when he decided to move the ark (2 Sam. 6), appears to have been close to the same temptation to manipulate

God's blessing. It is not obvious what Saul's sin was or why it was considered so much more serious than the various sins that David committed. The writers seem more concerned that readers understand that Saul was rejected than to explain the reason. The attempt to extend his power to include a priestly role as well as a military one might have encouraged later kings to add priestly power to their royal authority, and that could not be tolerated. Or his sin could be disobedience, in that he did not wait for Samuel as he had been told, or that he lost confidence that God was with him and failed to act in the assurance of the Spirit he had been given.

§12 Jonathan's Success (1 Sam. 13:23–14:23)

13:23–14:1 / The way in which chapter 14 is structured indicates that it is a written record of what was originally an oral story, perhaps one that was told around the campfire to young soldiers. These two verses set up the theme of the story, and then we have background information provided before the drama is revealed.

As chapter 13 indicated, the Philistines had sent out detachments to raid the countryside and in doing so left outposts to guard various passes. Jonathan, seeing an opportunity, seizes it. Waiting until the proper channels of communication had been used did not suit Jonathan's activist nature, and therefore Saul was not told. Saul's having not been informed is significant for the unfolding story.

14:2–5 / Saul was still based near his home at Gibeah with the **six hundred** troops who had remained loyal when Saul's defeat of the Ammonites was not repeated with the Philistines. One of the six hundred was Ahijah, Eli's great-grandson, who comes into the picture in verse 18. This fits the pattern of announcing characters prior to their involvement, but this complex introduction goes beyond what is usually considered necessary. We learn that Ahijah was **wearing an ephod,** that is, he was still functioning as a priest. The heavy judgment on Eli's family (1 Sam. 2:30–33) had not meant destruction. Human interpretation of God's intentions may go far beyond what God himself has envisaged. Eli's descendant was still able to function as a priest, and the thought is left that Saul's son could also have a future role in spite of Samuel's prophetic words (13:14).

Again the text says Jonathan's departure had remained unnoticed. The mention of the cliffs overlooking the path that Jonathan would have to travel reinforces the hazards of his venture, one that only the brave or the foolhardy would attempt. Any soldiers from the Philistine and the Israelite camps who happened to be looking would have been able to watch his progress. Perhaps the Philistine troops were too confident and the Israelite troops too disorganized for this to happen.

14:6–14 / The description of the actions of Jonathan and his armor-bearer draws the reader into the drama. The enthusiasm of both men and their confidence in God call to mind the young David when he was faced with an apparently impossible challenge. Jonathan's assured assumption that if God has decided to save then he can do it **by many or by few,** with "few" meaning the two of them, contrasts with Saul's reluctance to take his troops forward from Gilgal without Samuel's blessing. Even the request for a sign is loaded. The question is not whether they should or should not fight, but whether they should fight at the top of the cliffs or the bottom.

Both sides display supreme arrogance. The Philistines were so confident that they could defeat any Israelite in hand-to-hand combat that they allowed the two fighters to climb the cliff. They knew that there were Hebrews in the mountains, but none of them usually dared show themselves. Here was a chance for a fight.

Climbing the cliff required **hands and feet,** a detail that reminds readers that any of the weapons Jonathan might have carried could not be used. Thus anyone from above could have easily finished off Jonathan and his armor-bearer. But they ignored the risk, and the Philistines did not acknowledge that a risk was being taken. Jonathan's confidence in God, reemphasized in verse 12, is fully repaid: the cliff-top opponents and about **twenty** of their comrades in the surrounding area were killed. The description of Jonathan's victories, and his ascribing his success to God's help, may lead the reader to wonder whether Saul might be succeeded by his son after all.

14:15–19 / As news of these events spread, there were dramatic effects in both camps. The Philistine outposts became aware of their vulnerability and almost certainly headed back to their base, causing panic there. According to verse 15, **the ground shook,** adding to the panic. The writers state that God was involved.

Saul's reaction to the observable chaos in the Philistine ranks was twofold. First he carried out a head count, which revealed that Jonathan and his armor-bearer were missing. Then he sent for Ahijah and the ark to engage in some kind of ritual,

presumably to find out what he should do. The contrast between
Jonathan's confidence that God was on his side and his leaping
immediately into action and Saul's unconfident dithering is unmistakable. Using Ahijah's priestly skills, rather than sending for
Samuel, may reflect the fact that the former was present in the
camp; or it may indicate a deliberate avoiding of Samuel on
Saul's part. However, the need for action meant that Saul could
no longer delay, and the future-predicting ritual was aborted.

14:20–23 / When the battle was joined the success was
immediate and extensive. The Philistines were out of control.
Hebrews in their camp, whether prisoners of war or turncoats,
returned to the Israelite forces, and the small units that had cow-
ered in the hills came out into the open. The Philistines were **on
the run.** The **battle moved on beyond Beth Aven,** showing that a
significant amount of territory was recovered from Philistine
control and that the war was not over.

The victory was assigned to **the LORD** and his saving
power, a statement that may be general theologizing. Or the
writers may be pointing out that in the original action of Jonathan and in the ensuing confusion, the results were not those of
human power or skill, particularly not of Saul.

Additional Notes §12

14:1 / The armor-bearer acted as a squire, accompanying and
supporting his mentor and receiving training in warfare in exchange
for his services. The number of references to him indicate that he had
more significance than a golfer's caddy or a soldier assigned as a personal servant to a senior officer.

14:2 / The site of **Migron** is unknown. It is often suggested
that a slight alteration of the letters be made, which would then read
"on the threshing floor" (*bemo goren* as opposed to *bemigrôn*). Perhaps
Saul was holding some kind of justice court, for both trees and threshing floors have been mentioned in that context (e.g., Judg. 4:5; 1 Kgs.
22:10).

14:16 / It would be easier to see what was going on from Geba
than it would from **Gibeah,** and it is possible that the names have been
confused at this point.

14:17 / The literary structure of this chapter is complex, and the text as we have it involves some kind of compilation from different sources. However, some of the repetition in the narrative, as the reiteration that Jonathan's absence had not been noted (vv. 2–3, 17), is integral to this kind of storytelling and should not be seen as evidence of different sources.

14:18 / This reference to the **ark** is obscure. There is no other evidence for the ark being removed from Kiriath Jearim by Saul, and the order for the priest to **withdraw** his **hand,** implying some kind of ritual involving touching the ark, is also unclear. The LXX refers to bringing the ephod, which was at that time worn (by the priest) before the Israelites, and 23:9 and 30:7 use the same phraseology when the priest is called upon to bring the ephod. The ephod used to determine God's plans was different from the priestly garment. Translating "ephod" instead of "ark" makes sense of the reference to the hand being withdrawn, as the priest manipulated the sections of the ephod.

14:21–22 / The distinction between **Hebrews** and **Israelites** may again indicate that the Hebrews were outsiders brought in to support the Israelite army (cf. additional note on 13:3).

Although there is nothing contradictory between this section and the preceding verses, it does not follow smoothly. It may be that the writers gathered a range of stories concerning Saul and Jonathan to illustrate their contrasting characters and behavior, and then verses 47–52 may correct any imbalance in the earlier stories. The rest of chapter 14 to verse 46 describes two only partially interrelated accounts, a reflection on the sort of demands God makes and how God's actions should be understood. The reference to Ahijah as Eli's descendant at the beginning of the chapter (v. 3) prefaces this discussion.

14:24–30 / The first incident is Jonathan's unwitting breaking of an oath instituted by his father. The reference to the **distress** of the army indicates the writers' low opinion about the value of this oath, but the words of Jonathan illustrate how foolish it was. Saul again attempts to ensure that God is behind their action, but his understanding of what God requires (and presumably therefore of who God is) is limited. His use of the oath suggests that he thought that God could be bribed. However, Saul retains some charisma. Whether out of personal loyalty or out of superstitious fear, his troops, in spite of the difficulties that his oath will cause on a day of demanding military activity, follow the rigid fasting that Saul imposed upon them. Jonathan, who was not with the army when Saul's restrictions were imposed, enjoys what he probably saw as God-given refreshment. When he is informed of Saul's oath he feels no fear or guilt—he simply does not understand how his father could have been so misguided. Without the physical restrictions caused by the oath, they might have been able to drive the Philistines even farther back. God would have been able to do more for them, not less.

14:31–35 / Before there is any further comment on this incident, we learn that another breach of the law had taken place. The exhausted and hungry army, when they captured

Philistine animals, did not wait for proper ritual slaughter but ate meat with the blood still in it. There is no reference to Saul's oath; the problem is a straightforward breaking of the prohibition on eating blood (Lev. 3:17).

There were ways of dealing with this kind of sin. In this instance, Saul ensures that proper procedure is followed for future slaughtering. A primitive altar is set up on the battlefield. Animals, presumably plundered from the Philistines, are brought and sacrificed to the Lord. The statement in verse 35 that **it was the first time** Saul **had done this** is related to Saul's offering a burnt offering (ch. 13). But the relevance of this statement is obscure, particularly as the writers do not criticize Saul's action.

14:36–46 / Verse 36 may follow directly from verse 30, but even then the connection is not smooth. Saul, presumably encouraged by the progress that has been made, and in contrast to his previous delaying tactics, wants to press his advantage and engage in a night raid. The troops are willing, but this time the priest introduces a delay. Night fighting was unusual, and therefore seeking a special word from God is, in his mind, called for. But God does not provide that word. According to Saul, the lack of a reply must mean some sin had caused God's displeasure.

The account now links to Jonathan and the honey. Saul swears another oath, and again there is a hint that this is foolish. Even if it is Jonathan who has committed this supposed sin, he must die. The soldiers, who know that Jonathan had inadvertently contravened Saul's previous oath, loyally say **not a word.** This time the casting of lots works perfectly, and Jonathan is eventually picked out. He is incredulous that he should have to suffer the death penalty for something so trivial. But Saul swears again and insists that Jonathan must die. Swearing an oath almost certainly involved invoking God's name, and it is possible that Saul is desperately trying to recover God's favor, even at the expense of his son's life.

The army, however, cannot tolerate Saul's actions any longer. They intervene with their own oath that Jonathan will not die. Their confidence stems from a conviction that God had blessed Jonathan's action and therefore could not require his death. Their will prevails, Jonathan is spared, and there is no immediate effect from all this foolish swearing.

This section recalls both Jephthah's foolish oath and the common-sense attitude of Manoah's wife when she contradicted her husband's view that their having seen the angel was bound to lead to death (Judg. 11; 13). Whether or not the authors intended that reminder, this passage challenges readers to consider whether cursing or oath taking are appropriate ways to discover God's plans. The writers leave no impression that God has no plans, is incapable of making those plans known, or cannot ensure that they be carried out. Rather, God alone will decide what is sinful and will deal with sinners. Any action carried out in response to a curse or an oath cannot be assumed to have God's backing.

With the delay resulting from Saul's decisions the initiative was lost and the Philistines were left to withdraw at their own pace. The brief comment shows Saul's loss of control.

14:47–52 / This section, probably from another document, provides a summary of Saul's reign and, with its concern for the ongoing development of the community, is usually seen as coming from a Deuteronomic perspective. It portrays Saul positively and may be included as a way of indicating that the specific incidents concerning Saul's kingship do not give a complete picture of his reign. David is an example of Saul's co-opting into royal service any **mighty or brave man. Merab and Michal,** Saul's daughters, and **Abner,** his field commander, are introduced. This technique of introducing characters before they play a significant part in the narrative is used also in 2 Samuel 9:1–5 (cf. 2 Sam. 16:1–4; 17:27–29).

Additional Notes §13

14:35 / This was the first field altar that Saul built, and his action is seen as positive. His desire is to do what God requires, even if his conclusions about that requirement are to be doubted. The law does restrict sacrificial activity to priests, but this regulation was not fully applied until the temple cultus was set up. This makes it difficult to see the primary problem in 13:13 being that Saul offered a sacrifice. In that instance an altar existed at Gilgal.

14:40–42 / The normal methods of drawing lots or of predicting the future gave a yes/no answer or distinguished between two alternatives, as between Saul and Jonathan in v. 42. It is not known what method might have been used to request more complex information or could leave a situation in which no answer was provided, as in v. 37.

14:45 / If an animal was sacrificed as a ransom for Jonathan, that is not specified. It is feasible that Saul had become jealous of Jonathan, suspecting that Jonathan might intend to mount a coup, and was trying to manipulate the situation to ensure Jonathan's death. However, there is no hint that the writers point toward this conclusion. In certain societies surrounding Israel, life was governed by oaths and curses of this kind. There was in general a much more relaxed attitude in Israel, where the power of God, rather than the words of a curse, counted (see M. J. Evans, " 'A Plague on Both Your Houses': Cursing and Blessing Reviewed," *VE* 24 [1994], pp. 77–89).

14:50–51 / The discrepancy with 1 Chron. 9:36, 39, where Ner is apparently Saul's grandfather rather than his uncle, has been noted (cf. additional note on 9:1).

§14 Saul Is Rejected (1 Sam. 15:1–35)

15:1–3 / Verse 1 recalls Samuel's previous influence in Saul's life. Whether there is discord between them or in spite of any criticism he may have made since, Samuel reminds Saul that he had been appointed **to anoint** Saul as king. Now Samuel has a further task from God for Saul to carry out. He is to be entrusted with the punitive destruction of the Amalekites in a holy war. The reason given for this severe treatment is the Amalekites' attacks on the vulnerable Israelites coming out of Egypt (Exod. 17:8; Num. 14:43; Deut. 25:17–18).

In this instance nothing, whether human, animal, or property, is to be spared. The *herem,* dedication to God of an enemy, is hard for modern readers to understand but would have made sense to the cultures of Saul's time. The instruction is clear and could not be mistaken as a call for a simple raid against Amalek. The destruction was less than total, because the Amalekites remained a problem to Israel during David's time. However, the leaders of a group could not be allowed to survive. As Baldwin puts it, "the incident is a reminder that it is a fearful thing to fall into the hands of the living God" (*1 and 2 Samuel,* p. 113).

15:4–6 / This commission perhaps was a final chance for Saul to show his allegiance to Yahweh, and Saul took it seriously. He assembled the army, worked out a plan, and began to put the plan into motion. Because this holy war involved explicit punishment, it was inappropriate to involve in the action those who did not deserve this punishment. The Kenites, allies of the Amalekites, had not taken part in the activity for which the Amalekites were being punished, and so it was inappropriate for them to be attacked. How Saul persuaded the Kenites to move without alerting the Amalekites the text does not say.

15:7–9 / The Amalekites fled and were killed without mercy as the Israelite army chased them south. However, the element of carrying out a specific punishment on God's behalf was forgotten. The troops, with Saul's connivance, saw this battle as another mission to extend their power and territory. Thus, anyone who got in their way and anything they did not want was destroyed, but anything useful or valuable was kept, including Agag the Amalekite king. Their action became not simple disobedience but a refusal to acknowledge God and his rights. The property that they kept for themselves should have been dedicated to God and destroyed. The offense is similar to that of Achan and his family (Josh. 7).

15:10–11 / Samuel was upset when he heard that Saul had **grieved** God with his disobedience because he knew that Saul had finally burned all his bridges. In spite of any tension between them, Samuel had a great sense of affiliation with and affection for Saul. He had been responsible for Saul's appointment, and he wanted Saul to do well. Therefore, Samuel had a sense of personal grief that Saul should have failed. Samuel's long and desperate prayers were probably related to the knowledge that he would have to tell Saul that he had reached the end of the line. Samuel probably remembered another night when he had waited to tell another servant of God, old Eli, that his behavior was unacceptable to God.

15:12–15 / Samuel did not shirk his task. The news that Saul had **set up a monument in his own honor** is recorded without comment, but at a point when the honor of God had been forgotten, Saul was concerned about his own status. So far, Saul has been presented as seeking to serve God but being wrong through limitations in his theological understanding. Now his concern was to maintain his own reputation before the people. It may be that as the defeat of the Amalekites would mainly benefit Judah, Saul left behind a monument to remind the Judeans that he had done good things for them. This could be seen as a refusal to recognize God as the primary cause of his success.

Saul may have gone to Gilgal because Samuel had given him the task and he went back to their old meeting point to await Samuel's arrival. By his greeting, **The LORD bless you! I have carried out the LORD's instructions,** Saul may show lack of comprehension about his task or may be deliberately attempting to deceive Samuel. However, his response to Samuel's question makes clear that he was aware that total destruction had been called for. But it also seems unlikely that he would try to deceive Samuel, given that the army, with all their spoils, are with him.

It may be that Saul's response is the beginning of the mental problems that tormented him later. With a delusionary mentality he convinced himself that what he had done must have been what God had asked him to do. Nonetheless, Saul is fully responsible for his actions. His growing instability is pictured as more the result of his disobedience than the cause. Samuel's question brings him back to reality, and he then attempts to spiritualize the disobedience by suggesting that the preserved animals were for sacrifice.

15:16–23 / The story is vividly and realistically told. Samuel has had enough of Saul's prevarication and wants to deliver his unpalatable message. Saul had started off as humble— not the kind of person likely to set up a self-congratulatory monument—but the LORD anointed him as king. Without God he would have had no kingly role, but he had acted as if his own benefit was more significant than God's will, as if amassing plunder was more important than obedience. Saul's protest may be a natural defensiveness, or it may show that he had convinced himself that what he would like to be true was true. The animals were going to be sacrificed—what more could God require? But keeping the best of what was devoted to God—that is, devoted to destruction—even for sacrifice cannot be defended. His emphasizing that the soldiers took the animals only brings out his failure to act as king.

Samuel's response comes in the form of an oracle that reflects the interest (ch. 14) in the difference between ritual and attitude. God cannot be treated as if he were the same as an idol to be appeased by a nice present. Obedience must be seen as more significant than trying to pacify God with sacrifices. Saul's behavior was as bad as blatant idolatry; he proves himself to be not "a man after God's own heart" (13:14). Saul is the cause of his own rejection.

15:24–33 / Saul returns to reality. He accepts his disobedience, acknowledges that this had been conscious and deliberate, and admits the reason. He had been more concerned about what the people might think than what God might think. However, he has failed to grasp the permanent significance of his action and still hopes for forgiveness. But Samuel, concerned that his return with Saul may be seen as affirmation of Saul's position, repeats the words of his oracle. Saul has **rejected the word of the**

LORD and thus the Lord **has rejected** him **as king.** There can be no going back from this.

Saul's further attempt to hold on to Samuel only brings him more grief, the reminder that another will replace him. The description of God as **the Glory of Israel** is found elsewhere only in Micah 1:15. Using the language of Numbers 23:19, it not only stresses the transcendence of God and the vast difference between God and human beings, but also highlights Saul's arrogance in thinking he can manipulate this God.

Saul's final response adds to the pathos of the account. He pleads with Samuel to help him save face before the elders. There is no question of affirming Saul, just standing by him one more time, allowing him to **worship the LORD your God**—and the use of "your" is probably intentional. Samuel agrees to this request, but he makes sure that the people recognize the significance of obedience to God and his own lack of complicity in Saul's actions by putting the Amalekite king to death himself.

15:34–35 / The poignancy of the account continues with the statement that Saul and Samuel went their separate ways. This was the last time, apart from Saul's desperate descent into necromancy (1 Sam. 28), that they were to meet. But Samuel's recognition of the hard truth of God's judgment on Saul did not stop his mourning for lost potential and lost opportunities. As in verse 10, Samuel's personal grief for his protégé is set alongside God's grief that he had made Saul king. This dual mention of grief forms an *inclusio* for this section. God's grief is not that he had allowed a king to be appointed, but that that king had been Saul. The reader is left to meditate on how the God who does not change could nevertheless alter his opinion about Saul.

Additional Notes §14

It is impossible to tell how much time elapsed between the events of chs. 13 and 14 and ch. 15. The incidents are not directly related, but there is a continuing interest in obedience and disobedience, with an underlying reflection on why some apparent sins can be overlooked or atoned for and others cannot. D. Gunn has a full discussion of this issue (*The Fate of King Saul: An Analysis of a Biblical Story* [JSOTSup 14; Sheffield: Sheffield Academic Press, 1980], pp. 44–56, 123–31) that is worth following up.

15:2 / The language is parallel to that in Deut. 25:17, and this chapter is therefore often seen as being particularly influenced by Deuteronomistic thinking.

15:4 / Saul's taking more than two hundred thousand soldiers and David only four hundred (30:10) may mean that the numbers have been exaggerated here or that "thousand" is better translated "group" (cf. Klein, *1 Samuel*, p. 147). But it could indicate Saul's success in organizing and inspiring a national army.

15:5 / The Amalekites were primarily a nomadic tribe and had no major central city, so the reference to the city is unusual. It probably indicates the area that was the center of Amalekite activity.

15:10 / The reality and the cost of God's involvement with his people is often brought out by speaking in human terms of God's emotions, such as his grief. This technique, known as *anthropopathism*, is similar to *anthropomorphism*, which speaks of God having a human form (e.g., with hands or a face).

15:12 / Absalom's monument was set up as a memorial because he had no sons. There is no similar reason for Saul's action.

15:22 / Samuel's oracle forms the basis of several other reflections in the OT on the relationship between moral behavior and sacrifice (cf. Prov. 21:3; Hos. 6:6).

15:23 / How **the sin of divination,** which is condemned throughout the OT, relates to the use of the ephod (which seems to have been permitted) is not clear. Perhaps seeking to discover what was going to happen in the future was viewed differently from the attempt to discern God's will for the present.

15:24 / Saul failed to recognize the responsibility of the king as God's regent to direct the people to follow God. By seeking the approval of the people rather than leading them to obey God Saul abdicates as king. D. V. Edelman (*King Saul in the Historiography of Judah* [JSOTSup 121; Sheffield: Sheffield Academic Press, 1991], p. 321) makes some perceptive points relating to this issue. Saul continues as titular king of Israel until his death but is no longer spoken of as acting on God's behalf.

15:32 / Having been taken captive, Agag believed that the *herem* was not involved. Saul's action thus led the Israelites and the Amalekites to underestimate the significance of what God had said.

15:34–35 / V. P. Long (*The Reign and Rejection of King Saul: A Case for Literary and Theological Coherence* [SBLDS 118; Atlanta: Scholars, 1989]) sees 1 Sam. 13–15 as pro-monarchy or neutral but as anti-Saul.

§15 Introducing David (1 Sam. 16:1–23)

The focus again moves, this time from Saul to David. Saul remains in the picture up to 2 Samuel 1, and his influence is felt after that in the ongoing tensions between the north and the south in Israel. But from this point Saul is a secondary character. Samuel, who had resigned his commission as national leader (ch. 12), is recalled to anoint David. Samuel's return underlines the portrayal of Saul's reign as being a pause before the genuine new age arose in Israel with David's enthronement. The writers convey the impression that Saul's reign could have been the new beginning. But because Saul failed, at least in the view of the Deuteronomic historian, to grasp that kingship in a theocracy meant complete obedience to God, his reign became an intermission.

It is interesting to note that Samuel is presented as the primary decision maker in the appointments of both Saul and David. When Solomon came to power, David played a crucial role—his endorsement ensured Solomon's succession. The key influence was neither prophet nor priest although both were involved, as Nathan and Zadok supported Solomon and Abiathar acted for Adonijah. It is likely, therefore, that Samuel is pictured as having recovered his power from Saul and handing it over again, this time to David. Payne ("Apologetic Motifs in the Books of Samuel," pp. 57–66) argues that Samuel, Saul, David, and Solomon all had power handed to them and in none of these cases was that power usurped. In fact, all of these leaders, particularly the first three, are seen as being given to the nation by God.

The stress that each leader began well is represented as an important apologetic motif in these books. The early kings may have failed, but that failure was not because they lacked the potential to succeed. "In every generation, . . . Yahweh had not only overruled to benefit his people but had provided them with rulers of the right character and calibre and with every potential of success" (p. 65). Thus the failure of the monarchy was not to be blamed on any inadequacy in God's choice. It is possible that alongside this apologetic motivation is a further reflection that, in the case of human beings, all power corrupts.

16:1–3 / Samuel's grief that Saul had been **rejected** links this chapter with the previous one, but again it is not explained. Probably alongside the personal sorrow for Saul, Samuel felt a regret that the change in the system that he had reluctantly endorsed had not been successful. The call from God in verse 1 makes it clear that the problem was not with the system but with the personnel. God has made another choice, and the aging Samuel has yet another role to fulfill. The language is brisk and to the point. Samuel's response is reminiscent of the excuses brought by Moses (Exod. 3; 4). His fear of Saul shows the extent to which power had been handed over, and an indication that Samuel was about to remove that power could lead to a fierce and fatal reaction. Saul's apparent acceptance of his fate (15:30) does not mean that Samuel's fear was unjustified. Samuel was familiar with the turbulence of Saul's nature and with his determination to cling to power (cf. ch. 15).

God's response to Samuel, as that to Moses, takes his fear seriously, provides a way around the problem, and restates the calling. God reminds Samuel that the future for Israel is in God's hands, not in Saul's. The power is God's. The solution to the problem was for Samuel to carry out the anointing in the context of a normal sacrifice that Saul would have no reason to question. The firm **I have chosen** a **king** contrasts with the parallel circumstances regarding Saul when Samuel was told to **give them a king** (8:22).

For Jesse, unlike Elkanah and Kish, no genealogical information is given. He is simply Jesse of Bethlehem. Because geneologies were so important, this omission of information that would have been well known to all future readers highlights the ordinariness of David's background. It could be that because Jesse was well known it was unnecessary to give his credentials, but that would not reflect the usual practice of OT writers.

16:4–13 / Samuel gets on with his task and arrives in Bethlehem ready to sacrifice. The response of the elders implies that the tension between Samuel and Saul was well known among the people and these elders did not want to get involved. Samuel reassures them, and they all, including Jesse and his sons, prepare for the sacrifice. The statement that Samuel **consecrated**

Jesse and his sons implies that there was a separate meeting with that family prior to the town celebration. This would make sense of David's anointing being **in the presence of his brothers** and yet apparently kept a secret from the townspeople and therefore from Saul.

The description of the meeting when, presumably unaware of what was going on, Jesse's sons are introduced to Samuel, is evocative. Samuel wants to get away as soon as possible, and his conviction on being faced with the impressive Eliab that his task was done is understandable. Saul had also had an exceptional physique (1 Sam. 9:2). The intervention of God (v. 7) is portrayed more as a gentle reminder than as a rebuke. The choice is to be God's and is not made according to human criteria. The reminder stands as a clear lesson for future readers. Samuel, alert now for the word of the Lord, is presented with seven brothers, but in each case the Lord is silent. The only solution, having been given a clear indication that he was to anoint a son of Jesse, must be that there is another brother. Perhaps marveling at his prophetic insight, they send for David.

It is often assumed that David was not present because somebody had to stay at home to do the work. It is more probable that he had not reached the age of maturity; he may have been only eleven or twelve years old. However, Samuel insists that they will not be able to **sit down**, that is, to begin the sacrificial meal, until David arrives. The Lord speaks, David is anointed, and Samuel goes home to Ramah. There are none of the extensive conversations that Samuel had with Saul when he first anointed him (1 Sam. 9:25, 27) or hints that David or any of Jesse's family were made aware of the significance of this anointing.

Other than the statement in verse 1, that one of Jesse's sons is **to be king,** there is no reference to kingship in this chapter. Readers, however, know that from this time on **the Spirit of the LORD came upon David in power,** although there is no indication of how or whether this empowerment manifested itself. From this point David's kingship was assured.

16:14–23 / The next incident, providing one explanation of the first meeting between Saul and David and introducing David's skills as a musician, lacks the immediacy and the story-telling skill found in the previous verses and in chapter 17. The dialogue in 16:16–18, for example, is more stilted than that found elsewhere. It is almost as if the writers possess extra information that they want the readers to know about but are not sure how it fits with the rest.

The phrase **the Spirit of the LORD had departed from Saul** may mean that his spiritual or charismatic power had disappeared. However, the comment follows the statement that David had received the Lord's Spirit and may record that although Saul remained king, he could no longer function as a representative of God. David had replaced him in that role and would eventually replace him as king.

What characterizes Saul now are terrible depressive moods that are depicted as the result of an **evil spirit from the LORD**. All circumstances, good and evil, pleasant or unpleasant, were seen as coming from the all-powerful Lord. The evil spirit in this instance is as likely to be a bad temper as some supernatural intervention. However, given Saul's later uncontrollable or at least uncontrolled fits, the explanation of demon possession would be understandable. In either case the text never hints that this **evil spirit** provides an excuse. Saul remains responsible for his behavior. The problem is the effect of his disobedience resulting in a bad conscience and loss of any awareness of God's presence with him.

Saul's courtiers, concerned for his well-being, persuade him to look for a court musician, for music was recognized as having beneficial effects in some circumstances. David, apparently having some renown as a harpist, is sent for. The description of David as **a brave man and a warrior** does not fit with what immediately precedes or follows this section and fails to explain Saul's request that Jesse send **David, who is with the sheep,** which appears to indicate other prior knowledge. However, David, bringing appropriate gifts, joins Saul's service as an armor-bearer, or squire, who doubled as a music therapist. There is no inkling of any tension between Saul and David, but rather emphasis on the fact that Saul **liked** David and was **pleased with him**. The music therapy was apparently, if only temporarily, successful.

Additional Notes §15

16:1 / Animal horns were traditionally used as receptacles for anointing oil. Although the Chronicler provides a comprehensive list of

David's ancestors (1 Chron. 2) there is no genealogy for David in Samuel or Kings.

16:5 / Various kinds of purification, often using water, took place before sacrifices to ensure that the offerer was ritually clean. We cannot be sure what that consecration consisted of, but it is possible that oil was used in some way.

16:6–7 / The point of the discussion about **Eliab** is, as Klein suggests (*1 Samuel*, p. 160), to make sure that everybody understands that the decision concerning David came from God and was not Samuel's choice.

16:11–12 / The Lord is concerned with things other than outward appearance, but readers may nevertheless wonder what David looked like. He was good-looking, maybe with a country boy's tan, and it is easy to understand that David's attractiveness inspired great love and loyalty. Reference to height, which influenced the people's affirmation of Saul and Samuel's assumptions about Eliab, is omitted.

16:13–14 / D. M. Howard ("The Transfer of Power from Saul to David in 1 Samuel 16:13–14," *JETS* 32 [1989], pp. 473–83) discusses the relationship between movement and the transfer of power, and he concludes that in 1 Sam. 16:13–14, "the emphasis is upon the movements of the spirits and of Samuel and they serve to emphasize and symbolize this transfer of power" (p. 473).

16:14–23 / The perceived lack of cohesion in this section may indicate a conflation from two separate sources describing an older warrior David with poetic and musical skills known to have helped Saul and a young boy coming up from the country to enter court service, perhaps after his encounter with Goliath.

§16 David's Growing Fame (1 Sam. 17:1–18:5)

17:1–58 / This chapter, a single, coherent narrative, supplies an alternative introduction to David. Until he is anointed by the people of Judah (2 Sam. 2) there is no further reference to David's anointing. Nor does this chapter indicate that David might be widely known by the people.

The situation is familiar: two battle lines drawn up on nearby hills, with the intervening valley preventing any precipitous action. On this occasion the Philistines had commandeered a huge Gittite to act as champion, one who would fight on behalf of their army. If an equivalent champion from among the Israelites could defeat him, then the Philistine army agreed to surrender, not an unknown procedure. Goliath's physical presence— the weight of his armor suggests he was meant to frighten rather than fight—was intended to deter any Israelite from taking up the challenge. If the challenge was not taken up there was no gain for the Philistines apart from the psychological one. The tactic was effective, and the Israelites, while remaining in the field, had no alternative strategy and made no response.

For the first time the reader encounters David as a person rather than a soothing presence. David appears on the scene as a messenger boy carrying supplies to his soldier brothers and their unit commander and charged with bringing back a report. He arrives and sums up the situation. His innocent question brings out the fact that they have all, including the king, forgotten that however untenable the military position might appear to be, they are **the armies of the living God.** The plural may indicate that David assumed that unseen spiritual forces were also involved in the battle.

The encounter between the brothers, the skeptical embarrassment of the older and the confident defiance of the younger, rings true throughout the centuries. David is not to be put off and eventually comes before Saul, whose incredulity is understandable. That Saul allows David to take up Goliath's challenge indicates the despair felt by the Israelite troops. David's supreme confidence that God was on their side and was able to help may have influenced Saul, who had never been able to take hold of that confidence.

The incident with the armor, also easily envisaged, brings out Saul's need to depend on something other than divine protection and David's unwillingness to be something he was not. Given Saul's exceptional height, that he thought his armor would help David perhaps further indicates his inability to plan coherently. However, wearing another person's clothes is sometimes a sign of acting on that person's behalf or with the person's power (cf. Elisha taking up Elijah's cloak, 1 Kgs. 19; 2 Kgs. 2). David's refusal to wear Saul's armor could then be a symbolic affirmation that he needed God's power, not Saul's. David enters the field not as a soldier but as a young shepherd.

The two disparate figures approach; the giant offended by having an apparently unarmed boy sent to face him, David certain that God would not continue to allow his honor to be disgraced in the way that David felt it had been. The unwieldy giant is felled by a single stone to the forehead, and the Philistines are for the moment finished. Their confidence in Goliath had been such that they were not ready to fight, although their promise of immediate surrender is conveniently forgotten.

Saul's cousin Abner (introduced in 14:50), who acted as his general, is sent to further investigate David's origins and David, in the only link with the previous chapter, announces himself as the son of **Jesse of Bethlehem**. It is hard to reconcile Saul's lack of knowledge of David before this incident with their meeting in chapter 16, and the writers make no attempt to do so. It is possible that material from a number of original sources has been incorporated without subjecting them to a rigorous editing process.

18:1–5 / David's victory over the Philistine champion brought several major changes in his life. He ceased being a shepherd at his father's home in Bethlehem and joined Saul's service, becoming the squire who is described in 16:21. His service was appreciated by all, his military prowess indicating that his dramatic victory over Goliath had not been a fluke. Saul was so impressed that he gave David significant promotion within the armed forces, an action that officers and men approved.

Saul's heir apparent, Jonathan, shared the approval of David. His warm-hearted acceptance of David fits in well with the picture that has been conveyed. He was more than happy to welcome David as a kindred spirit, equally impulsive, equally brave, and equally confident that God was behind Israel. It was as if Jonathan from the beginning recognized that the Spirit of the Lord was with David and responded to this. There was never any question of jealousy, now or as Jonathan began to realize that David would replace his father. The text does not discuss this, but it is interesting to speculate whether Jonathan knew of Samuel's prophecy that Saul's would not be an enduring dynasty (13:14) or of the rejection of Saul by God (15:26).

The description of the beginning of this close relationship informs us that Jonathan loved David, that he made a covenant treaty with him, and that he gave him gifts. The terms of this treaty are not itemized, although later (ch. 20) Jonathan calls on David to look after his family. It seems to have been a mutual commitment to loyalty and friendship. It would be normal for Jonathan as the higher in status to take the initiative, but no indication is given at this stage of David's response. These verses seem to emphasize, before any conflict between David and Saul is introduced, that there was complete harmony. David is accepted as an equal by Jonathan, who does not see him as a threat to his own position.

Additional Notes §16

17:1 / **Socoh** and **Azekah** are south of previous Philistine incursions. This is thus a different stage in the ongoing conflict. The Philistines had been driven back but had not been defeated by Saul's and Jonathan's previous victories.

17:4–7 / **Gath** was on the east side of Philistia, close to Israelite territory. 2 Sam. 15:18 refers to a large Gittite group supporting David, possibly following his sojourn there (1 Sam. 27), but in general they were as opposed to Israel as the rest of the Philistines.

It is possible that Goliath suffered from a genetic defect causing giantism. Any exaggeration in the figures would be understandable given his clear difference from others. The references to other such giants in 2 Sam. 21:15–21, which mentions further genetic problems, may mean there was a significant problem in Gath. That Goliath's forehead was penetrated so easily may further indicate a bone deficiency causing the malformation.

Saul was exceptionally tall (1 Sam. 9:2; 10:23), and the text may reflect an implicit criticism that the tallest Israelite, Saul, did not take up the challenge. The relationship between this chapter and 2 Sam. 21:19, which states that Elhanan killed Goliath the Gittite, is discussed in §44, pp. 232–33.

17:12 / This is the nearest we get to a genealogy, but it is not in the standard form. To describe **Jesse** as an **Ephrathite** is probably the equivalent of saying he came from Bethlehem (cf. 1 Chron. 4:4).

17:54 / The mention of **Jerusalem** is strange, as Jerusalem was not taken from the control of the Jebusites until later. Perhaps a tradition that the **head** was kept as a trophy that eventually was stored at Jerusalem has crept into the text. 21:9 tells us that Goliath's armor was moved to the shrine at Nob.

17:55–58 / Certain manuscripts of the LXX omit various verses in this chapter, including these, probably to avoid the conflict with ch. 16. But the complete narrative within ch. 17 is coherent, and the arguments against such omission are strong.

18:3–4 / J. C. Exum (*Tragedy and Biblical Narrative: Arrows of the Almighty* [Cambridge: Cambridge University Press, 1992], p. 94) points out that although David treats Jonathan reasonably well, Jonathan seems to do all the giving in the relationship. An exchange of armor or clothing was a "common way of sealing a new friendship" (Caird, "1 and 2 Samuel," 2:981), but it is not clear whether there was an exchange or a gift. Jonathan's gifts contrast with the lack of gifts from Saul, despite his extravagant promises concerning the one who could defeat the Philistine. David did become Saul's son-in-law as promised, but not as a direct result of his victory in the valley of Elah.

18:5 / The timing is uncertain, but it must have taken some time for David to complete enough missions to gain the reputation that made it feasible for high military rank to be acceptably assigned.

§17 Saul's Resentful Fear of David (1 Sam. 18:6–19:24)

18:6–9 / David quickly became a popular hero. As has occurred throughout the centuries in countless places, folk songs were adapted and the returning soldiers were welcomed home to loud praises for Saul and David, but particularly for David. Saul, knowing that he no longer had the assurance of God's support and that his continued role as king depended on popular acclaim, was incensed by the way the credit was apportioned. His personal liking for David and his pride in David's successes turned into an obsessive jealousy. At this stage Saul may have realized that David was the shadowy figure mentioned by Samuel (15:28) who was waiting to replace him.

18:10–16 / Saul's first attack on David happens during a visit from **an evil spirit from God,** apparently a reference to the fits of depression that David had earlier been able to alleviate with music (cf. 16:14–23). While Saul's ecstatic behavior when he joined the prophetic band (10:10) is viewed positively, a sign that God's spirit was with him, here it is seen negatively, as part of his condition and related to his lack of fellowship with God. However, although there may be a hint that Saul was not thinking logically, the text nevertheless—by recording Saul's thoughts— presents Saul's throwing his spear as a conscious act with the intention of killing David. Twice Saul threw his spear at David, so this was not an impulsive loss of control.

It is feasible that Saul saw David's avoidance of death as a further sign that God was with David and not with Saul and that this added to his fear. In a calmer moment Saul's response was to send David away in charge of an army unit. Given what has been said of David's promotion, his being given command of a thousand, probably referring to a single troop unit rather than the literal figure, was likely a calculated insult and was meant to lead to

David's falling out of favor with people as well as with the king. If this was Saul's intention, it failed.

David's remarkable successes continued, and, although in one sense this bolstered Saul's position, it also confirmed the impression that God's hand was definitely on David. The people loved David **because he led them in their campaigns,** perhaps because Saul had ceased to take part in military activity. The approval came not just from David's own tribe but from across the whole nation, **all Israel and Judah;** this reinforced Saul's fear that the support of the populace, as well as that of the Lord, would be taken from him and given to David.

18:17–29 / Saul's obsessive plotting as to how he will deal with David becomes increasingly bizarre. He first decides to follow through, belatedly, on his promise that the national champion should marry his daughter; he intended that David's military activity would bring him to an early grave. David's question, **Who am I . . . that I should become the king's son-in-law?** should be interpreted not as rejecting Saul's suggestion but as a polite way of indicating interest. But when David continued to be successful, Saul withdrew his offer, and his elder daughter Merab was married elsewhere. Saul's change of mind when he heard that Michal, his younger daughter, loved David, fits well with the increasingly erratic nature of his decision making. Michal's love for David and Michal herself become mere tools in the ongoing power struggle. Saul thinks that that love may be the means of bringing David down, and David uses it to further his own desire to be the **king's son-in-law.** This is the only place in the OT narratives where a woman is described as loving a man.

As when Jonathan's love for David was introduced, there is no mention of David having any feelings for Michal. David's response to Saul's inquiries (v. 23) is this time part of a cultural game intended to keep the bride price low, as David's military successes would have elevated his position from a poor farmer with small resources. Saul picks up the suggestion of his inability to pay and asks for a grotesque bride price, again calculated to lead to David's death. However, this price, involving the killing of the Philistines (it is unlikely that they would agree to voluntary circumcision), is fully paid, and David achieves his ambition. Because Saul and David were playing a strategic game, it is possible that the task is symbolic or that the numbers are exaggerated. However, the numbers are small enough to be realistic, and the unusual nature of the task fits with Saul's erratic nature and David's relishing of a challenge. David's bringing two hundred foreskins preempts any attempt by Saul to change the bride price again.

The writers skillfully portray Saul's increasing frustration as everything goes right for David and everything goes wrong for himself. Far from Michal's love being able to be used against David, it strengthens his position as a possible successor to Saul. Jonathan, the people, and Michal all loved David—that this implied some kind of political support would be seen by Saul as inevitable. David could now be seen only as a permanent enemy (v. 29).

18:30 / This verse probably summarizes this period and comes from a document that did not include the detailed accounts of David's activity, but in the text as we have it the verse serves as a conclusion and stresses the failure of Saul's attempts to thwart David's growing popularity and power.

19:1–7 / In Saul's next attempt to destroy David he unrealistically tried to involve those around him who loved David. Jonathan's fondness for David is expressed by the same word as is used for the pleasure Saul had previously taken in David (18:22). It may be that Jonathan's calm good sense in removing David from the scene and then facing his father with the realities of David's support, through which **the LORD won a great victory for all Israel**, brought Saul back to one of his periods of reality. Jonathan must have had some awareness of Saul's fear that David would replace him, but his serene acceptance of the implications of David's victories was maybe a further factor in Saul's recovery of perspective. Jonathan's attempts to prevent his father from further damaging himself by his obsession are admirable. Saul was persuaded, and David, at least for a while, was able to return to court. Saul's confirmation of his word with an oath reflects the extremes of his mood swings.

19:8–10 / A further outbreak of hostilities gave David more opportunity to cause havoc among the Philistines. Whether David's further success caused Saul's further loss of his always vulnerable mental and emotional control is not clear. But in a replica of his previous action (18:10–11), Saul tries to **pin David to the wall with his spear**. However, David dodges and disappears. Saul was not to be given an opportunity to make a second attempt. David's **escape** appears first to have been from Saul's presence to his own home, although it became a permanent flight from Saul's court.

19:11–17 / This time Saul's violent anger did not die down, and he made premeditated arrangements to have David killed the next day. David's wife Michal, following her brother's example in acting on David's behalf, helped David to escape. The use of the **idol** as a ruse is reminiscent of Rachel's hiding of her father's household gods, where the same word is used (Gen. 31:19). Given the instability of Saul's nature, Michal risked her own life to ensure David's safety. Saul eventually discovered Michal's ruse, but she averted his wrath by suggesting that David had threatened to kill her (v. 17).

David seems to have left Michal without a thought. He returns to visit Jonathan (20:1) but not Michal and apparently does not see her again until he insists, for what seem to be political reasons, that she be taken from Paltiel, who loved her, and returned to David (2 Sam. 3:13–14). Maybe Michal's attitude to David the next time she looks **through a window** (v. 12) is understandable (2 Sam. 6:16). David continues to be portrayed as an attractive personality. It may be that his apparent disregard of the needs and feelings of others stems not so much from an uncaring nature as from a wholehearted involvement with the needs of the present that resulted in his overlooking other issues.

19:18–24 / David fled **to Samuel at Ramah,** possibly seeking to reassure Samuel that he had done nothing to precipitate Saul's action, but probably seeking sanctuary. Ramah was only a few miles from Gibeah, still well within Saul's reach. Saul's irrational enmity was not yet assuaged, and even the thought of Samuel's opposition did not deter him.

Three groups of soldiers and finally Saul himself attempted to capture David, but each was overtaken by some kind of ecstatic experience that prevented their taking further action. That this incident was also seen as a cause of the proverb about Saul's prophetic activity does not conflict with the explanation given in 10:11. Saul could easily have become known for his episodic ecstatic behavior, and the proverb perhaps had gradually changed its emphasis from affirmation to irony, from "Is the hand of God also on Saul?" to "Is Saul mad?" What is clear is that the method by which Saul was prevented from killing David is envisaged as being under the control of **the Spirit of God.**

Additional Notes §17

18:10 / Y. Ben-Nahum ("What Ailed the Son of Kish?") suggests that Saul suffered from a chemical imbalance that explains the ecstatic activity and the attacks on David. If such a condition was hereditary it could also explain Michal's personality and her infertility.

18:16–17 / There are strong parallels between Saul's behavior and David's behavior in 2 Sam. 11, when David neglected to lead his troops into battle, preferring to stay in Jerusalem. David hoped that the enemy would bring Uriah's death so that he would not have to raise a hand against him. For David, as for Saul, these tactics brought shame and disaster.

18:17–27 / Michal's exploitation by David and Saul is explored by R. G. Bowman ("The Fortune of King David/The Fate of Queen Michal: A Literary Critical Analysis of 2 Samuel 1–8," in *Telling Queen Michal's Story: An Experiment in Comparative Interpretation* [ed. D. J. A. Clines and T. C. Eskenazi; JSOTSup 119; Sheffield: JSOT Press, 1991], pp. 97–120). He concludes that David's character is "flawed but favoured" and the Michal is "ever victimized but never vindicated."

R. B. Lawton ("1 Samuel 18: David, Merob and Michal," *CBQ* 51 [1989]: pp. 423–25) suggests that the two sisters being offered to David sets up a parallel with Leah and Rachel being offered to Jacob. The parallel is strengthened by Michal's use of the idol (19:13, 16; cf. Gen. 31:34). This parallel may be deliberately set up to create an expectation of the statement that David loved Michal as Jacob loved Rachel. That this statement is missing therefore "underscores what David lacks in his relationship with Michal: love." Michal's later disdain for David's dancing should perhaps be seen in this context. However, the presence of the idols in David's household (19:13) indicates the extent of syncretism at this time and may indicate another reason why Michal was less than enthusiastic about David's unrestrained praise for the Lord. Or Michal's involvement with idols may have been part of the reason for David's cavalier treatment of her.

18:25 / Israelite men would have been circumcised as babies, and therefore there would be no doubt that adult foreskins would have come from the Philistines.

19:1–17 / There are significant parallels between events in this chapter and those in ch. 18 and ch. 20. It is possible to see this as evidence for different sources dealing with the same events (Caird, "1 and 2 Samuel," 2:986–87), but with Saul's condition repetition of previous behavior is believable, and nothing makes an ongoing narrative inconceivable.

19:3 / Jonathan's arrangement whereby David could see him **in the field** talking to his father is possibly to ensure that David could make a quick escape if necessary, prefacing the more complex arrangements in ch. 20, or it could be to provide David with an opportunity to judge Saul's mood for himself.

19:20 / Much of Samuel's ministry was as an independent priest and prophet, but major prophetic figures sometimes were associated with groups like this. Elisha was (2 Kgs. 2:15; 4:1; 6:1).

19:24 / Saul's stripping off his clothes is consistent with the behavior of known groups of ecstatic prophets. In this instance Saul's stripping off the trappings of his kingship in an unconscious parallel to Jonathan's presenting David with garments (18:4; cf. Gordon, *1 and 2 Samuel: A Commentary*, p. 165) creates a symbolism that is alien to Saul's purposes in being there.

Saul's prophesying **in Samuel's presence** does not appear to have led to any communication between them (cf. 15:35).

§18 Jonathan Is Faithful to His Covenant with David (1 Sam. 20:1–42)

20:1–4 / David seeks out Jonathan to clarify the situation before he decides on the next step. Jonathan is unaware of Saul's latest attack on David. This need not be seen as indicating a source that was unacquainted with the accounts of the previous attacks. Jonathan's uncomplicated nature means that he wanted to believe Saul's assurances about his attitude to David (19:6), and he finds it difficult to accept that Saul had regressed to his previous attitude. However, Jonathan accepts David's word and the explanation for his own lack of knowledge of Saul's intentions—namely, that Jonathan would **be grieved** (v. 3). Jonathan's willingness to take whatever action David considers necessary (v. 4) is an implicit statement that his loyalty would go to David rather than to Saul.

20:5–7 / David's concern about his attendance at **the New Moon festival** shows that he had not yet decided to remove himself permanently from the court. If his temporary absence is acceptable, then it is likely that Saul has calmed down and David will be safe, at least for a while. But if Saul is angered it will indicate that the failed attempt to capture David at Ramah had not brought Saul back to rationality. David and Jonathan understand Saul's capacity for intemperate rages. David's excuse, **an annual sacrifice** in **Bethlehem,** brings a reminder of the method Samuel used to avoid Saul's wrath (16:2) and raises the possibility that Samuel suggested this course of action.

20:8–17 / A dialogue about the relationship between David and Jonathan prefaces further discussion about their response to Saul's reactions. David seems unsure of Jonathan's loyalty; there is a hint that David suspects Jonathan of conspiring with Saul (v. 8). He therefore reminds him of the covenant that Jonathan had initiated (18:3). Jonathan's refutation of any suggestion of disloyalty causes David somewhat defensively to bring the conversation back to the problem of getting information about Saul's reaction. Jonathan's sensitivity to David's need for reassurance is profound. He will inform David within the first two days of the feast about Saul's response. Jonathan also gives a categoric assurance backed up by an oath that he will ensure David's safety if Saul's reactions are negative. Not only that, he is well aware that David will replace his father, gives his blessing to David, and asks only for **kindness** to be shown to himself and his **family.**

The **covenant** made on this occasion, backed by a prayer that the Lord should **call David's enemies to account,** is a deliberate, explicit statement that if Saul announces himself to be an enemy of David, then Jonathan is calling God's judgment on him. The insistence that David join him in this oath (v. 17) forces both of them to come into the open about their vision for the future of Israel. Jonathan abdicates all rights to, or hopes of, the throne. He is aware that a calling to account for David's enemies could involve himself as the son of David's enemy, but this does not prevent his action. His unselfish love in doing this and in making sure David knows that he had (v. 17), deserves the comment that the text makes about his love for David.

20:18–34 / The arrangements for getting the information to David are clarified, in case a meeting proves impossible. As if to reassure David that the return to more mundane matters does not mean that Jonathan regrets or is reneging on his commitment to David's cause, he reinforces that commitment by proclaiming that **the LORD is witness between** them **forever.**

The events at the New Moon feast progressed as had been feared. When Saul understood that David was not coming, his **anger flared up.** The excuse about the sacrifice was seen for what it was and Jonathan bore the brunt of Saul's rage, so much so that he too might have been killed. There was no longer any question as to whether Saul's enmity to David was implacable. Jonathan's anger at the unfair treatment of David and not at his own endangerment ties in with his character as it has been portrayed thus far.

20:35–42 / The prearranged signal was sent out, although it was possible for Jonathan and David to have a brief conversation before David's departure. That David wept the most may indicate his consciousness of the end of an era. Saul's call for David's death had been made at the New Moon festival. Abner was sitting next to Saul, and it is inconceivable that he and others would not have heard Saul's proclamation. David could not return to court; he had been proclaimed an enemy of the state, and the state's powers were likely to be used to seek his death.

Jonathan sent David off with his blessing and a reminder of the lasting nature of their friendship. The account of this friendship is reminiscent of tales of the kind of deep-seated friendship without any connotations of sexuality, described in Australia as mateship, that can take place between soldiers living in difficult conditions in wartime. The unselfish concern for the welfare of the other, involving at times great personal cost, and the request to care for a family that might be left behind, are familiar in such situations.

The statement that **David left** and Jonathan returned to town is poignant. Jonathan is still his father's son, and in spite of his loyalty to David and Saul's attack on him, he returns to support his father in the ongoing work of the kingdom. Although for Eli and Samuel the behavior of their sons is raised as a significant factor in their being replaced as national leaders, the same is not so for Saul. Given the questionable behavior of all of David's sons (e.g., Amnon in 2 Sam. 13; Absalom in 2 Sam. 15; Solomon in 1 Kgs. 11), the reader of the complete narrative in Samuel is left to reflect on the mystery of the choices that God makes.

Additional Notes §18

20:1 / How Saul reacted to his encounter with the prophetic group and how he returned from Ramah is not specified, but there was no change in his attitude. The question as to why Jonathan had not been present during Saul's latest outburst is also left unanswered.

20:5 / See additional note on 20:24–27.

20:7 / Both the young men were well aware of the increasing problem that Saul had in controlling his temper or in letting his anger dissipate. This increasing difficulty in keeping a hold on reality is a symptom of a number of psychological conditions.

20:14–15 / When one regime was replaced, all close allies and family members of those involved in the previous regime often were killed. The new regime sought to avoid any immediate threat of retaliation or rebellion. Jonathan seeks reassurance that when David replaces Saul that policy will not be carried out. David uses this incident to explain his interest in Mephibosheth (2 Sam. 9). It is sometimes assumed that Jonathan was unaware of involving Saul when he invoked God's judgment on David's enemies (e.g., Baldwin, *1 and 2 Samuel*, p. 135), but the explicit nature of Jonathan's other comments makes such naïveté unlikely.

20:24–27 / New Moon festivals played a key part in the ongoing religious life of Israel (Num. 10:10; 28:14; 2 Kgs. 4:23; Neh. 10:33). At a later stage these festivals were also heavily involved in the corruption of religious life (Isa. 1:14; Hos. 5:7). Any clean Israelite who was in the vicinity might be expected to attend, although it appears that in this instance a special arrangement had been made with David. The only excuse for missing such an occasion would be that some unforeseen incident had made a person **ceremonially unclean** and therefore unable to attend a sacrifice. But such uncleanness would not last overnight (vv. 26–27).

20:25 / The details of precise seating arrangements suggest that the account comes from an eyewitness.

20:30 / The epithet **(son of a perverse and rebellious woman)** that Saul ascribes to Jonathan idiomatically translates to "you rebel." The following reference to Jonathan bringing shame on his mother shows that no insult was intended to her. The introduction of contradictory phrases of this kind and the temporary disowning of a child with the equivalent of "look what your son has done" is consistent with a parent losing his or her temper and again suggests an eyewitness account.

See also additional note on 20:7.

20:41–42 / The text gives no reason to suppose that the relationship between David and Jonathan had any homosexual connotations. Their mutual commitment is based on their recognition of the trustworthy nature of the Lord and on a common allegiance to God's future for Israel.

§19 David's Flight—The Priests at Nob (1 Sam. 21:1–22:23)

21:1–9 / Having accepted that Saul's enmity was fixed and that exile was the only option, David sought initial supplies from the priest at Nob. Ahimelech's wariness on David's arrival may have reflected an awareness of Saul's antipathy toward David and a fear of getting involved in a power dispute. However, it is equally possible that Ahimelech's expression of ignorance in 22:14–15 was the truth and his fear was that David would bring Philistine troops in his wake. David's being unaccompanied would have added to Ahimelech's suspicion that he was being set up for an ambush. The choice to deceive Ahimelech by inventing a secret mission and a hidden troop adds to the impression that Ahimelech was unaware of the real situation, though David's deception may have been an attempt to protect Ahimelech from accusations of conspiracy.

Unleavened bread would remain edible for some time, and the nonexistent troop provides an excuse for David to ask for a good supply. The rule about no sex while on duty served as a way of alleviating any doubts that Ahimelech might have had about letting David use consecrated bread, which was normally restricted to priestly families. At a later stage, Uriah's adherence to the rule for troops under David's control brought disaster to both of them (2 Sam. 11).

Doeg's presence and the fact that he was Saul's man is noted by the writers and, as we are informed in 22:22, by David, although the fact is not detailed at this point. David was aware that Goliath's sword was at Nob and that it was probably the only weapon there; this would explain why he had headed for Nob. Metal weapons were scarce, and the chance of obtaining one was too good to miss. David's innocent-sounding question is thus a ruse to put Ahimelech off the scent. Any direct request for Goliath's sword would have raised suspicions.

21:10–15 / David's next step was to leave Israelite territory and seek sanctuary with **Achish king of Gath**. Verse 11 implies that David hoped to work as a mercenary soldier and that his being recognized by one of Achish's servants was an unfortunate accident. (Given that he was carrying Goliath's sword, his hopes for anonymity were unrealistic.) Achish had heard of David's reputation and was wary of his intentions. David feared for his life but managed, by feigning madness, to convince Achish that he presented no danger. The success of this ruse probably helped him to deceive Achish in other ways when sanctuary was provided (ch. 27). One wonders whether the boredom induced by having to sustain the deception contributed to David's decision to flee to Adullam in Judah (22:1).

22:1–5 / It would not have taken long for the news of David's disgrace to spread. Given Saul's instability, it is not surprising that David's family joined him in exile. Fear that Saul might take action against them was not unjustified, as is evidenced by Saul's treatment of the priests at Nob (22:18–19). It was also not surprising that a mixed group of other discontents quickly joined David. Some of these men were perhaps criminals, and it may be that most of them had also fallen afoul of Saul's intemperate nature, but they formed into a disciplined force. David, perhaps winning the support of the king of Moab by presenting himself as an opponent of the Israelite king, was able to leave his parents in safe custody. He remained for a while at a fortified base until a prophetic instruction sent him into Judean territory.

22:6–10 / Saul reacted predictably when he learned that David had surfaced and that a group had gathered around him. He took for granted that David's main aim was to win the hearts of even more people and draw them away from Saul by bribery. He smelled conspiracy even among the members of his own tribe. Specific mention of **men of Benjamin** may indicate that his paranoia had become such that he was afraid to have members of other tribes around. He was convinced that Jonathan's friendship with and defense of David meant betrayal. Verse 8 implies that Saul had only recently learned, perhaps from a courtier with a grudge, that the friendship between Jonathan and David had been reinforced by a covenant agreement. It says much for Jonathan that he stayed with his father throughout this period. Saul's ranting against him was just that, and in his saner moments Saul was well aware that Jonathan posed no direct danger to him.

Doeg the Edomite, seeing and seizing an opportunity for advancement in Saul's court, provides Saul with knowledge of where and from whom David obtained supplies. The information that Ahimelech **inquired of the LORD** for David, with the implication that he gave David his own and God's blessing, may or may not have been Doeg's invention. Any such enquiry is not mentioned in the earlier account but could have taken place. Saul, who by now sees conspiracy under every bush, interprets Ahimelech's helping David as a deliberate act of rebellion.

22:11–23 / Saul's interview with Ahimelech immediately becomes a trial with an inevitable verdict. In Saul's mind there is no question as to Ahimelech's guilt. Helping David could be nothing other than treasonable conspiracy. David's attempt to protect Ahimelech was unsuccessful. Ahimelech is seen as the one who has supplied David's whole force and enabled him to be the immediate threat to Saul's kingship that Saul was convinced he was. Ahimelech naturally protests that he had no idea David was fleeing from Saul and that as far as he knew by helping David he was helping Saul further his own plans for opposing the Philistines.

But Saul is too far gone to take any notice of what is said. So, contrary to any of the Israelite laws about trials and sentences (Num. 35:30; Deut. 17:6; 24:16), Ahimelech and his whole family, presumably including Saul's priest Ahijah, are put to death. The guards may have been unwilling to carry out this sentence because of a superstitious fear of harming priests, but they could also have been only too well aware of Saul's problems and had a clear perception of how unjust such action would be.

Doeg had no such qualms, and the destruction that Saul had been unwilling to apply to the Amalekites in response to God's command was applied without mercy to the little town of Nob. The repetition of *herem* language in verse 19 (cf. 15:3) shows that the writers were well aware of the irony of this parallel.

Only one of the priests, Ahimelech's son Abiathar, escapes to the relative safety of David's camp. David's reaction to Abiathar's news ties in with the ongoing portrait of his character in two ways. It presents us on the one hand with his inability to work through the consequences of any action he might take or to think through the relevance of information with which he has been provided. On the other hand there is a willingness to accept his own responsibility and to make reparation for his actions. He could not bring Abiathar's relatives back, but he can and does protect and provide for Abiathar.

Abiathar managed to rescue the ephod used for determining God's will and brought it with him on his flight (23:6). Thus Saul's actions again defeated his purposes and went further toward separating himself from contact with God. David now had the use of the ephod available to him and Saul did not—further evidence, perhaps, of God's ongoing support for David and rejection of Saul. The brief mention of the prophet Gad in 22:5 and this reference to the ephod reinforce the impression that God's servants, both priest and prophet, had abandoned Saul and were behind David.

Additional Notes §19

21:1 / **Nob** had become a shrine similar to the old priestly base at Shiloh, and the rest of Eli's family had moved there. Ahimelech is the brother of Ahijah, the priest who had been advising Saul (14:3; 22:9). Nob was a relatively short distance from Saul's camp. It was far enough away for it to be possible that Ahimelech had not yet heard of a definite break between Saul and David but near enough for him to be aware of Saul's problems and the existence of tension. As there had so far been no question of David opposing Saul, it would have been difficult to ascertain where Ahimelech's sympathies lay. David's unwillingness to tell Ahimelech the truth and Saul's suspicion of betrayal are understandable.

21:4 / Nothing in the law would have permitted Ahimelech to give consecrated bread (Lev. 24:5–9) to soldiers even if they were ritually clean. Whether Ahimelech was acting out of compassion for the needs of the soldiers or found himself unable to resist David's pressure is not clear. In Matt. 12:3–4 Jesus affirms Ahimelech's action and puts helping the needy as more significant than adhering to the precise details of the ritual law.

21:7 / The relevance of Doeg being **detained before the LORD** is not fully clear. It may be that he had to wait to become ritually pure before completing some ceremony, but that seems fairly unlikely for an Edomite. It is possible that he was being punished with a curfew or temporary imprisonment. If this is so it helps to explain Doeg's enthusiasm for helping Saul (22:9–10, 18–19) as a way of putting himself back in favor. The use of mercenary troops from surrounding nations has already been noted (cf. additional note on 13:3). The suggestion of P. T. Reis ("Collusion at Nob: A New Reading of 1 Samuel 21–22," *JSOT* 61 [1994], pp. 59–73), that both David and Ahimelech were aware of Doeg's presence and set out to deceive him, seems far-fetched. It would mean that they expected Doeg to report to Saul, and it is hard to see what advantage they could have gained from his reporting one story as opposed to another. The key issue was that David had fled and been helped.

21:11 / The people of Gath's description of David as **king of the land** goes some way to explaining Saul's fears that David intended to stage a takeover. For David this acknowledgment of his reputation for valor meant danger, and he reached the lowest point of his exile. The title of Ps. 34 gives this incident as its setting and, although the main emphasis is on trusting the Lord in all circumstances, it refers to someone who had been at a particularly low ebb.

22:1–5 / **Adullam** was a Canaanite city captured by Joshua (Josh. 12:15). It was situated halfway between Gath and Bethlehem, and its nearby caves were ideal for David's purposes. Whether or not the decision of his parents to stay in **Moab** indicates that contacts remained with Ruth's family there, Ruth being Jesse's grandmother, is speculation.

The site of David's next **stronghold** cannot be identified. It is not in Judah, and therefore it seems that he did not return to Adullam. The constant moving around for the kind of force that now accompanied David was essential, although **Hereth,** his next port of call, is also unidentifiable.

The **prophet Gad** appears without any introduction. He apparently remained with David throughout his long career as a significant adviser (2 Sam. 24; 2 Chron. 29:25), but we are told nothing of his background or origin.

22:6 / Virtually every reference to Saul in these chapters has him with **spear in hand.** His spear was a symbol of his kingship and possibly had some function in the court scene that was taking place. However, it is also possible that the writers repeatedly mention Saul's holding his spear because it gave him confidence in his own status and reminded those around him that he was to be taken seriously.

22:22 / The fact that David had recognized Doeg at the shrine could be seen as evidence that Doeg was a known troublemaker and supports the view of his detention as some kind of punishment.

§20 Saul Seeks Out David (1 Sam. 23:1–29)

23:1–6 / David's exile did not mean that he had lost his vision for Israel's security or his concern for the well-being of his fellow Israelites. The news of particular problems at Keilah stimulated his desire to continue fighting on behalf of God's people. The Philistines were not taking tribute from the Israelite farmers but were **looting the threshing floors.** They were waiting until the Israelites had done all the hard work and then depriving them of their livelihood for the next year. Such action could not be tolerated.

The situation was different from previous sorties when David had been working directly as Saul's representative, and it was important to ensure that his actions had God's approval. Therefore he **inquired of the LORD.** His makeshift army was understandably wary of moving from the relative security of the Judean hills back into territory where the Philistines had retained control. David did not ignore the fears of his men. He sought to reassure them by checking a second time that they could be confident that their action was within God's will and that God's presence with them could therefore be guaranteed. It is possible that the difference in the answers given to David signifies that different questions were asked. To the question **Shall I go?** the answer comes back **Go.** The addition of the phrase **and save Keilah** could indicate that the venture will be successful, but the request is primarily about the validity of the action, not about its outcome. The second question is not outlined, but the response, **Go . . . for I am going to give the Philistines into your hand,** may imply that the question was not just "Shall we go?" but also "And will we succeed?"

If this is so, we have an indication of David's leadership skills; he recognized that successful missions were more likely to occur when all those involved, not just the leader, believed in what they were doing and had confidence in their ability to succeed. There may also be a need here to convince the people with

David that alienation from Saul did not mean alienation from God. God's willingness to treat legitimate human fears seriously is a motif found throughout the OT narrative texts.

David and his men took action. Keilah was rescued, the looted grain was presumably recovered, and the Philistines were plundered of **their livestock.** David's team took up residence in the town, either to ensure ongoing security or because a town that has been rescued may be considered to be a place of safety.

23:7–14 / News of the victory reached the court probably not long after it happened. Saul's reaction that David had taken Keilah was one of delight—not that a defeat had been inflicted on the Philistines but that this might provide an opportunity, perhaps to Saul's deluded mind a God-given opportunity, for cornering and capturing David. David's advance knowledge of the projected siege indicated that he too was not short of informants, even among those in Saul's court. The ephod, which had been brought by Abiathar, was put to use. David was presumably disappointed by the news that the town he had rescued would not continue to provide him sanctuary when it meant facing Saul's siege forces. However, in stark contrast to Saul's intentions to destroy the town that sheltered David, David took action to protect not only himself and his forces but also the town that was ready to betray him. He wanted to make sure that the devastation he had caused at Nob was not repeated.

David and his men left quickly and commenced a nomadic existence mostly around the protected desert towns and isolated mountain hiding places of rural Judah. Saul's attention was focused on finding them. Even in such territory, news of the movements of more than six hundred men could not have been hard to obtain. David had good intelligence sources, and his skills in moving around the countryside, developed as a young shepherd and honed while fighting for Saul, were put to good use. But the writers are clear that Saul's inability to gain an advantage over David was a result of God's involvement (v. 14).

23:15–29 / One incident in Saul's relentless pursuit of David is described in detail. **Saul** was getting close and David was apparently beginning to panic. **Jonathan** bravely took the opportunity, perhaps coming over from his father's camp, unobserved in the rough territory, to visit his friend. Jonathan calmed David's fears and **helped him find strength in God.** Both men were convinced that the important thing for Israel was that

God's purposes should be fulfilled. Jonathan's conviction that David was to be the next **king over Israel** and that because this was God's plan there was no way Saul could succeed in killing him, must have given David renewed encouragement and strength. Jonathan again makes it clear not only that he is aware that David will replace Saul as king but also that he has no intention of opposing this. Saul's awareness of this is not unrealistic optimism on Jonathan's part; it is confirmed by Saul (24:20). Saul had heard God's word and knew Jonathan's perspective. His efforts to find and kill David are part of an attempt to change the future. If David is out of the picture surely Jonathan will take over. This desperate attempt to thwart God's known intentions ties in with the picture presented of Saul's obsessive paranoia, just as the sensitive good sense alongside the courageous if somewhat foolhardy risking of his own safety ties in with the ongoing portrait of Jonathan. This is the last recorded meeting between David and Jonathan.

The local residents' willingness to hand David over to Saul may result from fear for their own safety and an unwillingness to be embroiled in civil war. However, the emphasis on Saul as **king** (v. 20) may indicate that they were loyal subjects seeking to do their duty. Saul's unpopularity was largely a product of his own imagination. Even in this picture of self-interested betrayal in a text that depicts David rather than Saul as the hero, we find a glimpse of an alternative scenario in which Saul accepts David as heir and lives out his reign with the support of all the people.

However, it was not to be. Saul accepted the people's allegiance but was skeptical about their information. He did not want a fruitless chase. Although Saul had good sources, David's access to God's oracles would give him the edge. The information he could obtain (23:9–12) was always going to be more reliable than that from Saul's spies. Saul's local supporters searched on his behalf. The details included suggest an eyewitness account, although we cannot now identify the places named. Accurate information was provided, and Saul came very close to David before a Philistine invasion took him away. Saul's attention may have been diverted from national security, but he was not so far gone as to let his search for David lead to the destruction of the land. We are again given a hint of Saul's potential, the way in which he could have reigned if he had not been diverted from following God's path.

The two men separate before they have met. David retreats to **En Gedi** leaving Saul to deal with the latest incursion of
the Philistines. David's retreat may be a safety measure, since
hiding places and water could easily be found in the caves
around En Gedi in the Dead Sea region, but it could also indicate
a respect for Saul's abilities to defeat these raiders without David's help.

Additional Notes §20

23:3 / **Keilah,** the site of Khirbet Qila, is part of Judean tribal
land, but at this stage it was seen as outside of Judean control.

23:4 / David is not described as making inquiry of the Lord
before every action he takes, military or otherwise. The fact that from
now on he has the ephod available to him and that requests can easily
be made does not appear to be the deciding factor. It may be that in new
situations like this, such inquiry was considered appropriate. When instructions had already been given and assurance provided, as in the
case of Saul, then using the ephod or similar means of investigating
God's will was not warranted. In this instance David seems to have no
doubt about the necessity of dealing with the Philistine incursion. The
only question was whether he should get involved.

23:6 / Abiathar is described as joining David at Keilah and
bringing **the ephod down with him.** This means that the ephod would
not have been available for David to make his inquiries prior to leaving
Judah. He therefore must have used some other, unknown method of
inquiry, unless the phrase **at Keilah** has been misplaced.

23:13 / Saul's decision to abandon his project once David had
heard of it and moved on does not invalidate the oracle's prediction
that Saul would come to Keilah. Rather, it indicates the conditional nature of virtually all of OT predictive prophecies. When circumstances
alter, perhaps as a result of the prophecy, then the whole picture changes.
A good example of this is the overturning of the judgment on Nineveh
when, as a result of Jonah's prophecy, the city repented (Jonah 3:10).

23:17 / Jonathan's statement that Saul **will not lay a hand
on** David reflects not a naïve, ongoing belief in the basic goodness of
Saul's nature but rather a conviction that God will not permit Saul to
carry out his intentions. The repeated stress on Jonathan's endorsement of David's future kingship probably reflects the authors' intention to convince any doubters of the legitimacy of David's claim to the
throne.

23:19 / If the heading of Ps. 54 is accurate, then from David's perspective the **Ziphites** were ruthless, evil strangers, even though they were members of his own tribe. Ziph was a few miles southeast of Hebron, which later became David's capital when, on Saul's death, he took control of the southern region.

23:24–25 / It is hard to work out the exact movements. **Arabah** is the great rift valley around the Dead Sea and **Maon** part of the Judean wilderness, probably about five miles south of Ziph.

The dual reference to the **Desert of Maon** may be a scribal error and David moved from the Arabah (v. 24) to Maon (v. 25).

§21 Saul's First Escape (1 Sam. 24:1–22)

24:1–7 / Saul, having returned from an encounter with **the Philistines,** takes up his preoccupation with destroying David. He knows that David is located in **En Gedi** and can be looked for not too far away from the water source. With three battalions of crack soldiers Saul may expect to deal with David's six hundred scratch troops. It is greatly ironic that the only time that Saul came within reach of David he was unaware of it and utterly vulnerable.

The discussion between **David and his men** is vividly depicted. The men conclude this must be the fulfillment of God's promise that he would deliver David's **enemy into** his **hands** (v. 4). There is no record of this particular oracle being given, and it is probable that such an oracle was presupposed by David's rugged band, who by now must have known of his anointing as future king. David would have known the oracle was not valid, but in this emotionally charged situation he is easily persuaded and probably relishes the challenge.

David creeps **up unnoticed** and slices off **a corner of Saul's robe. Saul** moves off otherwise unharmed, but David immediately regrets what he has done. Royal garments have symbolic significance, and to take part of Saul's robe in this way, given the relationship between Saul and David, symbolizes seizing power. Jonathan has already made David a gift of garments (18:4), but David is aware that he can take over from Saul only when God makes it possible. Hence his anger with himself at succumbing to temptation in this way.

Saul was **the anointed of the LORD** and as such, in David's mind, could be dealt with only by the Lord. At this stage and in spite of their estrangement, Saul was still David's **master.** It is not hard to understand how David transferred his anger with himself to those who had encouraged him to take this action, although his rebuke of them seems harsh. He refused to allow any of them to take further advantage of Saul's weak position by attacking.

24:8–15 / It is difficult to gauge David's motivation in making himself known to Saul as soon as Saul had traveled a safe distance from the entrance to the cave. At face value his action was to try to persuade Saul that, in spite of his fears, David posed no direct threat to Saul's position. In fact the situation was the reverse because he had acted to keep Saul safe.

However, David's behavior may not be quite as disinterested as it first appears. There is something melodramatic in David's extravagant act of obeisance to Saul (v. 8), but Saul is not a stranger to melodramatic action, and the symbolism of David's prostration is clear. David is not seeking, and has never sought, to set himself up in opposition to Saul. In his own mind he remains in Saul's service; Saul is still **my lord the king.**

David, knowing the nature of Saul's jealousy and perhaps pandering to Saul's vanity, postulates that he must have been persuaded by convincing slanderers that David poses a threat. The implication is that Saul was far too sensible to come to this decision unaided. David has also suffered from unwise advisers who have tried to persuade him that Saul should be killed. But unlike Saul, David has refused to listen to them.

Cutting off the **corner of** Saul's **robe,** which a little while before David had seen as a reason to be conscience-stricken, now becomes a means of indicating his good faith. He could have killed Saul but he did not. Even his statements to his men about **the LORD's anointed** become transformed into a positive statement of good faith. David appears to be reinterpreting his own actions in an attempt to salve his conscience or in a highly skilled diplomatic tactic, using what comes to hand to further his own ends, perhaps much more effectively than a direct attack on Saul. There may be a little of both. Possibly David wants to reinterpret the robe-cutting episode before Saul discovers what he has done and interprets it as evidence that David is seeking to depose him.

However, although he may have manipulated Saul, there is no question that David was **not guilty of wrongdoing or rebellion.** He did not deserve to be **hunt**[ed] **down** in this way by Saul. He was willing to allow **the LORD** to be the **judge between** the two of them and the one who dealt with Saul, both for his unjustified attacks and, by implication, in any final removal from the throne.

The proverbial sayings of verses 13–14 may have some import that is now lost but seem to confirm that David was not a threat to Saul and that it was ridiculous for **the king of Israel,** which was how David viewed Saul, to bother about a **flea** on a **dog**'s carcass, which is how unimportant David portrayed himself to be. The point is that David trusted God to deal with Saul and to deliver himself from any danger.

24:16–22 / Whether or not David's whole appeal was carefully judged to reach through to the complex character that he knew so well, the appeal was successful. Saul was once again able to see David not as his enemy but as **my son,** perhaps responding to David's "my father" (v. 11). He regained his perspective concerning both God's activity and David's activity. He was convinced that an enemy would not have allowed him to escape so freely.

His assessment of David—**You are more righteous than I,** echoing Judah's comment about his daughter-in-law (Gen. 38:26)—means that if God were to judge between them as David had requested, the judgment would be given to David. **Saul wept aloud** as he acknowledged David's righteousness and allowed himself to face up to the truth of his own rejection by God. The horror with which David first reacted to his own action of taking a piece of Saul's robe was in no way reflected in Saul's reaction. Saul had been diverted from seeing that as a threat and persuaded that it was an act of mercy.

For the first time Saul acknowledges openly that he is well aware that David will be **king** and that **the kingdom of Israel will be established.** David will be able to achieve what Saul recognized was now beyond him, a stable and secure nation. Having acknowledged the inevitable, Saul repeats Jonathan's request that his family be protected rather than destroyed. With David's ready agreement to this—he has already given the same guarantee to Jonathan (20:14–15)—the two part. David is not so convinced by Saul's *volte-face* that he feels confident enough to accompany Saul. He knows that Saul's rational moments are neither regular nor extended. But for the moment he **and his men** are safe in their **stronghold,** which perhaps refers to Adullam (22:1).

Additional Notes §21

24:1 / The writers' purpose is not served by providing details concerning pursuit of **the Philistines**. However, incidental references like this support the view that the positive summary of Saul's reign (14:47–48) was not an unrealistic eulogy. He was able to take three thousand, or at least three battalions (see additional note on 4:10) with him to fight David. The whole army had not deserted.

24:2 / The **Crags of the Wild Goats** cannot be identified now, but the name is evocative. Wild ibex roamed freely not far from En Gedi, and the crags in question may have been a known grazing area. The ibex would have been a good source of food for David's men.

24:6 / The irony of v. 6 and v. 10 is pointed out by Edelman *(King Saul in the Historiography of Judah)*. Although David was well aware that neither he nor anyone else had any mandate to kill **the LORD's anointed**, Saul was trying to do that by seeking David's life.

24:8–13 / In that geographical setting sound would travel well over quite long distances. David's being able to **call out to Saul** (v. 8) does not mean that they had a face-to-face conversation.

Exum *(Tragedy and Biblical Narrative,* p. 94) considers that although David shows loyalty to Saul and does not kill him, nevertheless by "pointing out Saul's impotence" he humiliates him. Her suggestion, given David's questionable treatment of Michal and others, is that this humiliation is a calculated intention on David's part. David's speech does put himself in the right and therefore Saul in the wrong. However, Saul's response in this instance (vv. 16–21) shows that he feels remorse at misunderstanding David but not that he feels humiliated.

24:16 / David was Saul's son-in-law, but in the earlier stages of their contact the relationship between them was even closer than that (16:21–22). Saul did appear to regard David as a **son**. David sought to meet Saul's needs as a son for a father, and Saul furthered David's interests as a father for a son. It made the sense of betrayal felt by both when they became estranged particularly poignant.

Gros Louis ("The Difficulty of Ruling Well") makes a distinction between the public role and the private person. He argues that although the private Saul sees the private David as a son, Saul the king cannot cope with the threat posed by David.

J. D. Pleins ("Son-Slayers and Their Sons," *CBQ* 54 [1992], pp. 29–38) introduces an interesting parallel between Saul's attempts to kill David and Jonathan—his sons—and Abraham's sacrifice of Isaac. He posits a son-slaying "succession myth." "A structural analysis of the Genesis and Samuel narratives would yield the following basic scheme that we might term a succession myth: 1) God's demands impinge on the movement from one generation to the next. 2) The father attempts to kill the son. 3) The son is obedient. 4) The son does not die. 5) The son becomes the divinely supported heir. This is a myth that functions at levels of deep societal insecurity both biological and political" (p. 37). Using the term *myth* in this way may be questionable, and how Jonathan fits into this picture is not clear, but it is possible that the writers were conscious of the parallel as they wrote.

24:21 / The repeated stress on David's commitment not to destroy Saul's family may reflect that during David's reign he was repeatedly suspected of doing just that. The text thus serves an apologetic purpose to reinforce David's claim as king over the whole nation. Saul's supporters are being assured that there is no need for them to suspect and therefore reject David.

§22 David and Abigail (1 Sam. 25:1–44)

Sandwiched between the two parallel incidents in which David has the opportunity to destroy Saul but chooses to spare his life is this very different account of David's activities during this period. At first sight it appears out of place in the overall schema of the books of Samuel, where the focus is on the question of power, primarily in national leadership. But here too power is a key motif, and there are several reasons the writers might consider this incident to be relevant.

25:1a / Saul's open acknowledgment of David's claim to the throne (24:20) provides a turning point in the ongoing saga. Although his fight with reality continues unabated and David is again driven out of the country, the heart has gone out of Saul's desperate clinging to power. The reader is no longer in any doubt about the eventual outcome. It is appropriate, therefore, that the death of Samuel should be noted. Whatever vestige of power remained with Samuel has gone forever. Neither David nor Saul could seek out his advice. But Samuel had played a long, significant, and valued part in Israel's history, and the whole nation **mourned for him,** a fitting epitaph for a great Israelite. His burial **at his home in Ramah** reflects the refusal found throughout the OT to sacralize death. Even for a man of Samuel's caliber, to create a shrine around his tomb—in the way that was common in Egypt and other surrounding nations—was not appropriate. We can only speculate whether either David or Saul or both were present at the national assembly called to mourn Samuel's death.

25:1b–3 / David continued to move around the territory and returned to his old haunts in the **Desert of Maon** (23:24–25). The term *desert* can give a false impression. Parts of the land were able to provide grazing for animals, even if arable crops needed to be grown elsewhere.

Carmel was the place where Saul had set up a monument in his own honor (15:12). Near there a wealthy farmer conducted his business. **Nabal,** meaning "foolish," is almost certainly a nickname applied to suit his character. He had all the stamina and determination of his ancestor Caleb but had inherited none of his sterling qualities. Nabal was a selfish, unlikable brute. His wife, **Abigail,** is portrayed as an ideal partner, both **intelligent and beautiful.**

This chapter lets us know that in the dispute between David and Saul the people were beginning to take sides. Saul's paranoiac fear of conspiracy was beginning to have a basis in reality. Here we have even a husband and wife on opposite sides. That the one is portrayed as an ignorant boor and the other as a gifted and attractive personality increases the feeling that anybody with any sense would support David's cause. It was not in the interests of either David or the writers to present an overt criticism of Saul. However, Nabal, standing as Saul's representative, could be revealed to be as foolish as his name implied. Thus Saul's cause could be condemned without lessening the significance or the inviolability of being the Lord's anointed. The description of David as Nabal's son (v. 8), coming as it does after a chapter that reflects on David as Saul's son, subtly encourages the comparison, as does the fact that David could have killed Nabal but chose or was persuaded to leave his fate in God's hands. This "narrative analogy" is explored by Gordon ("David's Rise and Saul's Demise") and noted further by Exum (*Tragedy and Biblical Narrative,* p. 106).

25:4–9 / During their months of hiding David and his entourage sustained themselves by running a security unit, which could be viewed as a polite protection racket or as a semivoluntary neighborhood watch scheme. They did not engage in looting and prevented others from doing so, but at harvest time they expected to receive a reward for their forbearance and their protective activities. The very wealthy Nabal (v. 2) would have plenty to spare at the **sheep-shearing** celebratory feast, which was likely to be sumptuous. The message to Nabal is couched in typical Eastern flowery language. Even without any service they might have rendered, normal rules of hospitality would have brought them some kind of positive response.

25:10–13 / Nabal's reaction to their request is far from flowery. He refuses to accept any connection with David. "Your son David" of verse 8 is returned as **Who is this son of Jesse?** Nabal accepts Saul's assessment of David as a thankless rebel

accompanied by scalawags (22:13; 24:2), and he refuses to give
any help. The supply-seeking party returned to David, making
no attempt to remove supplies by force. This fact emphasizes the
discipline that David had instilled into his troops.

However, Nabal's reaction did not remain unchallenged.
The contribution to David's supplies may have been theoreti-
cally voluntary, but no contribution was unacceptable. Also, Nabal's aggressive support for Saul perhaps meant he was liable to
bring danger to them while they remained in that area. David,
following sensible tactics of not leaving his base camp unguarded,
went down to sort Nabal out.

25:14–31 / The characterization may be exaggerated, but
the picture is vivid and realistic. The farm workers who had
heard Nabal's tirade could envisage the consequences and went
to Abigail, expecting her to sort it out for them. In spite of her
husband's intransigence she had managed to build up such a
good relationship with the farm workers, a further tribute to her
character. They outline the situation, taking it for granted that
she knows that reasoning with Nabal is a waste of time, and
leave it in her hands.

Abigail takes immediate action and reaches David's raiding party in the nick of time. David's curse is reminiscent of earlier foolish vows made by Saul (1 Sam. 14), but in this instance
Abigail's intervention prevented David from carrying out his intentions. Her speech, although she refers to herself as a **servant,**
is masterly and has apologetic significance that goes beyond its
import in the unfolding events of the narrative. She takes the
blame for not having been aware of their visit, while disassociat-
ing herself from Nabal's action. She has brought the necessary
gift so that any action David might take could now be seen only
as revenge. Her knowledge of David seems enough to assure her
that he will consider revenge as God's prerogative, not his, and
that causing needless death is not his intention. She makes it
clear that her political views are diametrically opposed to those
of her husband. She is fully aware of what is involved in David's
dispute with Saul, and she associates herself with David, accepting unquestioningly his innocence, the rightness of his claim to
the throne of Israel, and the fact that God is behind him, who
fights the LORD's battles.

The details and clarity of her speech indicate that Abigail is
not simply protecting the farm staff from being harmed but also

expressing her own firmly held opinions. Her final request, that when he is in control he should **remember** her, parallels Saul's request in the previous chapter (24:21). David has an opportunity to grant her request sooner than might have been expected.

25:32–44 / David recognizes Abigail as a woman who has correctly identified his motives and concerns. He acknowledges that in the heat of the moment he would have taken hasty action to be regretted later. He is aware that Abigail has presented him with a challenge to nonviolent treatment of opponents within Israel that goes beyond her immediate request to spare Nabal and her own workers. He recognizes that Abigail's message is in line with what he knows God has been saying to him. Immediately he calms down, accepts the gift, and responds positively to her request for no further steps to be taken against the farm or its workers. David's response to Abigail's speech has some parallels with his reaction to what Nathan had to say to him in 2 Samuel 12, although that comes after rather than before he has taken unwise action.

Nabal, on hearing of his wife's action, suffered an apoplectic fit and within a fortnight was dead (vv. 37–38). David interpreted this death as vengeance taken by God on his behalf and thus a confirmation of all that Abigail said to him. Whether the marriage that then took place was one of convenience or reflected a loving relationship is not clear. It provided David with extra funding because Abigail almost certainly brought more than just the **five maids** with her. The marriage allowed David to fulfill any responsibility he might feel for protecting Abigail from Nabal's cohorts or even from Saul. It gave Abigail an opportunity to follow through her political convictions and a context in which to exercise her other gifts. The impression is that she enthusiastically accepted David's offer in spite of the fact that she was not his sole wife.

Additional Notes §22

25:3 / The Calebites were the descendants of Caleb, the spy who along with Joshua recommended entry to the promised land and who was still going strong well into his eighties (Num. 13:30; Josh. 14:6–15).

25:18–19 / The fact that Abigail was able to take away this amount of supplies, enough to supply six hundred men with a good meal (Baldwin, *1 and 2 Samuel*, pp. 149–50) without Nabal's noticing what she was doing, indicates how well-supplied the farm was and also perhaps demonstrates the extent of Nabal's denseness.

25:41 / Abigail's profession of willingness to do even menial tasks like foot-washing may be hyperbole or may indicate that this wealthy woman was well aware that life with a fugitive, even one with a guaranteed bright future, was not likely to be easy.

25:42–44 / **Abigail** and David apparently had one son, known as Kileab in 2 Sam. 3:3 and Daniel in 1 Chron. 3:1, but we read no more of him, and he may have died early.

Saul did not officially have the right to give **Michal** to another husband without David's consent, but the action is not surprising. The close connection between David and his family would have been anathema to Saul. He could not prevent Jonathan's friendship with David, but he could take Michal out of the picture. Whether Michal consented or not is impossible to determine. We do know that **Paltiel** loved her (2 Sam. 3:15–16).

We know nothing of **Ahinoam**'s background, but she was the mother of Amnon, David's firstborn son (2 Sam. 3:2).

§23 Saul's Second Escape (1 Sam. 26:1–25)

26:1–3 / The Ziphites, who nearly enabled Saul to find David once before, may have looked for a second chance. However, the wording in verse 1 is the same as that used on the previous occasion (23:19), which seems strange, even given the fact that David was likely to use the same hiding places on a number of occasions. Some scholars have concluded from this, from the similarity between the two occasions on which Saul's life was spared, and from the fact that the second account makes no direct reference to the first, that we have two alternative accounts of the same event.

However, there are also substantial differences between the two incidents. For example, in the first Saul strays into David's camp (24:3) and in the second David enters Saul's camp (26:5). The writers see the two as different yet with parallel significance. It is possible that a copyist's error led to some overlay between the accounts, but there is no reason to presuppose that in Saul's repeated searching through the mountainous wilderness for David, there was not more than one occasion when the hunter became the hunted. On this occasion Saul, again using his crack troops and having received good intelligence, moved quickly to the area where David could be found (26:2).

26:4–12 / David, also with a good intelligence network, was well aware of Saul's arrival. Having a vast knowledge of this territory David was able to get within eyesight of Saul's encampment without being seen by whatever sentries might have been posted. This time there is no question of coming across Saul by accident. David's small group is still too big to go down into the camp, so he asks for one volunteer, and **Abishai . . . , Joab's brother** goes with him. Saul and his army, with more confidence in their sentries than was warranted, are deeply asleep, a fact that verse 12 ascribes to God's direct action. This is perhaps included to provide a defense for Saul's general **Abner**, who is always presented as a good soldier (2 Sam. 2:1–30), as much as to explain how David and Abishai managed to get so close. Abishai, who may or may not have been present on the previous occasion, draws the same conclusion as his fellow soldiers had done (1 Sam. 24:4; 26:8). This was a God-given opportunity to remove Saul from the scene, and Abishai was willing to apply the single spear thrust that would be needed. David, however, is aware that opportunity is not evidence of God's purposes. This time he has worked through his conclusions and planned his tactics. He has no doubts that causing physical harm to Saul would lead to God's taking action to ensure that physical harm would in return come to the perpetrator (vv. 9–10). However, removing the water jug and the spear that was always by or in Saul's hand was a different matter.

26:13–16 / This time, having retreated across the valley, David calls out not to Saul but to **Abner,** who was wakened from the deep sleep. David, having got Abner's attention, acknowledges his reputation but lays charges, with some justification, that Abner and his men had not fulfilled their obligations to protect the king. Any bandit, which David was not, could have crept down and killed him. The evidence of the **spear** and the **water jug** was irrefutable. Abner and Saul's army in general were far more worthy of the death penalty for their lack of care for Saul than David had ever been.

26:17–20 / Saul, now awakened, either recognizes David's voice or, as the voice across the valley is likely to be distorted, assumes that anyone in this region daring to challenge Saul's camp must be David. On this occasion he calls David his **son** before rather than after David has presented his defense. This is far easier to explain if the previous incident did take place as recorded and is brought back to Saul's mind as he again hears David's voice across the wilderness.

Abner drops out of the picture, and David makes his final attempt to persuade Saul of the foolishness of his campaign against David. Unsurprisingly in the light of Saul's record, there is less conviction of a hearing than we find in chapter 24. David reiterates the arguments. He is **guilty** of nothing that could justify Saul's relentless pursuit. If the LORD **has incited** Saul then, even if David were guilty, **an offering** would be enough to make atonement. If human beings are responsible, and Saul is implicitly included, then they deserve to be **cursed before the** LORD, that is, put outside of covenant fellowship with God and his people. They deserve the punishment that they have in effect given to David, to be driven out of Israel. It is becoming clear to David, although it is not made explicit until 27:1, that his only option is to leave his native soil. He is no more harmful to Saul than a **flea**, so why should **the king of Israel** come after David as if on a game-bird hunting expedition?

26:21–25 / Saul, as he did on the earlier occasion (24:17), responds to the fact that David could have killed him and did not. He admits the wrongness of his behavior. He again calls David his **son** and this time explicitly calls on David to **come back**. David studiously ignores this request and makes no attempt to acknowledge Saul as his father, referring to him simply as **the king**. By recording Saul's description of himself as a **fool**, the writers draw attention to the parallels with Nabal's behavior in the previous chapter. David calls for someone to come over and recover Saul's property, although, because of its special significance, only the **spear** is mentioned. If the spear has symbolism as royal regalia, David wants to make it clear that he has no intention of removing it from Saul. Showing that he could have deprived Saul of his spear, and then very openly proclaiming that this was never his intention, makes a far more effective declaration of his acceptance of Saul's right to rule than not taking the spear in the first place. David's second speech to Saul makes it apparent that he views Saul's response with extreme skepticism, which is unsurprising given the short-lived nature of Saul's previous repentance. He picks up Abishai's assurance that God had given this opportunity but sees it as an opportunity to proclaim his innocence rather than to kill Saul, the LORD's **anointed**. Saul, as befits the king, takes the last word by giving David a blessing again, perhaps this time somewhat wistfully calling David his **son**. His acknowledgment of David's eventual **triumph** is less explicit than in chapter 24, but it is there nevertheless. The two men then part for the final time.

Additional Notes §23

The parallels between the account in 26:1–25 and that in 23:19–24:22 are undoubted and are ably set out by Klein (*1 Samuel*, pp.

236–37). Caird ("1 and 2 Samuel," 2:855–1176) and H. P. Smith (*A Critical and Exegetical Commentary on the Books of Samuel* [ICC; Edinburgh: Clark, 1951]) take for granted that the two accounts are different presentations of the same incident. Klein and Brueggemann *(First and Second Samuel)* also assume one event but think that the writers have different purposes as they present the two accounts. However, Gordon *(1 and 2 Samuel: A Commentary)* prefers to assume two events took place, arguing that the differences are significant and "it is probably easier to account for the similarities by assuming a degree of assimilation in their early transmission history" (p. 178). Baldwin *(1 and 2 Samuel)* takes it for granted that the two accounts record different events.

26:6 / **Ahimelech,** described as **the Hittite** to distinguish him from Ahimelech the priest, is unknown outside of this verse. A number of Hittites, like Uriah (2 Sam. 11:3), had joined David's forces.

Although this verse brings the first mention of both **Abishai** and **Joab,** any reader is expected to know the identity of Joab, who became David's military commander and played a significant part throughout his reign.

Along with Asahel, another brother, Abishai and Joab are known as the sons of **Zeruiah.** She was David's sister; presumably, as he was the youngest of the eight boys in the family, she was substantially older than he, making David's nephews around his own age. Why her three sons should be regularly identified by their mother rather than by their father or their birthplace is never clarified, although it may be because of the royal connection that she gave them. All three of them were named in David's elite group of "mighty men" (2 Sam. 23:8–39).

26:10 / David's statement to Abishai gives insight into the way in which he understood God to be involved in history. God's judgment on bloodguilt is seen as coming either through the natural processes of life **(his time will come and he will die)** or through the hand of an enemy in **battle.** God is in control of life and death even though the instrument used may be disease or enemy weapons. Saul's death in battle is possibly in the minds of the writers, as is the fact that Nabal died of natural causes (25:37–38).

26:11 / At first sight there seems to be a contradiction between David's being conscience-stricken about removing a small piece of Saul's clothes and his conscious decision on this occasion to take Saul's **spear.** Both of these items could be seen as related to Saul's kingship. The difference seems to be that on the first occasion, although he was able to transform the situation by presenting it differently to Saul, David saw it as a chance to do away with Saul. In contrast, this time his action was a deliberate ploy to make the point that he did not want to kill Saul and thus could in no way be seen as acting against **the LORD's anointed.** This strong sense of the importance of not taking action against the one whom God had put in place probably stemmed from David's genuine concern not to go against God's will. However, the concern of the writers, and maybe of David, to protect his future interests, could be coming into play. If the people could be imbued with the awesome nature of being anointed by God, they would be less likely to turn against David when he eventually came to power. Thus, patience with Saul was likely to bring great benefits to the security of David's regime later.

26:17 / On the previous occasion when Abner was instrumental in bringing David to Saul, the question of David's sonship was also an issue (17:57–58). The writers may have this in mind when they include Abner's participation in the account.

26:19 / It is conceivable that some of Saul's followers had said to David, **Go, serve other gods,** but his statement could be picking up his suspicion that he may be forced to leave the country. Outside the land, he had no **share in the LORD's inheritance,** to which land was intrinsic.

It was a common understanding in the ancient Near East that a god's power was geographically limited and that to enter another land almost inevitably meant serving another god. David's actions when he left Israel show that he did not hold this view, but it could be seen as the implication of Saul's men driving him out of his homeland. When he was outside the land he would have no access to the shrines where Yahweh was worshiped.

§24 The Philistine Campaign (1 Sam. 27–29)

27:1 / David's lack of trust in Saul's profession of sorrow and promise to cease harming David is made explicit. David assumes that Saul will try again and may eventually succeed in destroying him; he may envisage this destruction coming not through any military prowess on Saul's part but by David or his men being unable to resist another temptation to act against Saul. The destruction would then come not through death but through the kind of guilt that would destroy David's reign as certainly as it had destroyed Saul's.

To avoid this possibility David takes the dubious route of emigration into Philistine territory. He rightly predicts that Saul will not follow him there (v. 4). Saul may even think that since David has fled the country he has given up any chance to replace Saul on the throne.

27:2–7 / David's entourage moved with him to **Gath,** where **Achish** was still in control. The ability David had to stimulate trust and loyalty in his troops is evidenced at this early stage in his career. This voluntary exile must have been seen as a risky venture, but there appear to have been few dissenters. The fact that he had once before deceived Achish about his harmlessness (21:10–15) perhaps influenced David's choice of Gath as the site of his exile. Achish appears to have been a particularly guileless character, and David may have picked that up on his first visit; he takes advantage of that guilelessness now. For Achish, a recovered madman may even be seen as a token of good luck, which would perhaps explain his readiness to accept David at face value, as an enemy of Saul.

David, looking for a safe haven, skillfully manages to persuade Achish that his request for a **country town** is disinterested and for Achish's own benefit. These diplomatic tactics are similar to those used when David persuaded Saul that in cutting off part of his garment he was doing him a favor (24:11). Achish grants his request, and David, for **a year and four months,** has almost complete freedom. He and his men, living safely in **Ziklag** and without the threat of Saul hanging over them, can carry out raiding missions against Israelite enemies much as they have done before. In the overall narrative, verses 8–11 reassure any who heard that David had spent many months living safely within Philistine territory that he had not betrayed his own people but had benefited them by destroying groups of potential raiders. First Samuel 30:26 describes him as supplying his Judean friends with plunder.

27:8–12 / The account of the activities engaged in while based at Ziklag, like the accounts concerning Jonathan's exploits, could easily have been told as a campfire story, in this instance a humorous one, at least as far as Israelite soldiers were concerned. The community at Ziklag managed to wreak havoc among surrounding tribes that opposed Israel but were allies to Achish and the Philistines. Because the policy of total destruction, probably of fairly small groups at a time, left no witnesses, David was able to persuade Achish that the booty he was amassing came from desert communities belonging to Israel or to those in alliance with it. Some of this booty would have been paid in tribute to Achish, which made him happy to allow David's activities to continue unabated. Achish, even after many months, was oblivious to the truth and developed complete confidence in David as his own supporter.

28:1–2 / Achish's confidence was so strong that when a large-scale battle between the Philistines and the Israelites was being planned he took it for granted that David would join his own forces. His slightly tentative **you must understand** is perhaps an apology that David's forces will not be able to undertake an independent initiative in this battle. David's deliberately ambiguous reply reflects his knowledge that in this kind of battle Achish would discover his true colors. Achish, in his guileless innocence, does not recognize the irony and promises him a promotion with a lifetime guarantee.

The account, which continues in 29:1, is interrupted to give an insight into Saul's mindset during the time that David had been out of the country. The inclusion of this separate story at such a crucial moment is likely to be a deliberate tactic to increase suspense. The readers have to wait before they discover how David and his followers will avoid the inevitable discovery arising out of Achish's trust in him.

28:3–7 / For the purposes of this story it is important that the reader remembers that Samuel was dead and buried, that occult activity was forbidden in Israel, and that Saul had taken action to ensure that the law in this regard be kept. In an account that portrays Saul as at his lowest, there is still the underlying sense that he had on occasion fulfilled his responsibilities to keep the people in line with God's laws—that he had had the potential to be a good king.

The Philistines, on an occasion that is probably part of the campaign being planned in chapter 26, **set up camp at Shunem,** toward the north of Israelite territory but still south of Galilee. Saul's **gathered** army faced them from the slopes of **Gilboa.** Saul, a shadow of the noted warrior he had once been, was petrified. Given his fragile mental health, and having let go of his obsession that David was plotting to depose him, he may have had to face the reality of his own inadequacies. The need to protect Israel from Philistine attack remained as strong as ever, so seeking further instructions from God was unnecessary. But, crying out for the kind of confidence boosting that he had never been able to cope without, Saul tried every possible means to ensure confirmation of God's support except for the unavailable ephod now possessed by David (23:6; 30:7). This behavior shows Saul's desperation and perhaps an increasing lack of confidence in God's desire or ability to protect him. **Dreams, Urim,** and **prophets** all failed him; the only reply from God was silence. In desperation he turned to a source of information that he and all around him knew was not appropriate for those who were part of Yahweh's covenant nation (Deut. 18:9–14; Lev. 19:31). He asked for details of the whereabouts of a **medium** and was informed of the existence of a woman at **Endor,** a few miles to the northeast of Gilboa.

28:8–10 / The impropriety of Saul's action is emphasized by the need he felt to disguise himself and to trace this woman only by **night.** She does not recognize him at first but is cautious, fearing that any unknown potential customer may be a spy from Saul sent to ensure religious purity in the land. She is reassured by Saul's swearing in **the LORD**'s name that she will have immunity and agrees to practice her craft. It is ironic that anyone swearing in this way is unlikely to be concerned for the Lord's will and thus less likely to be a threat to her.

28:11–20 / Saul, when asked which dead person he wishes to consult, asks for **Samuel.** It seems that Saul wished to deny the reality of Samuel's death just as he had long tried to deny the reality of David's anointing. Whether or not the woman was a charlatan, what happened next was unexpected, and she was shocked and horrified. Whether this was because of what she saw or because whatever clairvoyant skills she may have had told her belatedly that her client was **Saul** is not clear. The sense of mystery within this account and the many unanswered questions are almost certainly an intentional strategy on the part of the writers. The woman's statement is vague, but by whatever means and with whatever reality, Saul became convinced that Samuel was there to give him the advice he so urgently needed. However, in addition to receiving confirmation of the things he already knew concerning his own sin and God's appointment of **David** as replacement, he became positive that death and defeat awaited himself, his sons, and the Israelite army. Not all Saul's sons were killed, for Ish-Bosheth remained to stand at least temporarily as a replacement for Saul, and although the army did suffer losses, subsequent events make it clear that those losses were not as great as Saul feared. However, Saul was left with utter, desolate hopelessness. Compounded by lack of food during his clandestine expedition, this led to his collapse.

28:21–25 / The **woman,** perhaps frightened by Saul's reaction to the night's events and unable to do anything to relieve his despair, sought to relieve his hunger. The fear that she would be blamed if Saul died at this point must have added force to her persuasive powers. Eventually Saul's attendants added their voices to hers, and he was persuaded to eat. The meal of meat with unleavened bread is reminiscent of other ceremonial meals, and perhaps even of the Passover, also eaten by **night.** This meal is eaten not in hope but in despair.

29:1 / The Philistine **forces** collected at **Aphek,** north of all the main Philistine towns but still well south of Gilboa, Shunem (28:4), and **Jezreel** before they regrouped to travel north to face Saul. The impression given is that Saul had already gathered his army around the **spring,** probably Harod (see Judg. 7:1), at the foot of Mount Gilboa. Saul's terror when he sees the Philistine army (28:5) does not at first sight support this impression. However, it could indicate that he had intended to wage a campaign against other northern groups and had not expected the

Philistines to challenge him in Gilboa. It may be that the Philistines were trying to prevent Saul from organizing a takeover of the northern area and thus gaining the strength to defeat them in the south. Saul's disorientation at this new, and from his point of view catastrophic, turn of events would then be easily explained. The willingness of the Philistine army commanders to take their forces so far out of their own territory is an indication of how confident they were at this time.

29:2–5 / As 28:1 has already suggested, **David and his men** marched alongside Achish's Gittite forces and arrived with them at the mustering area around Aphek. The other **Philistine commanders** were surprised that Achish had brought Hebrew troops with him when their expedition involved fighting against the **Hebrews.** Achish staunchly defends both David and his right to bring him, protesting that David has betrayed Saul and been loyal to Gath for more than **a year.**

However, Achish is overruled by the other commanders, who are correctly suspicious of David's motives. Unlike Achish, they are unconvinced that the one who had been such a scourge of their forces had changed his allegiance, or even if he had that he would not change again and be a destructive element as far as their campaign was concerned. Many of their men had heard David's name set before them as a taunt in the Israelite battle songs that could be heard across the fields and hillsides between their forces. They were probably wrong that David would attempt to regain Saul's favor, but they were right in every other way. Achish had no choice but to give in to their reservations. David was not to be attacked, but he must return to Ziklag.

29:6–11 / The unworldly Achish was caught between needing to accept the decision of the army leaders and his desire not to offend David. His naïve trust in David's loyalty remains unabated. He is confident of David's loyalty and would have had no qualms about having David **serve with** him **in the army.** In spite of the doubts of his comrades, he is not afraid that David might turn on him. But he is aware that the others are so wary that if David does not remove himself quickly he and his men might be harmed.

David reveals himself as a consummate actor, with no compunction about deceiving the one who had protected and supported him. His air of injured innocence masks the delight he must have felt at being so easily able to extricate himself from what might have been a disastrous situation. His protest that he is not to be allowed to **fight against the enemies of my lord the king** could be seen as genuine regret that he is not going to be able to act on Saul's behalf. Achish is convinced by what David says to him and for the third time proclaims his confidence in David's innocence. His comparing of David to **an angel of God** and his use of the name of Israel's God in verse 6 as part of an oath shows how much he wanted to back up his sincerity. But his trust is not enough, and David's party must leave for the south at once, which they did. Chapter 30 reveals that their early return to Ziklag was providential.

Additional Notes §24

27:2 / Gath was on the eastern side of Philistia, close to Judean territory but well south of Saul's base at Gibeah.

27:3 / The presence of whole families would indicate to Achish that this was meant to be a long-term visit and confirm the impression that the group had burned their bridges as far as Israel was concerned. It was a common occurrence for discontented groups from one tribe to hire themselves out as mercenaries to other groups, although joining in fights against their own tribes would be rarer—which explains the wariness of the other Philistine lords (29:3–5).

27:6 / **Ziklag,** one of the most distant of Gath's satellite towns, is in an area subject to attack from a number of different directions. Josh. 15:31 has it as part of Judah's territory, and it probably changed hands several times. It would have suited Achish's purposes to have an extra force, presumed to be acting for his benefit, guarding the border land, and it suited David's purposes to be far enough from Philistine population centers to be able to carry out his activities unchallenged.

27:8 / The **Geshurites** lived to the south of Philistia, and their home is to be distinguished from the Geshur across the Jordan, where Absalom spent his time of exile (2 Sam. 13:38).

Girzites are unknown outside of this verse.

The **Amalekites** had suffered great losses under the *herem* (15:3), but it had not been fully applied and they still remained a significant group. Whether the *herem* applied for a short time and then lost its force is not clear. Although David for other reasons kills all those he encounters, there is apparently no restriction on his taking plunder from them for his own use. Unlike Saul (15:7–26), David is not condemned for failing to destroy goods dedicated to God.

28:4 / 29:1 describes the Philistines gathering their forces at Aphek, where David left them, before going on to Jezreel, which is near Gilboa in the north, to meet Saul. If the same campaign is involved, the events recorded in ch. 28 must have taken place later than those in ch. 29.

The fact that Saul **gathered all the Israelites,** in other words organized a general call-up, shows that this was a major campaign and not part of the normal raiding activities of the standing army.

28:6–7 / God is described on a number of occasions as speaking through dreams, but unlike surrounding nations Israel did not have professional dream interpreters. If a dream was sent by God, and there is no assumption that every dream is God-given (Jer. 23:25, 28), then only God could interpret it.

The precise difference or relationship between the **Urim** and the ephod is not clear.

The existence of mediums in Israel further indicates the syncretism that plagued Israelite religion during the nation's history. Necromancy of this type was still flourishing in the reign of Manasseh (2 Kgs. 21:6).

It is interesting that Saul requests his attendants to find a female medium. Although Lev. 20:27 and Deut. 18:11 indicate that mediums could be of either sex, it is possible that more women than men were involved in necromancy. Or it may be that Saul felt safer with a woman, his paranoia perhaps leading him to assume that a woman would be less likely to betray him. Or he may take it for granted that any **medium** that might be found will be a **woman.**

28:11 / It has been suggested (e.g., Caird, "1 and 2 Samuel," 2:1028, following a few Greek manuscripts) that in v. 12 "Samuel" is a misprint for "Saul" and that the woman got a good look at Saul, perhaps recognizing him by his height, and this explains her horrified reaction. However, Saul believed Samuel had appeared to him.

28:15–16 / Samuel's complaint that he has been **disturbed** ties in with what we know of the early understanding of the fate of the dead. There was no real belief in ongoing life, but because nonexistence was incomprehensible they were seen as inhabiting the underworld, Sheol, in a kind of shadowy nonlife comparable to sleep.

Saul's statement that **God has turned away from** him is repeated by Samuel, indicating that Saul's own statement shows he should not expect Samuel to give him an answer on God's behalf. Part of the ambiguity of the passage is that an answer of sorts is nevertheless given.

28:21 / The woman's coming to Saul after his collapse suggests that she had not played any part in his encounter with Samuel.

29:1–11 / 1 Sam. 24–26 reflects on the question of bloodguilt and David's protection from it as he refrained from killing Saul, Nabal, and then Saul again. 2 Sam. 1–4 discusses the deaths of Saul and several members of his entourage and denies that David had any part in the killing. W. Brueggemann ("Narrative Intentionality in 1 Samuel 29,"

JSOT 43 [1989], pp. 21–35) sees ch. 29, which also reflects on the innocence or otherwise of David, as significantly placed between the two. He suggests that "the narrative may be designed to exhibit David's capacity for dishonesty, and his nervy effectiveness in conning the Philistines" (p. 28) but concludes that a more likely purpose is to show that although Achish's thrice-repeated statement of David's innocence was mistaken from his own perspective, nevertheless from an Israelite perspective David was innocent of all treason and betrayal in spite of living in enemy territory for so long.

29:2–3 / A distinction is made between the **rulers** of v. 2, probably the lords of the five cities of Philistia, and the army **commanders**. It is sometimes suggested that the rulers supported Achish and only the commanders were against David, but it makes no difference to the import of the chapter.

As noted in the additional note on 13:13, **Hebrews** was a term often used by foreigners to describe the Israelites, as here, and sometimes by Israelites to identify themselves to foreigners. It is rarely, if ever, used of Israelites among themselves. The term was also used for non-Israelite groups (cf. additional note on 13:3). The Philistines had previously suffered from desertion by Hebrew mercenary soldiers who may or may not have been Israelites, and these commanders were not about to allow the same thing to happen again (14:21).

29:6 / **Achish** uses the name of Yahweh, **the LORD**, probably out of respect for David rather than because he had given any allegiance to Yahweh.

§25 Victory and Defeat (1 Sam. 30:1–31:13)

30:1–5 / Although a small group could have traveled more quickly, it took David's army of about six hundred men three days to travel the fifty or so miles back to **Ziklag.** They almost certainly would have been away for at least a week, leaving plenty of time for **the Amalekites** to take advantage of their absence. David's previous activities against groups including the Amalekites (27:8) must have been noted, but his policy of destruction meant that there was no evidence against him. This attack on Ziklag appears to be opportunistic rather than special vengeance. The writers note that although all **the women** and children had been captured, no one had been killed. The approach of the Amalekite army was rather more forbearing than that of David's troops, which indicates that they had no idea of Ziklag's part in the attacks against them or that this was a group who had not been affected.

The attack may have been less comprehensive than it could have been; nevertheless to David's troops it was devastating. They had just engaged in a long march with great tension on the outward journey when they did not know if their duplicity would be discovered. With the relief of tension on the return trip was also probably a frustration that they had not been able to take any action, and the mixed emotions would have added to their exhaustion. To find that their sanctuary had been destroyed and their families, whom they had moved to Gath to keep them safe from Saul, had been captured, was more than they could cope with. The fact that David had been affected, losing his **two wives,** did not prevent them from blaming him for this tragedy (v. 6). The writers may also lead the reader to infer that if Saul had destroyed the Amalekites (15:3), then this tragedy would not have happened. Thus this incident provides a further reason for the need for David to take over as king.

30:6–10 / The men's heartache was primarily related to the loss of their families. David's wives are mentioned, and he wept alongside his men (v. 4), but in verse 6 his anguish seems to have stemmed more from the fact that his men were **talking of stoning him** than from the loss of his family. There appears to have been a general loss of perspective resulting from the trauma, but David's trust in **the LORD his God** enabled him and his men to regain perspective and find **strength** and courage. The sense of David standing alone with enemy and friend turning against him and only God to give succor is a common scenario in the Psalms.

The situation was bad but possibly not irreversible. Using **the ephod** was probably more for the men's sake than for David's. It turned their attention away from their loss, away from their perceptions of David's guilt, and toward God. The message given through the ephod convinced them in a way that David's own words were unlikely to have done that God was still with them and that there was hope that their families would be restored to them. It gave them the renewed confidence that was vital if any successful rescue campaign was to be mounted.

The tired troops therefore gathered their meager resources of energy and set off to pursue the raiders. The hike across the barren wastelands of this area would have been enough to tax the strength of fully fit troops. When they reached the major hurdle of the **Besor Ravine,** one-third of the men could not summon enough strength to cross. They stayed behind, presumably with any luggage that was too awkward to take over.

30:11–15 / It may be that the rescue of the dying **Egyptian** youth was a purely humanitarian act that happened to have good consequences for David. Giving food reflects a desire to fully restore the youth, not just to provide enough strength to enable him to speak. In that sparsely populated area anybody might have some knowledge of active raiding parties, but it is unlikely that there was evidence of a direct connection with the Amalekites until after the young man had eaten and recovered sufficiently to tell his story. He may have been captured, perhaps as a child, by a similar raiding party heading south rather than north. His being left to fend for himself when he **became ill** does not necessarily reflect cruelty on his master's part. There was no room in a raiding party for a sickly **slave;** to leave him was an alternative to his being summarily killed, and this way he had a chance.

The Egyptian said that he had come from an **Amalekite** party that had carried out raids against Israelites and Philistines and that had been responsible for the burning of Ziklag. He showed no particular loyalty to the Amalekites, and, seeking only an amnesty for himself, guided David's party over the Amalekite route. His knowledge of the route (v. 16) may indicate that his master had expected him to recover and catch up.

30:16–20 / The Amalekites proved to be an easy target even for David's small and exhausted band. They were **scattered over the countryside,** rejoicing in their success, and they had abandoned all defense strategies. Many were killed, and with deliberate irony the writers give the information that only **four hundred** escaped, the same number of men with which David had destroyed the rest. Every one of the people and every part of the property that had been taken from Ziklag was recovered alongside a great deal of valuable booty. The explicit mention that David's **two wives** had also been rescued suggests that they had more significance to him than the earlier reference indicated. David, who had been the scapegoat (v. 6), about to be stoned for failing to prevent such a loss, was now acclaimed as the author of a great victory. The capricious quality of human nature is evident in this chapter.

30:21–25 / David may not have had great success in personal relationships, but he had tremendous diplomatic skills. He knew how to inspire soldiers and how to create loyalty among his followers. The **two hundred men** left behind at **Besor** had recovered and were able to come out **to meet** the returning heroes. Many of David's troops were not professional soldiers, and it is to the credit of those who had not been able to continue that they had stayed with the baggage and had not drifted away.

The attitude of those who wanted to deprive the weaklings of a share in the **plunder** they had not been responsible for capturing is understandable. However, the text portrays such a selfish attitude as **evil** and its proponents as **troublemakers.** David in his rebuke calls them **brothers,** with an implicit reminder that those who were left behind were also members not only of David's personal army but of God's covenant family. God had given the victory to all of them. Because this was so, those who had been involved in the fighting were no more deserving than those who had not. The policy of equal sharing recognizes that all they have, particularly the plunder coming from victory in battle, is God-given. There is no indication that the two hundred who stayed behind did so for any other reason than exhaustion. However, David, in describing them as those **who stayed with the supplies,** gives them a function and in so doing restores their self-respect and makes them more likely to function well in the future. The principle that every soldier will gain the same reward whatever part he plays in the campaign fits well both with the covenant concept of brotherhood and with the concept of God as the one who is primarily responsible for each one of their victories. It is possible that Paul had been reflecting on passages such as this one when he developed his teaching about one body with many members (1 Cor. 12).

The reader is gradually being introduced to different aspects of David's role and the way in which he was carrying out kingly duties without having deposed the present king. In instituting the practice of sharing alike for all who take part in military campaigns in any way, David was already acting as king, making judgments and setting up new laws.

30:26–31 / It is hard to determine the motive behind David's action in sending a share of the substantial **plunder** to so many of the towns in **Judah.** It may have been a sense of natural justice, returning what had in many instances been taken from them. It may have been a sense of gratitude and obligation for helping him while he was seeking to evade Saul; there is specific mention of the places where **David and his men had roamed** before retreating to Philistine territory. It may have been political expediency, creating support for David by not only providing much-needed extra supplies for the towns but also reminding them of David's military prowess and of his loyalty to the tribes of Israel in spite of his present abode in Philistia. Probably it was a combination of all of these, but it was a shrewd move on David's part.

31:1–3 / The scene moves from David's successful reclamation of captives and property in the south to the major battle taking place in the north. There was no parallel success for the main Israelite army. Perhaps as a result of Saul's lack of conviction (ch. 28) lessening their confidence, the Israelite army was unable to repel the Philistine attack. Most **fled** and many were killed. Saul's family was targeted, following the maxim that an army without leaders is easier to defeat and harder to rebuild. Three of Saul's **sons,** including **Jonathan,** were **killed** in the fighting. Whatever Saul's mental state, he threw himself into the attack as far as he was able; there is no question of cowardice. His great fear had been not of the battle but of losing any sense of God's support. In the **fierce fighting,** indicating that by no means all of the Israelites had fled, Saul was **critically** wounded by Philistine **archers.**

31:4–5 / Saul's desire for a quick end avoiding any Philistine torturers is understandable, but so is the refusal of his **armor-bearer** to cooperate. It is probable that the terror of the armor-bearer was related to the results of being accused of killing the Lord's anointed king. However, he may have had qualms about taking life other than in battle. A third possibility is that with the obvious imminence of defeat he was paralyzed by fear. Saul had just enough strength left to use his **sword** to complete the work of the Philistine arrows. The armor-bearer could see no way out of the situation and took his own life. We can only speculate as to whether this indicates a loyalty to and a love for Saul, a recognition that he had failed to fulfill his role of protecting Saul and therefore deserved to die, or a sense that there was no hope and he too was only hastening a death that was inevitable anyway.

31:6–7 / The summary in verse 6 emphasizes the devastation in general and the decimation of the royal family in particular. It could be seen as a statement included by the editor from an alternative, shorter source. However, in the account as we have it this summary proves the determinative nature of this battle. Things for Israel would never be the same again. Their first king was dead. The northern territory that had been so hardly gained from the Philistines over the past few years was lost, reoccupied by Philistine troops and settlers. The remnants of the **Israelite army . . . fled** in disarray. Saul's reign, in spite of a few high points, had been a failure. His calling to deliver the people from the hand of the Philistines (9:16) had not been fulfilled, although to his credit he died in pursuit of that calling.

31:8–10 / The Philistines' plundering of the dead soldiers reflects standard practice. Metal weapons in particular could be made good use of by conquering armies. Their seizing the opportunity to use Saul's **head** and **armor** as trophies and his **body** as a signal of victory is not surprising. That they did so is recorded without comment. The writers manage to communicate a sense of hopelessness and of hope: hopelessness because the victory is total, hope because such a victory, with similar great national rejoicing on the Philistines' part, had been seen before when the longer-term result did not prove to justify such rejoicing. The hopelessness after the ark of God had been captured was followed by Israelite rejoicing when it was returned to Israel (chs. 4–6). The temple feasts after Samson was captured (Judg. 16:23–24) were followed by devastation for the Philistines. The enemy may not have remembered these things, but Israel should take heed and remember that God remained God.

31:11–13 / The hope is unstated, but the brave action of the **people of Jabesh Gilead** serves as a fitting epitaph for Saul. His reign had not been without its failures and disasters, but it had not been without achievements either. One of his first acts after being anointed as king was to rescue Jabesh Gilead from the Ammonites (ch. 11). Their gratitude remained strong, and they could not allow Saul's death to pass without a proper burial showing the respect that they felt he deserved.

Additional Notes §25

30:6 / David's attitude could indicate either his concern for himself rather than for his family or that his concern for his men's problems took precedence over his personal worries. In spite of his friendship with Jonathan, personal relationships, particularly within his family, were not David's strong point. But the stress here is on the community rather than on the individual, and the writers do not intend to emphasize David's inadequacies at this stage.

30:9 / **Besor** is quite likely to be identified as the Ghazzeh wadi, about twelve miles south of Ziklag. It is not surprising that a further twelve-mile march, on top of that day's section of the march down from the north, proved too much for some of David's men.

30:12 / The down-to-earth realism of this narrative, describing the exhaustion of the men and the details of the food given to the slave, provides support for the view that it originated as an eyewitness account.

30:14 / The **Kerethites,** allies of the Philistines, also originated from Crete. 2 Sam. 8:18 tells us that there was a Kerethite section in David's entourage. Possibly this defeat of their common enemy (the Amalekites) led to a developing alliance with and loyalty to David, which resulted in a group of them joining David's army.

30:20–31 / Unlike Saul's mission against the Amalekites (ch. 15), there is no question of David's having been sent on a holy war with all plunder to be destroyed. The booty obtained in this instance was the legitimate spoils of war. Klein (*1 Samuel,* p. 281) sees a possible conflict between David's taking the spoils as his own right and distributing this plunder among the Judean towns and the division of the spoils among the soldiers. However, there is no indication that the whole of the booty would be divided among the men, just that each one would receive his proper share. It would be extremely unusual in such circumstances if a significant portion of what was obtained (over and above the recovery of personal property) was not assigned to the military leader to distribute as he thought fit.

30:27–31 / Although some have modern counterparts (e.g., **Aroer** is Khirber ʿArʾareh), many of the southern towns mentioned cannot now be identified. **Bethel** cannot refer to the better-known town north of Jerusalem. There may have been another Bethel farther south, or the LXX alternative of Bethzur may be correct.

31:2 / In 14:49 Saul's **sons** are named as **Jonathan, Ishvi, and Malki-Shua.** 1 Chron. 8:33; 9:39 lists four sons: Jonathan, Malki-Shua, Abinadab, and Esh-Baal. It is usually assumed that Ishvi is another name for Esh-Baal, also known as Ish-Bosheth (2 Sam. 2:8). For some reason he was not present at this particular battle. In 2 Sam. 2–4 we learn of the way in which Ish-Bosheth ruled for a while over part of Saul's kingdom. The parallel account in Chronicles ignores this fact and moves from Saul's death to David's appointment. Although this was not straightforward, Ish-Bosheth's part receives no mention. His absence from this battle may be the reason the Chronicler, who is aware of his existence, saw him as irrelevant to the overall story.

31:7 / The Philistine occupation of the surrounding towns was not a result of direct conquest; they moved in after the Israelite residents fled in a mass panic arising from news that the Israelite army had failed.

31:9–10 / 1 Chron. 10 gives the further information that Saul's head was placed in the temple of Dagon. His armor was in the **temple of the Ashtoreths.** The term **idols**, indicating false gods, is pejorative, and Gordon (*1 and 2 Samuel: A Commentary,* p. 203) proposes that the writers ironically suggest that these idols needed to be informed of the Philistine victory as much as the people did.

Beth Shan (modern Tell el-Husn) was an old Canaanite town assigned to Manasseh (Josh. 17:11) but was then occupied by the Philistines. There is evidence that up until this time it had not come under Israelite control.

31:12 / Cremation was not usually practiced in Israel. Burning bones to lime was seen as a serious crime (cf. Amos 2:1), but as the bones remained to be buried that was not the practice being described here. In Amos 6:10, which is the only other reference to cremation that does not involve punishment or sacrifice, bodies were burned after plague. Disease was always a threat when bodies were left on a battle-field, and that may be the situation here. It is also possible that Saul's body had already decayed to the extent that normal burial was impossible. A further possibility is that the term refers to burning spices and not to cremation as such, but to interpret it in that way would involve an unusual grammatical construction. In any case, the emphasis of the text is that Saul's body was given a proper and respectful burial.

§26 The Report of Saul's Death (2 Sam. 1:1–16)

Despite the fact that modern Bibles present 2 Samuel as a separate book, there is no clear break from what goes before. First and Second Samuel must be seen as a unit (see pp. 1, 2 of the introduction).

1:1–3 / These verses clarify the timing of events. The opening phrase **after the death of Saul** is an editorial comment showing that a new section is beginning. Allowing for traveling time, the death of Saul in the north must, ironically, have taken place about the same time as David in the south was completing his victory over the Amalekite group—the group that had been the unwitting cause of Saul's fall from grace (1 Sam. 15).

Now the focus is on what is going to happen to David and the question of how long it will be before his promised kingship becomes a reality. David and his forces are not aware of Saul's death, although they were aware that the battle in the north was likely to have been a crucial one. They had seen the strength of the gathered Philistine army and had expected to play a part in the battle. They will undoubtedly have been eagerly awaiting news, and the arrival of a man showing travel weariness and mourning interested everyone.

The homage paid to David could have been that paid to any chieftain, but its extent, that the man **fell to the ground,** probably indicates that the man was acclaiming **David** as the new king of Israel. He knew well who David was and had traveled a great distance to seek out this group, presumably to gain the advantage of being the first to tell David of the new situation. His escape **from the Israelite camp** could mean that he had been a prisoner of war, but more likely he had been a member of the Israelite entourage, whether a slave or an ally, who had managed to avoid death.

1:4–10 / The Israelite army had been destroyed, and **Saul** and **Jonathan** were **dead.** The evidence was that the young Amalekite had been near Saul on the battlefield and had, at

Saul's request, ended the dying man's misery. He had then taken the royal insignia and brought it to David.

This account of Saul's death does not tally with that found in 1 Samuel 31. One solution to this discrepancy is that two separate traditions related Saul's death and the writers, unable to choose between them, included both (cf. P. R. Ackroyd, *The Second Book of Samuel* [Cambridge: Cambridge University Press, 1971], p. 20. Mauchline, *1 and 2 Samuel*, p. 197, also assumes two traditions and concludes that "the Amalekite's narrative rings true."). However, it is at least as likely that the Amalekite invented his story, that he came upon Saul's body after the battle but before the Philistines had taken plunder from the dead. He had then seized the opportunity to bring the **crown** and the royal armband to David, hoping to gain credit with what he expected to be the new government and to obtain a reward. Any person associated with the Israelite army who had been standing next to Saul **with the chariots and riders almost upon him** would not have avoided death. Nor does the Amalekite's story explain how he could have been sure of the death of Jonathan. The writers probably are well aware of this deception and include the discrepancies to make the Amalekite's lie clear to the reader.

1:11–12 / The first response of David and his followers is deep grief. Saul may have seen them as traitors and rebels, but they had a tremendous loyalty to Israel and **mourned** greatly, not just **for Saul** and **Jonathan,** but for the Israelite army and for what this defeat would mean for the **house of Israel.**

1:13–16 / On further investigation David discovered that the Amalekite was **the son of an alien,** that is, of a resident alien who had allied himself with Israel (cf. Exod. 12:48; 22:21; 23:9). The likelihood is that the young man had lived in Israel for many years, perhaps even from birth. This would explain his knowledge of Israelite politics. If David is quoting exactly when he cites the young man's words **I killed the LORD's anointed,** this would provide further evidence that the youth had some awareness of what was involved in killing Saul. If he had been close to the Israelite army, he was likely to have known something of David's belief in the inviolability of Saul's position as God's anointed.

In this section the writers show their ongoing interest in the question of how power was achieved and exercised. David could have had several motives in passing the death sentence on the Amalekite. Because he came to David directly from the battlefield, it could have been seen as a prearranged rendezvous. Given the suspicion of David by Saul and presumably by many of his entourage, this would have been interpreted as providing evidence of David's complicity in Saul's death; possession of the royal insignia would reinforce this view. In order to avoid any suggestion of such complicity, David had to act quickly and decisively.

David did not doubt that this young man deserved death—not because he had brought bad news, but because of the action that he had taken against Saul. Although the writers seem aware that the confession is dubious, David would have had no reason to doubt that the story was true. Whatever the political motivation, he was also concerned with justice. By confessing to the murder of Saul, the young Amalekite signed his own death warrant. It is probable that the result would have been the same whether or not the Amalekite had proved to be a resident alien, but his culpability would have been less and he might have avoided death. David, in pronouncing the death sentence on the killer of Saul, again takes on a royal role. Now that Saul is dead, his elevation to true kingly status must have been seen by his troops and himself as a foregone conclusion.

Additional Notes §26

1:1 / David's return to **Ziklag** may suggest that the town had not been as badly destroyed as 1 Sam. 30:3 seems to indicate. However, it could be that Ziklag had a water supply and was as good a place as any to start again.

1:2 / A dusty head and **torn clothes** could be as a result of the long trip at a fast pace but were also signs of mourning (cf. v. 11). If the man thought he was bringing good news (either telling David that Saul was dead and the way was clear for David to become king of Israel or providing the information that he had fulfilled Saul's last wish and expected a reward), he would not have adopted signs of mourning. Perhaps the story of his involvement in Saul's death had been a last-minute invention. If so, he badly miscalculated its results.

1:4 / **Jonathan**'s death is specifically mentioned whereas, unlike in 1 Sam. 31, that of his brothers is not referred to. This is probably because the lament later in the chapter focuses on Saul and Jonathan.

1:9–10 / B. T. Arnold ("The Amalekite Report of Saul's Death," *JETS* 32 [1989], pp. 289–98) has a detailed discussion of the relationship between 1 Sam. 31 and 2 Sam. 1. He argues that the concept of deception plays an important role in the narratives as a whole and that the deception that he suggests the Amalekite carried out is consistent with the motif throughout the book. If, however, this account is correct and the Amalekite did kill Saul, it could be seen as providing a reminder that one of the main factors in Saul's problems had been his failure to effectively carry out God's judgment on the Amalekites (1 Sam. 15).

1:13 / The question asked here is not the same as in v. 3 and does not use the same Hebrew wording. In v. 3 the question was about the origin of his journey; here it is about his background.

§27 David's Lament (2 Sam. 1:17–27)

1:17–18 / David's grief over the deaths of Saul, who had once been like a father to him, and of his friend Jonathan, was heartfelt. He found an outlet for that grief in writing poetry, and this lament is the result. The insistence that all the men of Judah learn the lament is likely to have been politically motivated. If the Judeans could be shown as paying proper respect to Saul's memory, there was a much greater likelihood of the northern tribes transferring their loyalty to David, who was Judean. The poem thus serves the dual purpose of paying homage to the dead king and introducing David as the obvious successor. The lament was officially recorded in the Book of Jashar, some kind of national record, perhaps of official poems.

1:19–22 / There is no underlying irony in David's opening words. The decimation of the army and the death of Saul were an unmitigated tragedy for Israel. It is not clear whether Saul or the whole army is being described as the **glory** of Israel and as **the mighty,** but the point is the same. The loss to those who remained behind, to the nation as a whole, was incalculable.

The forlorn hope that the news would not be spread among the Philistine cities and not become a matter for rejoicing there (v. 20) is unrealistic but heartfelt. Saul wanted to die before he could be mocked (1 Sam. 31:4); that mockery should take place in Philistia after his death added to David's sadness. The mourning of the nation was such that the land itself must share it (v. 21). It was unthinkable that the **mountains of Gilboa** carry on yielding crops as if nothing had happened when the prime of Israel's manhood had been slain on their slopes. In verse 22 the poem focuses on the fact that both Saul and Jonathan died bravely. Their weapons had been used to good effect before they were stopped short.

1:23–24 / Perhaps a grain of comfort could be found in memories of Saul and Jonathan and in the fact that in death they had been together. The point is not so much that they died at the same time and in the same place, but that at the end they had been united in purpose, both giving their lives trying to save the nation. They were brave soldiers, **swifter than eagles** and **stronger than lions,** a fact undoubted even by those who opposed Saul. They had inspired love and loyalty, and even if Saul's jealous rages meant that at times graciousness was hard to find, at other times it had been there and could now be brought to mind. Saul's reign had brought a certain amount of stability to Israel, at least enabling the economy to be better than it had previously been. For this and other reasons it was appropriate that, though the women of Philistia may be rejoicing, the women of Israel should **weep** for the death of their king.

1:25–26 / As the poem begins to focus on **Jonathan** the emphasis changes from the national mourning to David's personal grief for the friend who had been such a support to him in bad times as well as good. The care of **women** for him David perhaps took for granted, but that the son of the king who became his enemy should have done so was a constant wonder. David and Jonathan had made a covenant, so it was appropriate to refer to him as **brother.** There may be the underlying thought that, as Jonathan's brother, David was a natural choice to succeed Saul.

1:27 / The lament finishes with a further expression of desperation and grief. This was not a time for hope to be expressed. The evocative nature of the lament diverts attention from the fact that, unlike most of David's poetry, this is centered on human relationships. There is no reference to God in the lament. Perhaps at this early stage David was finding it hard to see what part God had played in these terrible events.

Additional Notes §27

There are a number of minor textual and linguistic problems in this lament in 1:17–27. For example, the meaning of the term translated **bow** in v. 18 is unclear, and the phrasing in v. 21 could be rendered in different ways. However, these problems do not affect the main sense of the poem or the force or depth of the emotions it conveys.

1:18 / The **Book of Jashar** was used to record the phenomenon described in Josh. 10:12–13 when the sun stood still in the sky, giving the Israelite army extra time to defeat the Amorites. The writers of Samuel and Kings made use of many different sources, some of which are named. Keeping proper records was a significant element in building up Israel's traditions. Prophets like Samuel, Nathan, and Gad kept records (1 Chron. 29:29; cf. 2 Chron. 9:29; 12:15), and there are around thirty references to the annals of the kings in the books of Kings. The significant thing is that Israel's records contained accounts that were not always complimentary to current rulers, a situation uncommon in official records of the ancient Near East. In this instance, however, the lament reflects positively on Saul and David, possibly providing support for David's authorship of the poem.

1:20 / The Hebrew word for **tell** *(taggîdû)* has a similar sound to the name **Gath** *(bᵉgat)*. The same phrase, used again because of its poetic assonance, is found in Mic. 1:10. Maybe by the time of Micah it had become a kind of proverb.

1:21 / Shields, in most instances made of leather, were **rubbed with oil** to keep them in top condition and ready for immediate use (Isa. 21:5). The oil stopped the leather from drying out and cracking. Perhaps Saul had had a reputation for keeping his armor ready, maybe related to his habit of always keeping his spear close by (1 Sam. 18:10; 19:9).

1:24 / The men of Judah are commanded to learn the poem, but it is equally addressed to the women.

1:26 / A. Cook (" 'Fiction' and History in Samuel and Kings," *JSOT* 36 [1986], p. 35) suggests that Jonathan's love is contrasted with that of his sister Michal, who could accept David the warrior but not David the dancing harpist. Saul had loved the harpist but did not cope with David the successful warrior. Only Jonathan accepted both.

§28 David's Rise to Power Begins
(2 Sam. 2:1–3:5)

Chronicles, which is primarily concerned with the history of the house of David, gives little detail about the reign of Saul. First Chronicles 10 records Saul's death in the same form as 1 Samuel 31 but with the addition of a negative summary of Saul's reign. Chapter 11 of 1 Chronicles then moves to the meeting of the whole nation with David at Hebron that is described in 2 Samuel 5:1. The pains and struggles that accompanied the birth of David's reign and the role of Ish-Bosheth are ignored. However, for the writers of Samuel these struggles were significant, forming part of the ongoing, underlying debate about the nature of power and the way in which power was exercised in Israel.

2:1–4a / How much time elapsed before it was considered appropriate for David to return to his homeland is not clear. But **in the course of time** and after making sure that he was not stepping outside God's purposes (v. 1), David returned to Judah and set up a base in **Hebron.** The **two wives** who had been with him in exile and his originally makeshift army, now a force to be reckoned with, accompanied him. Once he was **settled,** the leaders of **Judah** came and officially recognized David as their **king.** Whether or not there was a widespread knowledge of David's anointing by Samuel—and such news has a way of creeping out—they would have been aware of Saul's fear of, and Jonathan's backing for, David. It would have been dangerous for them to have done anything other than acknowledge as king the skilled warrior chieftain now living among them. However, there is no suggestion other than that they did so freely and gladly. David was the choice of the people as far as Judah was concerned.

2:4b–7 / Having returned to Judah, David was able to obtain full details of what had happened to Saul and his army.

The message sent to **Jabesh Gilead** reflects the two aspects of David's character that made him such a good king. On the one hand, his gratitude to them for what they had done for **Saul** was sincere. He was genuinely moved by their bravery and their **kindness.** His blessing and his assertions of **favor** toward them were unfeigned. On the other hand, he was politically astute and well aware that making friends of those outside of Judah was no bad thing for him. If David could win the hearts of a town that had been so unquestionably loyal to Saul, then his chances of quickly gaining the loyalty of the whole nation would be immensely strengthened. He was conscious of their loyalty to Saul and praised them for it. But he makes the point that **Saul . . . is dead** and thus implies that to support David would not express disloyalty to Saul.

David's arguments are subtle. First he associates his own blessing with the blessing that God gives (v. 6), implying that God's blessing can be manifested through David and that David is God's choice. Second, by stating that **Judah** has crowned him as **king** in place of Saul, he shrewdly introduces the idea that to do the same thing might be in their interest.

2:8–11 / **Meanwhile, Abner,** Saul's cousin (1 Sam. 14:50), had taken action in the north. **Ish-Bosheth** was **forty years old,** but it seems that Abner was the driving force in the attempt to maintain power within the Saulide dynasty. Saul was dead, but this did not mean that support for his son's claim to the throne disappeared. Whereas David was acknowledged by the men of Judah (v. 4), Ish-Bosheth was **made . . . king** by Abner, who apparently took Ish-Bosheth around the tribes, perhaps conducting ceremonies throughout the land in **Gilead, Ashuri and Jezreel** as well as at **Mahanaim.**

Abner was a gifted general and it may be that the primary loyalty of the troops was to him rather than to Ish-Bosheth, but loyalty there was and none of the northern tribes were ready to change their allegiance from Saul's son to David.

Verses 10 and 11 provide a summary of the years before David became king over the whole nation. If Abner had ambitions to be king, the text has no indication of this. Given Ish-Bosheth's weakness and Abner's royal connections, there would have been no major obstacle to his taking over at this stage.

2:12–32 / **Gibeon** was a few miles north of Jerusalem, in Benjamite territory but within reach of Judah. It may be that the discussions there were originally intended as a summit meeting to work out whether or not compromise was possible. **Joab,** David's nephew and general, and **Abner** arrange an intriguing competition between **twelve** of the young men on either side that ended in a grisly draw. The twenty-four young soldiers were killed, and instead of saving further bloodshed, the unsatisfactory contest led to an extended battle.

There is no sign of the careful persuasion with which David had sought to win over Jabesh Gilead. Instead we have a power struggle between Joab and Abner. Although Abner is presented as being on the losing side and the writers have no doubts about the rightness of David's claim, nevertheless Abner is more sympathetically portrayed within these verses than is Joab. Joab is consistently more interested in victory than in the needs of individual people. Abner seems to have much more of a natural compassion.

Three hundred and eighty Israelites were killed that day, the vast majority of them coming from the tribe of Benjamin, as Judah had the best of the fierce fighting. The most significant incident from the writers' point of view, however, was the death of a Judean, Joab's young brother **Asahel,** who shared Joab's arrogant confidence. Although he had speed, Asahel had not developed tactical abilities. He decided that he would put an end to the fighting by defeating Abner, and he used his speed to catch up with him. Abner, knowing that to kill Asahel would lead to further trouble, tried to persuade the young Judean to abandon his task. When this was unsuccessful he killed him by a ruse, allowing Asahel to come up close behind him and then suddenly stopping, thrusting the back end of his spear into Asahel's stomach.

This appears to have been a turning point in the battle. The Judeans were slowed by the sight of Asahel's body, and the Benjamites, who formed the bulk of Abner's forces at this stage, took courage and **rallied behind Abner.** Abner, who had common sense and no desire to kill fellow Israelites, even those from Judah, called for a truce. Joab, sensing that for that day his success had run its course, agreed, and both armies returned to their base—Abner's troops to Ish-Bosheth at **Mahanaim** and Joab's to David at **Hebron.**

3:1–5 / Verse 1, an editorial comment, establishes that the truce declared in 2:28 was not permanent. The outcome of the power struggles between David and Ish-Bosheth and between Joab and Abner was not yet clear, although David's supporters were constantly strengthening their position. While this struggle went on life continued, and we are told of six sons who were born to David while he was based in Hebron. Three of these six, **Kileab, Shephatiah,** and **Ithream,** are mentioned elsewhere only in 1 Chronicles 3:1–3, where Kileab is called Daniel. It may be that they died in childhood, as even if they had done nothing that the writers considered worth mentioning one might expect that their names would have occurred more often in genealogical lists. **Amnon, Absalom,** and **Adonijah** play a significant, if not always glorious, part in the later narratives. Of David's four new wives we know nothing, although **Haggith** is referred to three times in 1 Kings 1–2 as Adonijah's mother and therefore appears to have been known in the court.

Additional Notes §28

2:2 / David's **wives** both came from Judean towns and that may further emphasize David's links with the tribe. The **Carmel** where **Nabal** had lived was in the Judean hills and is not to be confused with the mountain range in the north.

The mention of the wives also makes it clear that this was not a temporary encampment. David's exile in Philistia was over.

2:4a / This anointing is a public, political act very different from David's first, secret anointing by Samuel. There do not seem to be any specifically religious considerations, although in general the historical books see public acclamation and religious affirmation as being crucial elements in the appointment of a king (e.g., 1 Kgs. 1:39; 2 Kgs. 11:12).

2:4–7 / **Jabesh Gilead** was in Transjordan and although the people from that area remained loyal to Saul's family for some time, it was in David's interests to create positive relationships within the region. Much of the Ephraimite territory, including Jezreel, was in Philistine hands and could only in theory be identified as Ish-Bosheth's territory.

2:8 / Ish-Bosheth is also known as Esh-Baal (1 Chron. 8:33; 9:39). The practice of having *baal*, meaning "lord," as part of a name became unacceptable when this ordinary word was inseparably associated with the god Baal. It was thus replaced by *bosheth*, meaning "shame." In a similar way we have Mephibosheth as an alternative name for Meribbaal (1 Chron. 8:34; 9:40). Given the perspective of the text as favoring the Davidic dynasty, the choice to use the altered name may have made a conscious criticism about Ish-Bosheth. However, the fact that the attitude to Mephibosheth is not negative makes that possibility less likely.

Ish-Bosheth's capital **Mahanaim** is, like Jabesh Gilead, situated in Transjordan.

2:10–11 / The figures given in these verses can be interpreted in various ways. It is not clear how much time passed after Ish-Bosheth's death before the Israelite tribes came to invite David to lead them (5:1). If the start of David's reign over Judah at Hebron was around the same time as the start of Ish-Bosheth's reign over the northern tribes at Mahanaim, then the extra five and a half years that David spent at Hebron must be either before the Israelites accepted his leadership or before he moved his capital to Jerusalem. The later text does not suggest such a long a time gap before either of these events, but neither does it preclude it. David was thirty years old when he became king (5:4). If Jonathan, who was the eldest son of Saul, was around the same age as David (which their friendship suggests), then it is hard to know how Ish-Bosheth could have been forty years old at this time. A. A. Anderson (*2 Samuel* [WBC; Waco: Word, 1989], p. 35) suggests that the number forty may have been included as "a round figure in the absence of the exact figure."

3:2–5 / Each of David's six wives is mentioned as having one, and only one, **son**. There could be many reasons for this, and Hertzberg (*I and II Samuel*, p. 253) may be right in suggesting that only the firstborn son is mentioned. It is also possible that this is an indication of the difficulty David appears to have had in maintaining good long-term relationships within his family (cf. D. J. A. Clines, "The Story of Michal, Wife of David, in Its Sequential Unfolding," in Clines and Eskenazi, *Telling Queen Michal's Story*, pp. 129–40). Even Bathsheba, after the birth of Solomon, is mentioned again only as Solomon's mother—not as David's wife.

§29 The Murders of Abner and Ish-Bosheth (2 Sam. 3:6–4:12)

3:6–11 / Although **Ish-Bosheth** was titular head of the northern tribes and Abner seemingly made no attempt to change that, real power centered around Abner. The fate of the country lay in his hands, and verse 6 implies that he took action to ensure that this remained the case. It is not surprising that Ish-Bosheth, who seems to have left all the decision making to his general (3:8–17), felt threatened by Abner (v. 11). Whether or not Abner had a relationship with Saul's **concubine Rizpah,** the phrasing of Ish-Bosheth's accusation is significant. To take over the wife of a previous monarch was tantamount to claiming his throne, and Ish-Bosheth was accusing Abner of disloyalty. Abner, who had been loyal to Saul and his house, saw the accusation as an unacceptable insult (v. 8).

At this point Abner decided that his single-handed maintenance of the Saulide cause was no longer worthwhile. Without his support Ish-Bosheth could not retain even the appearance of power, and Ish-Bosheth recognized this (v. 11). It may be that Abner had already seen his support for Ish-Bosheth as only delaying the inevitable. He was aware that God had **promised** the whole land to David, although only after David's crowning at Hebron (2:4) did the original promise became known. Possibly Abner had been searching for an acceptable way of allowing David to take over the country, and Ish-Bosheth's accusation provided the justification for such an action. In any case, Abner decided that Israel should join with Judah, and Ish-Bosheth went along with that decision.

3:12–21 / Without any further discussion, Abner sent a delegation to David to discuss terms for a merger between the two Israelite groups. David had no doubts that Abner was able to carry out his promise of bringing **all Israel over to** David. Nevertheless, he introduced one condition that would serve as a sign of Abner's and Ish-Bosheth's good faith and would also provide a continuing link with Saul's family that could help David to unite the country. He insisted on the return of his **wife Michal.** Nothing in the text indicates that David still had feelings for Michal, and it is hard to see this as anything other than a political move. Her return as part of the royal entourage would give the supporters of Saul's family a focus for allegiance to the new regime without betraying their original loyalties. David was aware of the benefit of such moves and maybe felt that personal wishes had to be subordinated to the national good.

Ish-Bosheth, as head of Saul's family, **gave orders** that Michal should be returned to David. Ish-Bosheth's role in this indicates that Abner was not simply deserting Ish-Bosheth but rather advocating that the nation, including Ish-Bosheth, become reunited. In this scenario Ish-Bosheth would become a tribal leader under David's kingship. Although Ish-Bosheth may have had no choice, he did not oppose the course of action that Abner had taken. By agreeing to Michal's return, Ish-Bosheth gave tacit approval. Neither Michal nor her current husband was given any choice in this, nor were their feelings taken into account. Michal's reaction is unrecorded, but the picture of **Paltiel's** distress is poignant and shows signs of being an eyewitness account.

So far the negotiations seem to have been a private matter. Abner had tested David's reaction by messengers before committing either himself or the nation (v. 12). However, at this stage (v. 17), the elders are involved. Although Abner had carried the day, his policy of keeping Israel and Judah separate had not had universal approval. **For some time** a significant party had **wanted to make David king.** Abner informs them that his opposition to that action has been removed and they may go ahead. He has a special meeting with **the Benjamites,** who as Saul's relatives were perhaps least likely to approve of the new situation.

The **twenty men** who accompanied Abner to Hebron were there to arrange for the official handover, that is, for David's coronation as king of all Israel. Abner's suggestion was that this should take place **at once** and should involve a clearly defined protocol between the king and the people. This **compact** would make it clear that David's kingship of the northern tribes was freely accepted and was not imposed as a result of conquest. It would set out the agreed rights and responsibilities of both sides. Abner continues to be portrayed positively as a soldier and a diplomat. Abner and David parted on good terms; it was important to the writers that David was seen as playing no part in what happened next.

3:22–39 / Joab had been absent while these negotiations had been proceeding. The story of his successful **raid,** in which **a great deal of plunder** was taken, reminds readers that the struggles against the Philistine enemies had not ceased. Joab's reaction to David's having made **peace** with Abner was shocked horror. Joab saw Abner as his enemy. The rivalry of two skilled generals had been exacerbated by Abner's having killed Joab's brother Asahel. Joab could not envisage that anyone whom he viewed with such enmity could be seeking peace (v. 25). Joab appears to have viewed conquest in war as the only secure way of obtaining or reclaiming territory. He was extremely suspicious of any kind of diplomatic compromise, although he was a skilled negotiator or at least a skilled manipulator of people (cf. 2 Sam. 11:18–22; 12:27–28; 14:1–3).

Unbeknownst to David, Joab sent **messengers** to call Abner back, on the pretext of further negotiations but in reality to kill him. The motivation for this killing was pure revenge (vv. 27, 30). The effect that Abner's death may have had on David's attempt to take control of the whole kingdom does not seem to have entered into the equation for Joab. However, David was aware that without Abner and with the suspicion that David had abused the negotiation process in having Abner killed, his kingship of Israel could be delayed, even prevented. In order to avoid this David took immediate and decisive action. He cursed Joab (v. 29), making it clear that not only did he not instigate Joab's action but also he did not approve of it. He instituted full mourning procedures for Abner within Judah and insisted that Joab take part in this mourning (v. 31). He **sang** a **lament for Abner** and fasted in the way he might have done for a close relative. In effect, he treated Abner as royalty and his death as a tragedy.

David's policy was successful. The people of the country, Israel as well as Judah, believed him and were impressed and satisfied by the action he had taken. The question of power again comes to the fore. David was king, but he had not had the power to prevent the death even of a great soldier-prince like Abner. Given the treatment handed out to the Amalekite who had claimed to kill Saul (1:15) and to the slayers of Ish-Bosheth (4:12), it is not clear why David felt unable, or at least reluctant, to handle Joab and his brothers. Perhaps there is some degree of self-interest in this. Joab was a great general, and David benefited greatly from his skill and his loyalty. Perhaps David could not bring himself to destroy his nephew. This explanation ties in with his later inability to deal properly with his sons.

In this instance, handing over Joab to God's justice (v. 39) recognizes that something ought to be done about Joab's high-handed killing of Abner but makes it possible for David to avoid the consequences of doing anything himself. Abner's death was murder. Legitimate killing to avenge the death of Asahel did not apply in this case because Asahel's death took place in a battle situation and he had been given an opportunity to escape (2:22). Justice therefore demanded that Joab should be executed—the same justice that resulted in the execution of Ish-Bosheth's slayers (ch. 4). There seems to be implicit criticism from the writers regarding David's lack of action in this case.

4:1–12 / If Abner's death was likely to cause problems for David, for Ish-Bosheth it was a disaster. Abner had been strong and capable enough to ensure guarantees of safety for Saul's remaining family. Now there could be no guarantees for anybody, and the specter of a bloodbath, when the north was taken by force and the leaderless northern army decimated, loomed large. Ish-Bosheth **lost** what little **courage** he might have had, and **all Israel became alarmed.** In the context of that panic two of Ish-Bosheth's soldiers decided to take action. **Baanah and Recab were leaders of raiding bands;** that is, they were not bandits but had charge of semi-independent military units engaging in constant guerrilla warfare against the Philistines. As patriotic soldiers, but without Abner's loyalty to Saul's family, they probably had little time for the weak Ish-Bosheth and decided that the best thing for Israel was for any remaining barriers to David's leadership to be removed.

The reference to **Mephibosheth** seems slightly out of place and is often considered to be an insertion from elsewhere. Some versions, including the NIV, place verse 4 in brackets to indicate that it is considered as an interruption to the main text. This may be so, but it serves to show that because of his handicap and possibly his youth, Mephibosheth was not considered to be a threat and explains why he escaped death.

Ish-Bosheth was not so fortunate. The two conspirators **set out for** his house. As guerrilla leaders, part of Ish-Bosheth's forces, they had no problems in gaining access, and they **killed** Ish-Bosheth. The removal of his **head** seems gruesome but would provide evidence of what they had done.

The account of Ish-Bosheth's death is fairly detailed and makes sense as a description given to David's court by Recab and Baanah. Like the Amalekite who had killed Saul, Recab and Baanah expected to be well received, thinking that they brought David good news and a quick means of uniting the country. It appears that they had not heard of the Amalekite's execution in Ziklag. This seems unusual, but is possible if they had been engaged in battle, since Ziklag is quite a distance from Hebron and even further away from the site of their fighting. On the other hand, the news of Abner's death and the aborted negotiations concerning unity seems to have reached them.

Their ignorance of previous events was soon remedied. They were informed now of the action David had taken with the Amalekite. Their killing of Ish-Bosheth could only be considered murder and in David's mind could in no way be excused. Even though to have Ish-Bosheth out of the way was advantageous to David, his death was further likely to cause resentment among the tribes that had remained loyal to Saul's line. Yet again David needed to distance himself from the killing. In this instance he had no qualms about carrying out the death sentence. The two men were executed as traitors, and Ish-Bosheth's head was given a decent burial. There was now no barrier to David's becoming king of the whole country.

Additional Notes §29

3:8 / Dogs were almost always portrayed as despised animals, and therefore the term was commonly used in insults. Goliath felt he was being shown disrespect, treated as a dog, by being faced with the boy David (1 Sam. 17:43). In most OT instances, the image occurs when people refer to themselves as dogs—expressing either their feeling of being insulted, as here, or their humility (1 Sam. 24:14; 2 Sam. 9:8; 2 Kgs. 8:13). The only exception is when Abishai, Joab's brother, calls the Saulide Shimei a "dead dog" (2 Sam. 16:9).

3:15 / Z. Ben-Barak ("The Legal Background to the Restoration of Michal to David," in Clines and Eskenazi, *Telling Queen Michal's Story*, pp. 74–90) sees Michal being married to Paltiel when David disappeared, and subsequently returned to David as based on known legal procedures in Israel and Mesopotamia. David may have deserted Michal, but he had not officially sent her away. They were not therefore divorced, and this means he had a right to demand her return. Her return did not count as a remarriage, which would have been forbidden under the normal rules of divorce (Deut. 24:4). David, in making this request, perhaps deliberately involves Ish-Bosheth and thus makes it impossible for Ish-Bosheth to say later that Abner removed him from power without his consent.

3:17–18 / Abner felt that he had enough influence to persuade Israel to accept David's kingship, but the people were ultimately responsible for deciding whether David should be accepted. Again the writers's interest in the mechanisms of power and power brokering is apparent.

3:21–23 / The repetition that Abner was sent away **in peace** emphasizes that he was given legal sanction to pass through David's territory unharmed. David had guaranteed his safety. Thus Abner's death was inevitably a slur on David's integrity. This again makes it difficult to understand why David did not call for the execution of Joab.

3:29 / David's cursing of Joab's family, here and in v. 39, was not insignificant. Its content is fierce, and it stood as an open, public rebuke to Joab. However, there is no provision in the law for cursing to be seen as an alternative to proper prescribed punishments. In that sense David could be seen as avoiding the proper responsibilities of kingship to ensure that justice was done and was seen to be done.

3:30 / It is possible that the problem for **Joab** was not just that **Abner** had killed **Asahel** but that he had done so by a ruse. Asahel's death was not heroic. Abner's death, also by a ruse, perhaps was seen, at least by Joab and Abishai, as poetic justice. However, the writers consider Abner's death to be murder.

3:33 / **The lawless** translates the Hb. word *nābāl*, which is translated as "fool" in 1 Sam. 25:25. The great soldier Abner is thus associated with the far from great Nabal, and David rightly asserts that this is not just.

4:2 / **Beeroth** is a Canaanite town that had apparently been absorbed into the tribe of **Benjamin**. We cannot be sure whether **Baanah** and **Recab** were Benjamites living in Beeroth or native Canaanites. If they were Canaanites their killing of Ish-Bosheth may have settled an old grudge, but it seems unlikely that they would be described as **leaders of raiding bands** if they were known to be disgruntled. The wording makes it clear that their bands fought for, not against, Ish-Bosheth. It seems more likely that their act was out of loyalty, however misguided, to a united Israel.

4:4 / **Mephibosheth**'s name was originally Meribbaal. See additional note on 2:8.

4:6–7 / The text in these two verses is difficult. It is not clear whether we have two accounts of the same event or an extended description with **slipped away** (v. 6) better translated as "slipped in." Many scholars and several Bible translations (including JB and RSV) take as authentic the textual tradition followed by the LXX, which translates v. 6 as "The woman at the door had become drowsy while she was sifting wheat and had fallen asleep so Rechab and Baanah slipped in" (GNB). If this is correct then we have evidence of the low-key arrangements at Ish-Bosheth's court with only one woman doorkeeper on duty. The impression is of a fairly impoverished lifestyle rather than a lavish palace. However, the NIV may be correct in following the MT, where v. 7 appears to reinforce what has been described in v. 6.

4:8–9 / The men's claim that through their action **the LORD has avenged** David may or may not have been true, but it makes no difference to the rightness or wrongness of their action. God can use wrong actions, a fact demonstrated when Judas betrayed Jesus. In this case David benefited in the long term from Ish-Bosheth's death, although in the short term it may have caused him problems. David's reply to their claim affirms his conviction that now, as always, Yahweh alone had delivered him, and their implicit assumption that they had a part in that could not be accepted.

4:12 / Exposing the bodies of criminals was a known practice, acting as a warning to those who might be tempted to similar behavior. The cutting off of the **hands and feet** emphasized that these men were traitors to David and should in no sense be seen as his allies.

§30 Confirmation and Consolidation (2 Sam. 5:1–25)

5:1–5 / This section provides an editorial summary of what may have been protracted and at times tense negotiations. The delay between Ish-Bosheth's death and David's enthronement over Israel is not known. It was seven years and six months before the capital was moved to Jerusalem, and verse 5 could imply that the two events were simultaneous. However, although it is likely that the negotiations took longer than they would have if Ish-Bosheth had lived, it is unlikely that Israel was left kingless for more than five years. The timing was not vital to the writers, but the fact that David's kingship over Israel was at the initiative and with the full affirmation of the nation was crucial.

The **compact** that David made with the people would have included mutual obligations, making explicit his responsibilities to them and the support he could expect from them. This is the first time (v. 2) the **shepherd** image is used to describe David's God-given calling, but it became a well-used motif in the psalms and in the prophets for the role of national leaders, particularly the king. God is described as the shepherd of his people (e.g., Gen. 49:24), and David's background (1 Sam. 16:11) makes it not surprising that the writers pick up the imagery.

David is acknowledged as one of the people, their **own flesh and blood**, as a competent **military** leader, and as appointed by God. All three are key elements in the Israelite understanding of kingship. In a ceremony at Hebron the contract that had been envisaged by Abner (3:21) was finally ratified, and David was **anointed** as **king** over the whole nation. He was in his early thirties, at the height of his powers.

5:6–8 / Hebron had been a useful center for David, but it was too far south and too closely identified with Judah to serve as capital for the whole country. **Jerusalem**, occupied by **the Jebusites**, was seen as much more suitable. It was inside the area assigned to Benjamin, but it had never yet been conquered. It was not far from David's home area and was probably well known to him. It had good communication routes and yet was easily defensible. The decision to move there was taken, and David marched his troops against the city.

The description of David's conquering of Jerusalem reads like a précis of a much longer account, with more attention given to the origin of the proverb about **the blind and lame** than to the conquest. The Jebusites had a warranted confidence in the security systems of their fortress city, but it was not impregnable. It is possible that David had for many years envisaged Jerusalem as his capital and had identified a way of breaking through the defenses. As well as providing David with a more central capital, the conquest would also add to his reputation as a brilliant soldier, improving his status and the security of the nation. The Jebusites discovered that no army, let alone the despised blind and the lame, could prevent David's taking the city from them.

5:9–16 / Having successfully captured the city, David instituted a building program and bolstered his power base in every area. The writers identify the increasing strength of David's power as resulting from the fact that **the LORD God Almighty was with him.** David's sense of God's presence with him was reinforced by the growing stability of his reign, evidenced not least by the increase in trade relationships with surrounding powers. He was able to have a **palace** worthy of the name, and he could pay for it and defend it.

However, the link between these narratives and the Deuteronomic kingship code that was so positively seen in verse 2 continues more negatively. The ideal king was forbidden to take many wives (Deut. 17:17), but David did exactly that, for national political reasons or as a boost to his own status. We are told that he had many children.

5:17–25 / This is the last battle against the **Philistines** that is described in detail; apart from retrospective references in chapters 21 and 23, the Philistines play little part in the rest of 2 Samuel. Their concern that David's appointment would bring trouble for them was warranted (v. 17). Either as part of a longer campaign or on two separate occasions they came in force to the **Valley of Rephaim** and were so comprehensively defeated that they no longer posed any real threat to Israel.

David, presumably still taking advantage of the ephod that had been in his possession for so long, **inquired of the LORD** and was guaranteed success. The first incident was memorable and led to the name of the place where it happened being changed or given a new significance. The impotence of the Philistine gods to protect even themselves, let alone their people, brings the power of God's help into focus. In the second incident the sound of the wind in the treetops confirmed God's presence with the Israelites as they fought.

Additional Notes §30

5:1–3 / There are strong links between this section and the regulations for kingship set out in Deut. 17:14–20. The dual recognition of leaders by God and by the people led is a common motif in the OT. This second anointing of David, this time as king over Israel, not just Judah (2 Sam. 2:4), makes sense within that context (the original anointing of David by Samuel in 1 Sam. 16:13 indicated future potential rather than position). Theologically, David was king because God had chosen him as king. Sociologically, he was king (at least of the northern tribes) because he and the tribes signed and sealed a covenant agreeing to terms of kingship. The writers do not see a conflict between these two perspectives.

5:4–5 / Giving David's regnal dates emphasizes that what was promised has now come to pass. For further discussion of the delay see the additional note on 2:10–11.

5:6 / The **Jebusites** are the final tribe in the list of those whose land God covenanted to give to Abraham's descendants (Gen. 15:18–21).

The references to **the blind and the lame,** so prominent here, are omitted in 1 Chron. 11:1–9, which includes a reference to Joab's part in the conquest of Jerusalem (omitted here). It seems that David was offended by the implication that even the weakest would be able to defeat him, and he therefore picked up the taunt and turned it against the Jebusites.

5:7 / This is the first reference in the OT to **Zion,** the hill on which the city was built. Zion became an alternative name for Jerusalem and was used metaphorically to refer to God's heavenly city. The ancient Zion was to the southeast of the Temple Mount and is distinct from the modern Mount Zion, which is farther to the west.

5:8 / The method David used to breach the city's defenses is unclear. The word translated **water shaft** occurs elsewhere in the OT only in Ps. 42:7, where it is translated "waterfall." Other meanings for the word have been suggested, as in the NIV margin's "scaling hooks." The picture of David climbing up the water tunnel with a small group of men may be correct but can never be more than speculative. T. Kleven discusses this issue in "Up the Waterspout: How David's General Joab Got Inside Jerusalem," *BAR* 20, no. 4 (1994), pp. 34–35.

5:11 / **Hiram** did not come to power until later in David's reign, so although he could have acted as agent for **Tyre** before he was king, it may also be that the building program did not come into full play immediately after David entered Jerusalem.

5:14–16 / The names of David's daughters are not given here, although the Chronicler names Tamar. 1 Chron. lists two other sons, Nogah and a second Eliphelet (1 Chron. 3:5–9) or Elpelet (1 Chron. 14:4–7) but goes on to say that these thirteen were only the sons of his official wives. Many more children were born to David's concubines. We are also informed in 1 Chron. that the first four in this list were Bathsheba's children. Apart from Solomon, the only one from this list to be mentioned again is Nathan, who in the genealogy given by Luke, was one of the ancestors of Jesus (Luke 3:31).

5:17–25 / Anderson (*2 Samuel*, p. 77) suggests that this Philistine campaign occupied the five-year gap before David took possession of Jerusalem and that the two incidents mentioned are only a summary.

5:20 / Baal Perazim means "the lord who breaks out." This is a further indication that the word *baal* ("lord") at one time had no idolatrous connotations and was applied to God (cf. additional note on 2:8).

5:21 / The account in Chronicles has almost identical wording and obviously uses the same source but adds that David had the idols, abandoned by the Philistines, destroyed by fire. 1 Chron. 14:17 also stresses the way in which these battles brought fame to David. The defeat of the Philistines was one of David's greatest achievements, and the writers here choose to emphasize God's help for David rather than David's increase in fame. The Chronicler presents the Davidic monarchy in as good a light as possible. The writers of Samuel share a profound interest in David and his descendants but present the story from a more objective viewpoint.

§31 The Ark Comes to Jerusalem (2 Sam. 6:1–23)

6:1–5 / The story begins at **Baalah of Judah,** where **the ark** had been kept since its recovery from the Philistines twenty years before. To take a party of **thirty thousand** men for a ceremonial duty sounds excessive, and the accuracy of the text has been seriously questioned. It is possible that the "thousand" refers to a military grouping (cf. additional note on 1 Sam. 4:10). However, Baalah, although Judean territory, was still within the range of Philistine influence. Thus, by bringing the ark to Jerusalem, David made a political statement as well as a theological one. The huge army could be seen as flaunting David's growing power over the diminishing influence of the Philistines. Or, particularly if this incident took place in the early years of his reign, it could be that David made certain that the Philistines could not stop him from taking this action.

Although 1 Chronicles 13 sheds more light on the process of decision making, this text gives no hint of David's motivation for bringing the ark to Jerusalem. But the significance of the ark is undoubted. For Israel it was the most potent sign of God's presence with them; it was called by God's **name,** and its lid provided a symbolic throne for him. **The LORD Almighty,** invisible and not limited by time and space, had in the time of Moses chosen to give the ark significance. If Jerusalem was to be the heart of the newly united nation of Israel, then the heart of their faith, represented by the **ark of God,** was to be there as well. It would provide a vital link between the new state and what had gone before. The ark was taken from its resting place, which had never been seen as permanent, and put on a **new cart.** Its newness symbolized holiness, and it had probably been built for this purpose. The Philistines had also used a new cart to transport the ark (1 Sam. 6). The writers make no comment, but the subsequent narrative may cause the reader to reflect that following local cultural customs rather than looking to the law is a dangerous procedure.

The cart was provided with guards and, accompanied by a huge and noisy procession, set off for Jerusalem. They used all kinds of musical instruments to celebrate this indication of the stability and security that David had brought to the nation.

6:6–11 / After a while **the oxen stumbled,** and **Uzzah** naturally took action to prevent the ark from falling, but that action resulted in his death. The Hebrew in verse 7 is unclear, and most translations rely on the parallel passage in 1 Chronicles 13:1–14 to make sense of it. Uzzah's act was seen as **irreverent** and deserving of this severe penalty. First Chronicles 15:2, 15 refer to the importance of Levites carrying the ark, and perhaps this is presented as the cause of Uzzah's death. The Israelites in general and David in particular had been guilty of trying to use the ark for their own purposes—in effect, they were trying to manipulate God. They had rejoiced at the demonstration of God's power, but they had not taken either his power or his holiness seriously. There is no record of the kind of warning being given here that was given to those Israelites who might have strayed too close to the mountain where God was going to speak to Moses (Exod. 19). Maybe the writers intend to show the ignorance within the Israelite community concerning religious traditions, in particular regarding how they should properly treat the ark.

David's first reaction to Uzzah's death was fury, either because his plans for a glorious affirmation of his new capital had been ruined or because he had genuinely been trying to do the right thing and saw God's action as unfair. However, as he began to realize the enormity of his own behavior his anger was replaced by fear. He realized that the ark—indeed God—was unpredictable and awesome. David abandoned the project and the ark. The ark was given for safe keeping into the hands of **Obed-Edom.** It remained with him **for three months** and to his **household** brought nothing but blessing. This apparently convinced David that not the ark but a wrong attitude and approach to it was a danger—although it could also be that God's anger had turned to blessing.

6:12–15 / The procession and the celebrations began again. Chronicles confirms the implication of verse 13 that this time the ark was carried by Levites rather than on a cart drawn by oxen. This time also, as a precaution and a sign that the people took God's holiness seriously, a sacrifice was carried out after **six steps.**

David wore **a linen ephod,** a priestly garment, which may indicate that David deliberately accepted a priestly role. The ephod was short, and in the enthusiasm of his dancing David exposed himself (v. 20). His dancing **before the LORD** indicates cultic activity, possibly involving some kind of ecstatic trance. Legitimate cultic dancing of this kind is not mentioned again after the time of David. Shouting and trumpet blowing were used both in festivals and as a call to war, and in this instance there may be an element of both. The text conveys the excitement of the occasion.

6:16 / We have here an insert preparing for verses 20–23. **Michal,** perhaps still unable to come to terms with the way she had been treated by David, **despised him** because he forgot his dignity. Her part in the ritual is often assumed to be parallel to that of the queen in the sacred marriage ceremonies of the ancient Near East. Looking out of the **window** is typical of the goddess in ancient myths where "the woman looks out on the world to see what men have accomplished" (Exum, *Tragedy and Biblical Narrative,* p. 89).

6:17–19 / When **the ark** reached Jerusalem, the celebrations continued. The ark was given its place inside a **tent,** parallel to but not the same as the wilderness tabernacle. David again appears to take a priestly role. Although the Levitical priests may have actually carried out the sacrifices, David as the anointed king gave a royal and perhaps priestly blessing to the people. All Israel were now involved, not in the sacrifice as such but in the accompanying celebration. All were given a gift, either as a natural part of the celebrations or as a shrewd political move to create good public relations.

The ark was settled in its new home, and Jerusalem was established as the accepted center of Israel's worship. There is no sign of prophetic opposition to this move. The dangers of the people's viewing Jerusalem, particularly once the temple was built, as an indication that God dwelt there and not elsewhere (cf. 1 Kgs. 8:27–30) were perhaps outweighed by the advantages of having a geographical religious focus.

6:20–23 / Michal explains her attitude using very blunt language. She is concerned not so much to shame David as with the fact that he has shamed his position. David's point is that she has misunderstood his position and the concept of shame. He contrasts Michal's **in the sight of,** or "before" **the slave girls of his servants,** with **it was before the LORD.** David recognized that before God any status he might have was of no significance. He was willing to make himself as less than nothing if it would bring glory to the God who had chosen him, above Michal's father and his family, as **ruler** (Hb. *nagîd,* "prince") over Israel. Kingly status was not about being aloof from the people but about serving God.

The implication is that Michal's childlessness was a punishment for her presumption. It is not clear whether this was a barrenness sent by Yahweh or a choice made by David or Michal to avoid sexual relations. In either case it indicates that Saul's house was to have no ongoing part in the kingship of Israel. The writers' purpose may be to emphasize that David's heir was not to come from Michal.

Additional Notes §31

---

2 Sam. 5 brings to an end a long series of related stories, combined in a fairly coherent and consistent way and sometimes known as the History of David's Rise. 2 Sam. 9 begins another such related series that is sometimes known as the Succession Narrative or the Court History. Chs. 6, 7, and 8 have proved less easy to classify. Ch. 6 is clearly related to the Ark Narratives found in 1 Sam. 4:1–7:2, but in this context in 2 Sam. the chapter stands alone. The further developments in David's reign described in ch. 7 follow from ch. 6, but the style and structure are very different. Ch. 8 provides a summary of military actions but again has a different style and structure from other chapters and almost certainly refers to battles that took place before the events described in chs. 6 and 7.

These chapters reveal the overall editorial policy of the books of Samuel, detailing the links between theological and political concerns for the development of life for God's people within the covenant and the way in which power is reinforced. Maybe those who formulated that policy were less concerned with literary cohesion than we would have liked, and these chapters, in a similar way to chs. 21–24, contain material that is considered to be important for readers to know and that fits best at this point in the generally chronologically based narrative.

Bringing the ark of God into Jerusalem took place after Jerusalem had been captured, but there is no way of determining how long after David began to reign in Jerusalem this occurred.

6:1 / It has been suggested that v. 1 has been detached from its original context, perhaps as an introduction to ch. 8. But it is, as Gordon (*1 and 2 Samuel: A Commentary,* p. 231) argues, unnecessary to see it in that way.

6:2 / **Baalah of Judah** is the alternative name for Kiriath Jearim (1 Sam. 7:1), a small town a few miles inside the borders of Israel on the route between Philistia and Jerusalem.

The ark's being **called by the Name** may mean "named after" or "over which the name is called." Using the concept of the name of God in this way reinforces the idea that God was not localized in the ark without taking away from the concept that the ark was a place where God could be found. The repetition of **the name,** a common Hb. idiom indicating significance, is omitted in the Gk. LXX and the Latin Vulgate.

The **cherubim** were carved into the lid of the ark and the outstretched wings formed a kind of seat. In Exod. 25:22, God promises to meet with the Israelites from "above" this place.

6:3 / Neither **Uzzah** nor **Ahio** is mentioned in 1 Sam. 7:1, where Eleazar is the ark's sole guardian, but they may be younger sons or grandsons of **Abinadab.** The name **Ahio** may mean "his brother," and some scholars identify this with Zadok (2 Sam. 8:17), which could explain the importance later given to Zadok. But this is speculation, based on the fact that in 2 Sam. 15:24–29 Zadok appears to be in charge of the ark.

6:8 / The name **Perez Uzzah,** or "outbreak against Uzzah," may be linked to the name Baal Perazim (5:20), although there is no connection between the two places other than the meaning of their name.

6:10 / **Obed-Edom the Gittite:** It seems unlikely that even in this emergency the ark would be entrusted to a Philistine. It may be that Obed-Edom was a Levite who had resided for some time in Gath and is therefore described as a Gittite. Perhaps he was there as part of David's exiled group. It is possible, however, that his family had been long-term resident aliens within Israel and he, although still known as a Gittite, was a fully accepted member of the Israelite community.

6:12–15 / This account is sometimes taken not as describing a particular event taking the ark to Jerusalem but as a description of a regular ceremony taking place each year at new year, when the ark was brought anew into the temple. Some of those who take this view assume that sacrifices took place after every six steps and see this as a confirmation of a regular ritual. However, there had to be a time when the ark was first taken to Jerusalem, and nothing in the text as we have it precludes this from being an account of that first occasion.

6:16 / Bowman ("The Fortune of King David/The Fate of Queen Michal") argues that both Saul and David sought to exploit Michal's love for their own benefit. Saul tried unsuccessfully to use her to defeat David. David used her, in claiming and then reclaiming her, to bolster his status. If the only thing Michal gained when she was taken from Paltiel was the somewhat dubious privilege of her status and dignity as the king's wife, it is not surprising that she was concerned that David's uncontrolled dancing might cause him, and therefore her, to lose all that she had left (v. 20).

6:18 / David's actions are sometimes seen as indicating an early tradition of priest-king, perhaps linked to the Melchizedek tradition (Ps. 110:4). In 2 Sam. 8:18 David's own sons are described as priests, although the NIV prefers to interpret this as "royal advisers." The relationship between kingship and priesthood is not always clear within the OT. Saul was apparently condemned for engaging in priestly activity (1 Sam. 13) and so was Uzziah (2 Chron. 26:16–21), but David's priestly activity does not seem to incur the same rebuke. We cannot be sure of the reason for this disparity, although it may relate to the motivation behind the various activities. Saul was motivated by fear and Uzziah by pride, whereas at this point David's motivation appears to be to encourage the people in their service of God.

§32 God's Covenant with David (2 Sam. 7:1–29)

This chapter forms the climax of the whole Davidic tradition and brings together two themes, the foundation of the Davidic dynasty and the building of the temple. These themes are not fully integrated (vv. 1–7 and vv. 8–29 can each stand alone), and scholars have debated the structure and origins of the material. However, the fact that we have the origin of two institutions that dominated Israel's history shows how vital this chapter is. The connection between the two themes is the word "house," used in two different ways. David is not to build a house (building) for the Lord, but the Lord will establish a house (dynasty) for David. All the positive and beneficial aspects of kingship presented in the rest of Scripture center on the Davidic line. David was the one with whom God made a personal covenant.

7:1–4 / Verse 1 sets the scene. David had **rest from all his enemies.** He therefore, perhaps reflecting on Deuteronomy 12:10–11 or the tradition on which it was based, decided that it was time to build a permanent temple in Jerusalem in which to house the ark of God. The divine guarantee and endorsement of David's throne comes only after David had been proclaimed king by popular acclaim (5:3) and by conquest. In spite of his initial anointing by Samuel (1 Sam. 16), up to this stage he had been a soldier-king. Only in this chapter is the concept of sacral consecration formulated.

David recognized the part that God has played in his life so far, for **the LORD had given him** rest. He consulted **Nathan the prophet** to confirm that the planned temple was the right thing to do in God's eyes as well as his own, and Nathan initially gave him that confirmation.

Sometimes prophets were given a direct revelation from God, but a lack of such direct revelation did not mean that they were unable to speak for God. They could assess a situation in the light of their knowledge of God and make a judgment about it. That is what Nathan did in this case. However, the judgment even of a true prophet like Nathan may be flawed. There is no condemnation of Nathan for assuring David that his plans were in accordance with God's purposes. David's idea was good, but the timing and the personnel were not right. God then spoke directly to Nathan, and under those circumstances Nathan showed no hesitation in coming back to David with a different response. There is no room for pride when God speaks, and Nathan was not afraid to change his position. Jeremiah 28 offers some parallels to this story, but in that instance Hananiah's refusal to change his position resulted in his being branded as a false prophet.

7:5–7 / **My servant David** (also v. 8) illustrates the special relationship between God and David. Although Israel as a nation is described as God's servant, the ascription is rarely given to individuals. "My servant," however, becomes almost a title for David as it had been for Moses. Perhaps we are being introduced to a new phase in David's ministry. Two reasons are given for not building the temple at this stage. The Lord was not to be limited by a building, and the Lord had not yet asked for such a house to be built. The tendency to localize God could weaken the sense of his all-pervading presence, and Israel was perhaps not yet ready to resist that tendency. In the OT the uniqueness of Israel's God is always safeguarded.

7:8–11 / These verses begin to state God's positive intentions for David. He is to be reminded again of God's gracious delivering acts and can have confidence for the future based on his knowledge of the way in which God has been with him in the past. God speaks of his particular choice and election of David—he has already been appointed as *nagîd,* ruler or prince. God gives him a personal promise of a great **name** and a great **house.** Verse 10 shows that this personal promise to David is in the context of God's concern for all the people. The well-being of the people is secured within the Davidic covenant.

7:12–16 / Three lines of fulfillment of these promises have been identified. First is the **offspring** who will be permitted to **build a house** for God. Offspring may mean a son or posterity. It probably refers to Solomon, although he is not named. Second, a Davidic dynasty will be established, and third, a messianic king is promised. The understanding of the latter idea is not explicit in this text and comes primarily from historic hindsight (cf. Jer. 33:14), although the repeated **forever** is seen as making the implication. This messianic extension of the Davidic line is said to be more obvious in the parallel passage in 1 Chronicles 17, though in both cases the thought is clearer from a retrospective position.

Although the Davidic king became the ideal (e.g., as in Ps. 72), the view here is realistic. Verse 14 in particular shows that David's descendants were not expected to be ideal. The Davidic dynasty will endure, but it is to be a "dynasty under discipline" (Ackroyd, *The Second Book of Samuel*, p. 78). The intimate father-son relationship between God and the king will necessarily include chastisement. The word *covenant* is not used in this chapter, but the language reflects that of other covenants. God's ḥesed, covenant **love**, will **never be taken away** from David and his descendants.

7:17–29 / **Nathan,** having received this detailed message, reports it fully to **David.** David recognizes Nathan's words as coming from God and responds to the promises contained in the prophecy by sitting down in God's presence and speaking out in what is part prayer and part hymn of praise. David's initial response is awed wonder. He is so overwhelmed by the honor that God is showing to him, on top of the marvelous way that God has led him and protected him so far, that any disappointment relating to building a temple pales into insignificance. Perhaps he remembered that Saul, fairly early on in his reign, had had any hopes of a dynasty taken away (1 Sam. 13:13–14). David was given a promise of an enduring dynasty.

From his sense of the honor God has done to him, David reflects, in praise and worship, on the nature of Israel's **great** God. He marvels that the unique **Sovereign LORD** who controls all of history is able to give assurances about the future in this way. He relates the new idea of a Davidic dynasty to the old ideas of the Sinaitic covenant. This stresses the historical continuity of God's control and shows that the original covenant may be developed but is not superseded. God's choice of David and **his house** stands alongside God's choice of **Israel.** This God was able to deliver Israel and can therefore be trusted to deliver David.

In the final section of his prayer, David asks for confirmation that God will keep these promises. Verse 28 makes it clear that this reflects not doubt in God's word but a continuing incredulity that David is the recipient of such **blessing.** This section echoes Abraham's prayer in Genesis 18, with its confidence in speaking out before God alongside an awed recognition of God's greatness and a wonder that such communication is possible.

The stress in this chapter on the importance of the Davidic dynasty and the responsibilities of David's descendants reinforced other messianic passages (e.g., Pss. 2, 110; Isa. 9:1–7; 11:1–16; Mic. 5:1–5) and led to the conviction that the Messiah would be a descendant of David. The NT proclaims that the **offspring to succeed** David (v. 12) and fulfill these messianic predictions was Jesus Christ. This explains the desire of both Matthew and Luke to emphasize the authenticity of Jesus' descent from David (Matt. 1:1–17; Luke 3:23–37).

Additional Notes §32

7:1 / The strong links between Deut. and the so-called Deuteronomic History, of which the books of Samuel are a part, are clear in this chapter. However, debate continues as to whether Deut. forms the background that shaped that history or was written as late as the 7th century B.C. in the light of that history. This chapter presupposes peace in Israel, which indicates that the wars and victories of ch. 8 should precede this chapter chronologically. But the material in ch. 8 is placed later because the content in ch. 7 follows directly from the content of ch. 6.

7:2 / Although this is the first reference to **Nathan,** and in spite of his major significance here and later as the main but not the only prophetic adviser to the king (the prophet Gad also played an important role, 1 Sam. 22:5; 2 Sam. 24), Nathan appears without any introduction. This may be because his family was not seen as significant, or it may deliberately introduce an element of mystery so that the emphasis is on Nathan's role as God's spokesman rather than on his background.

7:6 / God's mobility and guidance were emphasized in the period of the judges when the ark was located at Bethel, Shechem, and Shiloh. Perhaps the use of the Hb. *yshb,* meaning to dwell permanently, rathar than *shkn,* meaning to dwell for the time being, is significant. The latter could have been applied to Shiloh (a substantial structure; 1 Sam. 1:9; 3:15), whereas the former, used here, could not. In any case, God is not bound to one place.

The danger of the temple building and its city becoming the basis of a false superstitious trust is seen in Jer. 7:4, 20, 24. There is little evidence that a religiously motivated "anti-Jerusalem-Temple" group was responsible for this passage or that such a group existed. Even Ezekiel, who saw the glory of the Lord departing from Jerusalem, envisaged that glory returning to a purified temple (Ezek. 11:23; 43:1–4; 44:4).

In 1 Kgs. 5:3 and 1 Chron. 22:8; 28:2, David's pollution by wars and killing is given as the reason for his not being permitted to build the temple, but there is no hint of that here.

7:8 / David was called to be the prince (Hb. *nagîd*) of Israel. Although *melek*, the word for king, is used often elsewhere, particularly in the Psalms, it is not normally used in the historical books as an ascription of individual monarchs. This is probably to safeguard the concept of Yahweh's remaining the true king, a concept that Psalms safeguards in other ways.

7:11 / I and **The LORD** are used interchangeably in this verse. This is a fairly common literary practice with only stylistic significance. It is not evidence that this passage was compiled from two separate sources.

7:13 / **Name** is probably used here as a synonym for God but retaining that sense of distinction already seen (6:2). The temple, like the ark, will be a place where Israel can meet with God but not a place to which God can be restricted.

7:14–15 / The covenantal relationship between David and Yahweh is made explicit in Ps. 89 (see also 2 Sam. 23:5; Ps. 132:12). This covenant, primarily between God and David but also involving the people, follows from the covenant between David and the people but involving God (5:3). In 2 Kgs. 11:17, where Joash was made king, the priest Jehoida instigates covenants between God and the king with his people and between the king and the people. Such a double covenant pattern may have been common.

7:18 / David presumably entered into the tent where the ark was kept. His ambition may have been to build a beautiful building for the ark, but he knew that such a building was not essential for meeting with God.

Absence of any reference to the temple within this prayer is perhaps evidence that there were originally two documents, one relating to the temple and one initiating the Davidic covenant. It could equally be evidence that David accepted God's decree without question. The Chronicler tells us that David made detailed provisions for the temple that he believed Solomon would build, but the writers of Samuel do not mention this. It has been suggested that the writers composed this prayer to summarize what has gone before, but there is no reason why it should not be seen as a prayer of David.

§33 War and Peace—Enemies and Friends (2 Sam. 8:1–9:13)

8:1–14 / In contrast to the relaxed narrative style of the surrounding chapters, this is a terse summary of David's military successes against the surrounding tribes. These verse fill in the background and explain how **the LORD** gave him rest from all his enemies (7:1).

David's victories eventually led to the stage where the Philistines no longer posed a serious threat. In a similar way, the other tribes surrounding Israel were subdued and often subjugated. Some, like **Hamath** (a tribe from the northwest of Israel above the Aramean region), who were not defeated in battle, nevertheless brought tribute (v. 9). **Edom** in the south, **Ammon** and **Moab** in the east, and the **Arameans** in the north ceased to cause any major problems for some time.

Not only were Israel's borders now well protected, but also **garrisons** were placed at key bases outside, in the north (v. 6) and the south (v. 14). Of course, none of the great powers were interested in this region at the time. But the writers emphasize God as the key influence in Israel's success and resultant stability: **the LORD gave David victory wherever he went** (vv. 6, 14). This dual reference to the Lord's help shows how remarkable this transformation of the fortunes of Israel was. David recognizes God's part in his victories by dedicating to God all the treasures taken in tribute.

The gruesome lottery (v. 2) perhaps shows not the extent of David's cruelty but his mercy. Destroying the army would devastate any nation, but a **third,** even of the fighting men, were **allowed to live.**

8:15–18 / David's kingship was not just a matter of providing a national defense system. He also assumed responsibility for internal government, so that probably for the first time in Israel there was some kind of centralized justice and administration system. Religion also began to be centralized, with the focus of worship not around local shrines but around the central temple. What amounts to David's first cabinet is described briefly, including senior religious representatives alongside the military and organizational leaders. In this kind of theocratic state there was no separation between religious and secular affairs. Verse 15 implies that David headed the justice department. This provides the background to Nathan's presentation to David of a case that needed to be judged (ch. 12).

Now that the nation was at peace and the government established, the account can continue with the story of life in David's kingdom and in particular life in the royal court.

9:1–13 / The story of David's first encounter with **Mephibosheth** is told without editorial comment. It can be read as a charming picture of life at court, emphasizing David's **kindness** and sense of responsibility. However, it can also be read as a further example of David's political opportunism, using Saul's family to bolster his own position within the country.

There has been a long delay between David's promise to care for Jonathan's family (1 Sam. 20:14–16) and the events of this chapter. Mephibosheth was five years old at the time of Jonathan's death (4:4), and now he has a **young son** of his own (v. 12). Mauchline (*1 and 2 Samuel*, p. 244) suggests that these events took place early in David's reign and the reference to Mica is a later addition, but Mephibosheth appears to be an adult in this account. This delay lessens the impact of David's desire to show kindness to Jonathan's descendants.

However, the writers have no qualms about ascribing negative motives to David in other contexts (as in 2 Sam. 11), so perhaps it is best to take David's actions at face value. He may be blameworthy in forgetting about Jonathan's family for this period of time, but when the thought eventually comes to mind he seeks to make amends and genuinely wants to help Mephibosheth. Chapters 9 through 20 build up the picture of many characters in David's circle. Mephibosheth, **Ziba**, and Mephibosheth's patron **Makir** all come into the story again later.

Ziba, **a servant of Saul's household,** acted as the estate manager for Saul's property. This was an important position, and in the absence of the owners he had made substantial financial gain out of it. He may or may not have been pleased to acknowledge Mephibosheth's claim to the estate or have Mephibosheth close at hand rather than safely ensconced in **Lo Debar** on the other side of the Jordan. He is well aware of Mephibosheth's existence and condition, but that he does not give a name perhaps indicates his attitude that Mephibosheth, as crippled, was a nobody. Given that most dynasties in the ancient Near East were wiped out when a new one emerged, it is likely that Mephibosheth and any other of Saul's heirs would have hesitated to claim their property rights for fear of endangering their lives.

Makir son of Ammiel lived in a disputed area east of the Jordan (v. 4), far enough away from court life for Mephibosheth to be safe. During Absalom's rebellion Makir helped David (17:27). It is likely that his support for David then was influenced by David's kindness to his ward at this point.

Verses 3 and 13 describe Mephibosheth as **crippled in both feet.** This could mean only that he limped, but the problem severely hindered his movement. Mephibosheth was invited to eat at **the king's table,** that is, to be an official member of the court, but he would still need the use of Saul's lands to support his family and his household.

David's initial assurance to Mephibosheth (v. 7), **Don't be afraid,** shows that David recognized that Mephibosheth might have perceived himself to be in danger. Mephibosheth's reference to himself as a **dead dog,** undeserving of David's kindness, which parallels David's assurance to Saul in 1 Samuel 24:14, may again stress that he is not a threat. It may also show a low self-image related to his physical problems. At this point Mephibosheth was disabled politically and emotionally as well as physically. In either case, Mephibosheth seems genuinely grateful that David has taken this action and, in spite of Ziba's later accusations (16:1–4), genuine in his protestations of loyalty to David. Both will have been thinking of **Jonathan.** David, aware of the time when as an endangered fugitive he had been shown kindness by the royal prince, perhaps felt that a debt has been repaid. Mephibosheth, no doubt aware of the relationship between David and his father and perhaps inheriting his father's generous spirit, was more than willing to become a loyal courtier to his father's friend.

The mention of **Mica** in verse 12 may be incidental or a hint of a possible future threat to David's security. However, again the writers seem to have deliberately avoided implying that David's motivation was political. Mica never developed into a threat; there is no further reference to him.

Additional Notes §33

8:1 / The significance of **Metheg Ammah** is unclear. It could be a place name, but there is no other known reference to it. The literal meaning of the words, "bridle of the forearm," may mean that the leading reins of Philistia were now in the hands of David (Mauchline, *1 and 2 Samuel*, p. 233). However, because the term is not in common usage its significance remains in doubt. Removal of the Philistine threat is clear.

8:3 / **Zobah** is in the north, probably even farther north than Damascus and possibly part of a regular alliance of Aramean tribes. The defeats of the Aramean kingdoms were not as comprehensive as that of the Philistines; they returned to fight another day. But for the moment peace was achieved.

8:4 / Damaging the hamstrings of the vast majority of the captured **chariot horses** removed them as a threat. It may be that David did not want the problem of transporting these horses back to Israel, where they could not be used in the rough hills where most defensive fighting took place. However, it could be that David was aware of and took seriously the prohibition against amassing many horses (Deut. 17:16). Joshua is also described as hamstringing enemy horses in response to a command from God (Josh. 11:6, 9). David's copying his actions may be evidence that he saw these campaigns as part of a holy war.

8:9 / The son of **Tou king of Hamath** has an Israelite name meaning "Yahweh is exalted." David probably gave him this name to indicate vassal status. 1 Chron. 18:10 calls him Hadoram ("exalted Hadd").

8:16–17 / We cannot be sure of the exact duties of these officials, although the main structure is clear. **Joab** had responsibility for the main Israelite **army** and Benaiah for the foreign mercenary troops, who were usually kept separate.

The **recorder,** a new figure in Israel's government, maintained the essential national records and possibly ensured efficient communication among the king, his officials, and the nation.

The role of the **secretary** was probably comparable to that of a secretary of state, or the most senior civil servant.

This is the first mention of the priest **Zadok**. Throughout the rest of 2 Sam. Zadok's partner is named as **Abiathar,** and in 1 Sam. 22:20 Abiathar is named as the son of Ahimelech. It is therefore possible that the names of father and son have been transposed in this verse and should be reversed.

8:18 / **David's sons** are described as priests (Hb. *kōhⁿnîm*), which the NIV interprets as **royal advisers**. The king's role was considered to some degree sacred, but there are no other indications that the royal princes took part in traditional priestly activities. Their role here is clearly separated from that of Zadok and his colleague.

9:1 / It is possible that David's question arose after the death of another seven of Saul's descendants, described in 21:1–14. It is hard to understand, if it was before the death of these seven—and the timing of that is unclear—how David could be unaware of Saul's descendants. However, the arguments about the relative timing of these two incidents go both ways, and it does not affect the interpretation of either incident as to which came first.

In spite of the awareness of human nature that is apparent in David's poetry, and in spite of his passionate commitment to the matter occupying his mind, David is not renowned for thoughtfulness about other people's feelings and concerns. The sudden recollection of a responsibility to Jonathan ties in with what we see elsewhere of David's character.

Baldwin argues that David's attention has been occupied with securing the kingdom and only now can he honor his promise to Jonathan (*1 and 2 Samuel*, p. 226). L. G. Perdue (" 'Is There Anyone Left of the House of Saul . . . ?' Ambiguity and Characterization of David in the Succession Narrative," *JSOT* 30 [1984], pp. 67–84) argues that "the narrator's characterization of David is intentionally ambiguous so that two very different interpretations of David may emerge, depending on the reader's own assessment of the motives resting behind the king's actions and motives" (p. 71).

This ambiguity reflects many Israelites' ambivalent attitude toward the monarchy. Thus the reader is not necessarily being asked to choose between the "David who valiantly attempts to rule his kingdom with compassion and forgiveness, changing only at the end of his life when, as an old embittered and dying man, he comes to recognize that ruthless force is the only way to suppress revolution" and the David who "is consistently deceitful, treacherous and ruthless, demanding loyalty from his subjects but repaying it only if it promotes his own self interests" (Perdue, p. 80). Rather one must accept the ambiguity, acknowledging an element of truth in both pictures.

The Hb. word translated as "kindness" is *ḥesed,* which indicates a close relationship of personal giving, love, and loyalty. It is used for God's covenant love for his people, involving total commitment as well as deep love and affection. In v. 3 David makes it explicit he is talking about this kindness, God's *ḥesed.*

9:2 / Both Ziba and Mephibosheth (v. 6) refer to themselves as David's **servant**, or, in modern terms, his loyal subject. This is probably a polite response to the king's greeting but may be a deliberate attempt to set themselves apart from any group that might oppose David.

9:6 / 21:8 speaks of **Mephibosheth** as Saul's son by Rizpah, one of the seven who were killed to satisfy the Gibeonites' vengeance. It has been suggested that this Mephibosheth is referred to here and the references to Jonathan are added to emphasize David's loyalty to Jonathan. However, the same name recurs in families, and Jonathan had descendants (1 Sam. 20:15 makes no sense otherwise). There is no reason to assume anything other than that the text describes Mephibosheth, Jonathan's son.

See additional note on 9:2.

9:11 / We have no record of what David's sons felt about having Mephibosheth added to their number.

§34 The Ammonites Are Defeated (2 Sam. 10:1–19)

10:1–19 / The relationship between Israel and Ammon around this time is unclear. In 8:12 the Ammonites are one of the peoples subdued by David, but the relationship between David and the Ammonite king Nahash had been good. Chapter 8, which gives a brief summary of all the campaigns and battles that helped David to consolidate and extend his power, perhaps was written after the events described. This kind of detailed account of a particular military campaign is somewhat unusual and may be included as an illustration of David's dealings with others and of how such battles were fought and won. But the main purpose in this case is probably to provide background and context for the story of Bathsheba and Uriah (ch. 11). It is possible that the stage of the war described in verses 15–21 is a more detailed account of the battle referred to in 8:3–6.

Verses 1–5 introduce the reasons for this confrontation. When the young prince **Hanun** took over from his father **Nahash** as king of Ammon, David sent a **delegation** to mourn with the people and to make preliminary negotiations with the new regime. The time of transfer of power is always difficult in any country, and surrounding tribes needed to consolidate or renew relationships to ensure their own security. Whether the parallel with Mephibosheth was in David's mind is impossible to ascertain, but it was in the mind of those who compiled the material. The writers show David as a trustworthy king who repays loyalty, whether it comes from a great friend or a foreign rival.

Nahash's past kindness to David cannot be determined. Perhaps Nahash had paid a voluntary tribute to Israel in exchange for military protection. If this was so, one purpose of the delegation would have been to renew the terms of the agreement. In this case, Hanun's suspicion of the motives of David's ambassadors would have been unjust but understandable. He did not want vassal status to remain, and he rejected David's kindness, which presupposed some kind of relationship. His actions, however, were less than wise, given David's growing reputation. Hanun not only **sent** the delegation **away** without agreeing to any terms but also insulted them. Shaving off **half** the **beard** and cutting **off their garments** were shameful indignities. Hertzberg (*I and II Samuel*, p. 304) suggests that this was "an unconsidered act of a young king prone to making coarse jokes." However, it is perhaps better seen as a deliberate attempt by a confident young ruler to assert his independence and even to provoke war. There are parallels to the foolish advice that Rehoboam received from his contemporaries when he took office after Solomon's death (1 Kgs. 12).

For David, this episode could be seen as the first real test of his reign. The response he made would enable those within and without the nation to judge the stability and strength of his own regime and also his own capabilities in handling people and situations. The details reflect the writers' ongoing interest in the use and abuse of power.

Hanun had intended to humiliate David and his men, but when the consequences of his actions dawned on the Ammonites they became perturbed. Backing up the supremacy that Hanun had sought to demonstrate was not going to be easy. Verses 6–19 describe the course of the war. Ammon collected a substantial military force of mercenary soldiers from the Aramean tribes of **Beth Rehob, Zobah, Maacah,** and **Tob** to reinforce its army. The Israelite forces were vastly outnumbered, but Joab's tactics were masterly in terms of military strategy and morale boosting. The forces were divided—one select group under his command faced the more dangerous Arameans, and the rest with Abishai faced the Ammonites' army. But they were organized in such a way that either of the two groups could reinforce the other. Joab's rallying speech was brilliant. He called them, in a similar way to Gideon's call to another vastly outnumbered force (Judg. 7:15–18), to **fight** for **God** and the **people,** that is, their own families. He reassured them, and apparently convinced them, that the result could safely be left in God's hands.

The Aramean forces were **routed,** and the Ammonite troops were forced back into the confines of **the city. Joab returned** temporarily to **Jerusalem.** Leaving over the final stage of the siege was probably related to the time of year (cf. 11:1). The Aramean ruler took the defeat of the mercenaries from his army

as a personal affront (v. 15). The whole Aramean army therefore
regrouped and came to fight Israel in their own right. Again they
suffered an ignominious defeat, this time with David command-
ing the whole Israelite force. A number of other small tribes who
had been **vassals of** the Aramean king **Hadadezer** changed their
allegiance and made their own **peace** treaties with Israel. Ammon now had no outside support and for a long time the threat
to Israel from Ammon and Aram was removed (ch. 8).

Additional Notes §34

10:1 / Dating the events in the early chapters of 2 Sam. is often
difficult. Although chronology was significant, it was not the only factor in deciding how the accounts of different events should be fitted together. If ch. 8 includes the Ammonite wars of chs. 10–12 in its summary
of David's battles, this is a further indication of how hard it can be to be
precise about the timing of events.

10:2 / Saul had earlier soundly defeated **Nahash** (1 Sam. 11),
and it may be that David, as Saul's known enemy, had received good
treatment from the Ammonites. The emphasis on David's loyal kindness in chs. 9 and 10 brings into sharp contrast his betrayal of the loyal
Uriah in ch. 11. By this juxtaposition the writers want this contrast to
be understood. David's strengths and his weaknesses must be seen
together.

10:4 / A beard was often interpreted as a sign of mature manhood, and this forced shaving would indicate that David's embassy was
not to be treated seriously. David's recognition of how humiliating their
treatment was is shown in his allowing them to avoid facing their
friends and family until the beards had regrown. **Jericho** would have
been the first stopping place within recognized Israelite territory.

Such embassies would travel lightly, probably with no easily obtained change of clothes. Garments cut off **at the buttocks** would thus
leave the soldiers exposed as they moved away through the crowds
outside the new king's palace. It was an insult that no Eastern soldier
could tolerate.

10:6 / In the accounts found here, in ch. 8, and in 1 Chron. 19,
there are slight differences as to the numbers taking part and the numbers killed. This possibly arises out of confusion between the numbers
of footmen, chariots, and horsemen or between the mercenary forces of
this encounter and the full Aramean force (vv. 17–18). Discrepancies
with ch. 8 can be ignored if the two chapters are talking about two different encounters, but it is hard to see how the Aramean forces could
have endured two such devastating defeats within a relatively short

time. Whichever came first, there is hardly time for a new army to be formed.

10:12 / The phrase **the cities of our God** is unusual. It seems as if Joab is introducing the idea of a national community. They were fighting not just as isolated groups uniting to defend themselves but as a community of cities that all belonged to God.

§35 David and Bathsheba (2 Sam. 11:1–12:31)

The mopping-up operation to complete the siege of the Syrian capital Rabbah is described in 11:1, but the completion is not recorded until 12:26–31. In between is the story of David's involvement in adultery, betrayal, and murder.

11:1 / The writers make it clear that David's presence in Jerusalem at this time was unusual. The fighting season has begun, but **at the time when kings go off to war, David sent Joab.** That is, he did not go himself, and the verse stresses that while the army was destroying **Rabbah, . . . David remained in Jerusalem.** While his men risked their lives on his behalf, he was "killing time" (Baldwin, *1 and 2 Samuel*, p. 231) as he walked around on the roof. Joab's feelings about this are revealed in 12:27–28, when he eventually managed to persuade David to come to the battlefield. The reader is left to decide whether the king's inactivity was the cause of the events that followed.

11:2–5 / The story is told without embellishment. A powerful man **saw a woman bathing, sent** for her, and **slept with her,** and she became **pregnant.** It has been suggested that **Bathsheba** was not blameless, that this was a consenting affair rather than what amounts to rape (see additional notes). This account, however, is concerned with David and his guilt. Although the case against Bathsheba is unproven, the case against David is clear, and later David takes full responsibility for his sin (12:13). Bathsheba was notable as the daughter and the wife of national heroes (23:34, 39) and the granddaughter of David's adviser Ahithophel. David's conduct was bound to have repercussions. It is possible that disillusionment with David over this issue led to Ahithophel's support for Absalom in the later rebellion (15:12). Nonetheless, the news that Bathsheba was married did nothing to stifle David's lust. The significance of this account, and the reason it is included, are twofold. First, it shows that David, in spite of being God's anointed king, is not removed from the failures and sins of ordinary mortals. His nature, throwing himself passionately into things without thought for the consequences, can be used for good when the task in hand is fighting for God's honor or keeping his band of outcasts safe from Saul's obsessive revenge. But his passionate nature can equally be used for ill when the only motive is satisfying his own lust. Second, the account shows that David acted like any other oriental despot. He behaved as if he was above the law. The account makes it clear that both king and people must realize that it is unacceptable to God for power to be abused in this way. Verse 5 tells us that a child was **conceived**. It was thus David's responsibility to do something about it.

11:6–13 / The easiest way to solve David's problem was for **Uriah** to be made to think that the child that had been conceived was his. So Uriah was recalled from active service, used by Joab to send dispatches to David, and then encouraged by David to take a few days leave, to **go home** and spend time with his wife. It adds to the sad irony of the text that David's stratagem did not work because of Uriah's transparent integrity. His refusal to go home may have been because he had heard rumors about David and Bathsheba, but the account does not present Uriah as a suspicious or jealous husband. Rather, he is depicted as a straightforward man of principle, a soldier with a strong sense of duty. The country was at war, the army was on active service, **camped in the open fields,** and he would not take leave while his fellow soldiers were still at risk. His commitment to the **ark** of God, uppermost in his mind, would not allow it. Uriah, the foreigner, had a greater concern for covenant principles than the one who had been anointed as protector of the covenant. The "no sex while at war" rule was a basic battle principle (Deut. 23:10–15; 1 Sam. 21:4–5), and Uriah took this seriously. He refused to go home, even after **David made him drunk.**

The writers' interest in the use and abuse of power again comes to the fore. David has been flaunting his power, assuming that he can obtain anything he wants. But he lacks the power to deprive Uriah of his integrity. Thus Uriah returned to Ammon without having slept with Bathsheba, and there was no possibility that the unborn child could be passed off as his. Uriah's honor contrasts with David's underhanded behavior.

11:14–17 / For David, there seems to be no question as to what must happen next. The only way that he can be protected from the results of inevitable exposure is for Uriah to die, so David writes to Joab and arranges Uriah's death. The account portrays this as murder even if, strictly speaking, the letter of the law has not been broken. And the blame for this murder is placed securely on the shoulders of David, not of Joab, who made the arrangements. Joab was an excellent and successful general with an unquestioning and unquestioned loyalty to David. However, as other passages show (3:22–30; 18:14), he was a hard man and saw no problem in getting rid of an embarrassment, even when that meant losing a brave warrior. It is possible that Joab was glad to have an excuse to take some active measures against Rabbah. David's letter provided him with freedom from the usual restraint that David placed on his military enthusiasm (see additional note). Verse 17 makes it clear that other soldiers fell in what was a suicide mission. Other families also suffered to protect David's "honor."

11:18–27 / The record of Joab's dispatches showed that David was usually a careful general concerned to avoid unnecessary deaths even if it meant taking a longer time to defeat the enemy. He would normally have been angry at the risk Joab took. Perhaps David had not envisaged the death of other soldiers, though his instructions made it inevitable. However, the news of Uriah's death, as Joab had foreseen, cut off any angry reaction. The incident was dismissed as part of the normal course of war (v. 25). Perhaps David was trying to convince himself.

The text gives no indication that Bathsheba's mourning for Uriah was anything other than genuine. We are told explicitly that **she mourned for him,** in addition to the mention of the **time of mourning** required by the law. How one reads verse 26 depends on the extent to which one sees Bathsheba's complicity to be voluntary. David ties up loose ends and perhaps salves his conscience by marrying Bathsheba. The child is born in wedlock. But the chapter finishes with an understatement that indicates the incident is not yet closed: **the thing that David had done displeased the LORD.**

12:1–6 / The Lord therefore takes action. It was important that David and the readers of this account should realize the significance and unacceptability of what he had done. Hence, **the LORD sent Nathan.** What happens may be a working out of the "discipline" for David's dynasty that had been described in 2 Samuel 7. Monarchy was new to Israel, and it was vital that a standard relating to God's expectations for the behavior of kings was set up and understood. Their authority as kings in no way exempted them from the requirement to keep God's law for themselves.

Nathan, as in 1 Kings 1, appears suddenly. He seems to have been a trusted adviser and a recognized prophet (ch. 7), but there is no indication that he was present regularly at court. This visit to David took place probably about a year after the main events of chapter 11. There are indications that David's conscience has spoken during the intervening period. He was prepared for the prophet's reproaches.

Nathan tells David a story, a recognized method of presenting a case study (used also by Joab via the woman from Tekoa in 2 Sam. 14), and David understood it in that way. In David's capacity as the head of the justice department (8:15), it would not be unusual for such cases to be brought before him. Nor would David have assumed that Nathan was there to deal with David's own sins. With a parable like this it is unnecessary to make every detail of the story fit what happened among David, Bathsheba, and Uriah. In Nathan's tale the **rich man**'s crime was the abuse of power involving greed, gross injustice, and sheer meanness. How could a man who owned so much deprive a **poor man** of his one pet **ewe lamb**? This cold-blooded meanness was the most shocking. David was concerned in general about justice, and he was enraged that anybody could have behaved in any way that could be seen as fitting this story. We are told that he **burned with anger.** He made a legal pronouncement that a man who did such a thing **deserve**[d] **to die** and should be made to pay substantial compensation. It says much for David's character and his basic sense of justice that his outrage remained, even when he came to realize that the story was about himself.

12:7–9 / Nathan's statement, **You are the man!** must have shocked David. Surely he had never done anything vaguely resembling that. But Nathan presses the point and recounts David's sin in detail. David's horror may at first have been related to the realization that everything was known, that all his efforts to protect his reputation had been in vain. But it became horror that he had behaved in that way. David, in spite of his great privileges, had misused his position. He had had everything he could have wanted, and yet he despised **the word of the LORD** and committed both adultery and murder. The

meanness and selfishness of David's sin are emphasized as much
as if not more than the aspects of sexuality or immorality, but the
worst part is scorning God's word. David had acted as if God's
word counted for nothing.

12:10–14 / The question of judgment is dealt with. As
a consequence of David's violence and adultery, violence and
adultery would plague his house. There would be open rebellion
in the country, his family would be destroyed by **the sword** and
would turn against David, his **wives** would be taken, and his
child with Bathsheba would **die.** David had worked hard to save
himself from shame, but he would be openly shamed. Verse 13
records David's acknowledgment of his sin. Because of this confession and the presupposed repentance, and in spite of his own
pronouncement that death was deserved, he will not die. But
the consequences of his actions remain, and the child born to
Bathsheba will die. David had caused the enemies of the Lord to
blaspheme, to think of God wrongly. Hence the NIV's translation
that he had **made the enemies of the LORD show utter contempt.**
Outsiders would look to God's anointed king to show what God
was like. David's behavior could make them believe that God
does not care about justice. The death of the child showed that
God cannot and does not let David do as he pleases just because
he is king.

12:15–25 / The description of the child's illness and
death is interesting, particularly insofar as it relates David's conduct. It would have been unusual for an Eastern monarch to behave in this way. Harem children had little significance. There
were many of them, infant mortality was common, and this was
not an only or an eldest son. So David's excessive mourning,
which made his entourage fear that news of the child's death
might cause suicide, was as unexpected as his later behavior. But
the writers wanted to portray David's relationship with and understanding of God and possibly to bring out the differences
from Saul's reactions to his sin, where Saul tried to excuse his actions (1 Sam. 13:11–12; 15:13–21). David knew that God was not
an arbitrary dictator but that he did relate with and respond to
the actions and attitudes of his people. Thus while the child
lived, it was always possible that God would **be gracious,** that
the child could be saved and the consequences of David's sin
worked out in a different way. However, when the child died,
this was not to be. For the moment it was over, the death could

not be reversed, and there was no need for further mourning. The **I will go to him** (v. 23) could imply some sort of belief in immortality. However, such a belief is never strongly worked out in the OT, and it is probably a recognition of the inevitability of death.

Under the circumstances, the greatest comfort that Bathsheba could have would be to have another child to love. David's original behavior was inexcusable, but it would only compound his sin toward Bathsheba to divorce her now. The name **Jedidiah** ("loved by God"), which Nathan gave to **Solomon,** confirmed that David's sin can be put behind him. This name for Solomon is not repeated elsewhere, which lessens the likelihood that it should be seen as the equivalent of an anointing, a divine validation of Solomon's later claims to kingship.

12:26–31 / These verses make it clear that the campaign against **Rabbah** in which Uriah had lost his life was completed and the **Ammonites** defeated. The lower city was taken first by Joab. This cut off the **water supply** to the main **citadel** and made defeat inevitable. David himself was brought in to finish the task. The words of Joab (vv. 27–28) rebuke David, implying that he should have been there all along. In spite of his faults, Joab was never a usurper and always acted in what he saw as David's best interests. The Ammonite land was incorporated as part of David's territory and the Ammonite population used as slave labor. Hanun's cruel joke (10:4) had had disastrous consequences for Ammon.

Additional Notes §35

11:1 / Wars tended to be seasonal. Armies were not equipped to move in the times of heavy rains, and supply lines could too easily be cut in the winter, even in Mediterranean lands. A token siege force probably had been left outside of Rabbah, but any active fighting ceased for the winter. A modern equivalent is the mountainous areas of Kashmir, where even with all the advantages of modern technology, the conditions in winter drive armies back to the safety of their own bases.

11:2–5 / This account of David's adultery and its consequences is omitted by Chronicles, which is more concerned with David's royal role and less interested in his personal successes or failures.

It is impossible to know whether or not Bathsheba was aware that the courtyard of her house could be seen from the palace roof. Most such courtyards are private, and although we cannot be sure of the customs of the time, it would not be unusual today for women in parallel circumstances to bathe outdoors in secluded courtyards. It is unlikely that she was bathing in the seductive manner assumed in some paintings. She may not even have been naked.

The point of the bathing was to cleanse herself after the ritual impurity of her monthly period, making it clear that she was not pregnant. It is ironic that this attempt to fulfill the demands of the law led to such a gross transgression of the law. Technically and legally Bathsheba would have had the right to refuse the king's request. In practice such a refusal would have been difficult. The balance of probability seems to lie with Bathsheba's innocence.

There is no evidence that the adultery was repeated or that there was an ongoing relationship between David and Bathsheba. Once she has been identified (v. 3), Bathsheba is not referred to by name in this passage. She is simply **the woman** (v. 5) who could satisfy David's lust and "Uriah's wife." The writers present this not as a great romance but as a rather seedy action on David's part that led to consequences with which he must now deal.

11:8 / **Wash your feet** may mean "make yourself comfortable after a long journey," but it may also be a euphemism for sexual intercourse. If it is the latter, then David would be blatantly encouraging Uriah to break the ritual law. Sexual activity caused ritual impurity, and soldiers on active duty were required to remain ritually pure (Lev. 15:18; Deut. 23:9–11). Even if David was not trying to manufacture a legitimate reason to destroy Uriah (Anderson, *2 Samuel*, p. 154), the suggestion nevertheless implies that David was above the law and could give dispensation to ignore it.

11:9 / Uriah's ethnic origin was Hittite. (The Hittite empire in Asia Minor no longer existed, but their descendants remained in the eastern Mediterranean region, particularly in Syria.) However, his name is an Israelite one meaning "Yahweh is light." Although he was ethnically foreign, either he or his parents had become converts. He fought as a full and significant member of the Israelite army. Perhaps the lack of an Israelite heritage caused him to be especially rigorous in keeping the law.

11:14–25 / Once a city was besieged, military activity became extremely limited. The surrounding army only had to wait until the city's stores ran out. Unless the general decided to finish the situation quickly and attack the city, casualties were unnecessary. If the surrounding troops got too close to the walls, casualties were inevitable. Joab's instincts were to attack and bear the cost of the casualties; David's were to avoid the death of as many of his troops as possible.

From this point on, David found it increasingly hard to manage Joab and impossible to replace him. David's actions had consequences that went far beyond protecting his good name. Joab had a hold over

David that he could use to manipulate David into taking further actions that may have been against his better judgment.

The NIV follows the Hebrew MT at this point. The LXX has a longer version in which David reacts as Joab predicted, by getting angry and then being pacified by news of Uriah's death. On occasions where accounts in the MT and the LXX differ in length, the longer version is usually seen as the original. In this instance the extra material reiterates what is known. It is difficult to be sure whether it was added to clarify Joab's words or omitted to simplify the passage. In either case it has no effect on the meaning of the chapter.

11:21 / This incident is recorded in Judges 9 when Gideon's son **Abimelech** was killed through going too close to the wall. Baldwin makes a credible suggestion that Joab's stress on the involvement of a **woman** in Abimelech's death gives a subtle hint that he knows what is going on (*1 and 2 Samuel*, p. 234).

12:1 / For comment on Nathan, see additional notes on 7:2.

12:1–7 / Pss. 51 and 32 are indications of how well David learned the lessons about the horrific nature of sin, responsibility, and the need for and the possibility of repentance and forgiveness. The heading of Ps. 51 states that it was written after Nathan's visit and, although the headings of the psalms are not part of the original text, there is no reason to doubt the authenticity of their claims in this instance.

12:8 / It was common practice for a new ruler to take over the **wives** of the previous ruler as a sign of supremacy and control. Although this was not permitted under the law of Moses, it happened in Israel as elsewhere. Thus Absalom, for example, made a major political statement when he openly slept with his father's concubines (16:21–22).

12:9 / Nathan ignores that Uriah was killed by the besieged Ammonites and bluntly states that David **struck down Uriah the Hittite with the sword.** David was as much responsible for that action as for the more direct taking of Uriah's **wife to be** his **own.**

12:10–12 / Punishment for sin and the consequences of an action are not the same thing. Part of what is described is punishment and part is the unavoidable consequences of David's behavior. Friction between the children of different mothers is not in itself a punishment for unwise multiple marriages, but it is a regular consequence. Three of David's sons, Amnon, Absalom, and Adonijah, died violent deaths, and all, including Solomon, seemed to have learned more from David's example of behaving as if he was above the law than they did from David's repentance.

Polak ("David's Kingship: A Precarious Equilibrium") sees the threat that **the sword will never depart from your house** (v. 10) as contrasting with the promise "My love shall never be taken away from him" (7:15) and reflecting the constant tension between positive and negative views of David and his monarchy.

12:13 / The relationship between justice and mercy in the OT is an interesting one. The importance of the law, and the necessity of obedience to the law, is clear. However, punishments are not always carried out in the way the law requires, and sometimes God allows or encourages such mercy to be exercised. In this instance it could be argued that although David had committed murder morally, he had not done so legally and therefore the death penalty does not apply. However, the text has no indication that this line of argument is being followed. As far as the writers were concerned David had killed Uriah, but he was not to die. G. W. Coats ("2 Samuel 12:1–7a," *Int* 40 [1986], pp. 170–73), sees God's compassion to David as a deliberate contrast to the lack of compassion shown by the rich man in the parable and by David in relation to Uriah.

12:14 / For modern readers this is one of the most difficult verses in the Bible. Was the guilty David to be freed, while the innocent baby was punished on his behalf? Again the difference between consequence and punishment must be maintained. One could say that although the child's death was interpreted as being directly related to David's sin, the child was going to die anyway and God used the timing to make the point. Equally one could argue that for the infant, death was a better option than being faced with the inevitable traumas that would have ensued for him. However, the writers do not explore these options, and although we have to beware of introducing modern dilemmas into a context that would not have understood them, the difficulties remain.

12:18 / The normal seven days of mourning rituals that David might have been expected to take part in had been completed before the child died. Thus David's cheerfulness is not as heartless as it might seem to contemporary readers.

12:25 / There is no mention of any oath made by David promising that Solomon would be his eventual heir. It is not clear whether this oath, mentioned by Nathan in 1 Kgs. 1, occurred but is not mentioned in any of the texts that we have or was an invention created to manipulate the aged David and ensure Solomon's succession. It is possible that Nathan, himself fairly aged by that time, had come to believe that God's love for Solomon, which he had been told to proclaim, was a promissory statement concerning the succession. G. H. Jones (*The Nathan Narratives* [JSOTSup 80; Sheffield: Sheffield Academic Press, 1990]) suggests that Nathan was a Jebusite, an original inhabitant of Jerusalem, who had joined David's service. Nathan sought to do his best for the Jebusite community by ensuring the succession of Solomon, who was born in Jerusalem. However, Jones's theory depends on fairly radical source criticism, including the assumption that all the theologizing within the text is a later Deuteronomic addition to a basic narrative.

12:30 / The weight of the plundered crown (between 65 and 75 pounds [30–34 kilograms]) is excessive. It might have been the crown of the local god, Milcom, rather than the king's crown, but there is no direct evidence for this. As the crown would have been far too heavy for a man to wear, McCarter suggests (*I Samuel*, p. 313) that the precious stones, rather than the crown itself, were placed on David's head. Saul had been condemned for taking plunder (1 Sam. 15:19) whereas David **took a great quantity of plunder from the city.** The difference is that Saul had been told in advance that all the plunder from his campaign was to be dedicated to the Lord and destroyed. David's campaign did not have the aura of the *herem* instruction, and taking booty was not forbidden.

12:31 / The Hebrew in this verse is unclear. It may refer to the torture of Ammonite men using the implements mentioned or making them "pass through" brick kilns. However, such torture would probably have used military weapons, and the general understanding is that the Ammonites were put to forced labor.

§36 Amnon, Tamar, and Absalom (2 Sam. 13:1–39)

13:1–11 / The story of Amnon's abuse of Tamar, when he treats her solely as the object of his desires with no rights or value of her own, follows directly from the story of David's abuse of his power. Amnon followed his father's example. For a parent there is no private morality. Behavior and attitudes have repercussions within the family, and the repercussions of David's actions were manifesting themselves, although not in a way that he would have wished for or envisaged.

Amnon was David's eldest son by Ahinoam from Jezreel, the first woman David married after he had left Michal. The text states that Amnon **fell in love with Tamar** but makes clear that love in any meaningful sense had no part in his actions.

Jonadab, Amnon's cousin and friend, was **a very shrewd man,** whose friendship meant helping Amnon to gratify his passions rather than encouraging him to resist them. Presenting Amnon with a carefully worked out plan, Jonadab demonstrates his shrewdness in his understanding of David's nature. He assumes that David will visit his loved son when he is ill and also that his concern for Amnon's health will allow normal convention to be dropped so that Tamar can visit.

Tamar, when specifically requested by David, would have had no choice but to go. Her feelings are seen as irrelevant and therefore ignored by David and Amnon. It was a common custom to prepare a special meal for the sick, in this case probably a particularly nutritious kind of cake. When the meal is prepared, the servants are dismissed. They would have been reluctant to cross this petulant prince, and therefore Tamar is left alone with him. He then wastes no time in letting her know the real purpose of her presence as far as he is concerned.

13:12–19 / Tamar recognizes the sin involved. Her protests could indicate an awareness of a law against incest, but the

narrative does not emphasize that. The issue seems to be that fornication would lead to **disgrace**, although Tamar's words could
imply that the use of force itself was so wrong. If Amnon behaved in this way he would prove himself to be a **wicked fool.**
Amnon is not to be restrained, and Tamar is **raped.** The text
makes clear that the sexual encounter is against her will and that
Amnon sins against her as well as against the law. The writers' interest in the use and abuse of power is again illustrated. Amnon
compounds his crime by his subsequent rejection of Tamar. His
lust once satisfied, he wanted nothing more to do with her. Again
the parallels with the way that David treated Uriah, acting as if
his life was a matter of no import, are clear.

Mention of Tamar's special dress, which would have marked
her out as an eligible young woman, adds great pathos to the
story. Amnon's treatment of her, apart from the trauma of the
rape, means that she will be unwanted. The prized dress becomes a mockery to her. Her desolation is feelingly described. As
so often happens in OT narratives, the writers are well aware of
the attitudes of society toward women and yet present alongside
this an implicit critique of those values. To Amnon, Tamar was
now simply **this woman,** to be summarily dismissed. But to the
writers, Tamar's distress, and the fact that she remained a desolate woman, were significant.

13:20–29 / **Absalom** seeks to comfort Tamar, and he
takes his responsibilities toward her seriously. But he also plans
revenge, perhaps using this incident as an excuse for getting rid
of Amnon on his own account. Absalom was an ambitious young
man, and there was no love lost between the two brothers. Verse
21 tells us that **David** was **furious,** but apparently he took no action concerning Amnon's behavior. Even if he was unwilling to
put Amnon to death it would have been within his power to
force him to marry Tamar. It may be that, being well aware of his
own guilt, David felt unable to condemn Amnon. It may also be
that in spite of David's great military and diplomatic successes
he found taking disciplinary action against members of his family impossible.

But the effect was that David too treated Tamar's desolation,
which Absalom was forced to observe every day, as unimportant. David's lack of action increased Absalom's desire for
revenge. The bitterness in Absalom was just as strong after
two years. He shared his father's ability to create loyalty in his

followers but not the nature that could leave the past behind and be passionately involved only in the present. Absalom's revenge was even more well-planned than Amnon's campaign to take Tamar. It was not an impulsive outburst but a premeditated execution. Amnon, well aware of Absalom's hatred, took steps to avoid him, but a special party with the king's sanction, even given against his better judgment (v. 26), was difficult to avoid. At the party Amnon, on Absalom's instructions, was killed. Absalom also followed his father's example in assuming that he had a right to arrange events and manipulate others for his own purposes. The other brothers feared for their own lives **and fled.**

13:30–39 / The first report brought to David, that **all the king's sons are dead,** was devastating, but **Jonadab** was able to put him right. It may be that Jonadab was now supporting Absalom and that the way in which the news reached David was planned to lessen the impact of Absalom's guilt. However, Hertzberg may be right to see Jonadab's intervention as the result of a guilty conscience (*I and II Samuel,* p. 327). Even when it is apparent that the disaster was not as major as was first supposed, David was again and understandably upset at Amnon's death. But again he takes no action against his son, although Absalom recognized the need to flee. Sanctuary for murder was not permitted in Israel, and Absalom therefore retreated to his grandfather's house at **Geshur,** on the edge of Aramean territory, northeast of Galilee. **David mourned** extensively for Amnon (v. 37) and possibly for Absalom as well.

Additional Notes §36

13:3 / It is possible that **Jonadab** thought he was supporting a romance and that he had no idea of how **Amnon** would react, but Tamar's welfare did not enter into his mind.

13:7 / Ackerman ("Knowing Good and Evil") suggests that David hoped for a liaison between Amnon and Tamar and encouraged them toward it. If this were so, it might have added to David's sense of personal responsibility when it all went wrong. However, such a theory is speculation.

13:11–13 / Sexual relations between brother and sister, including half-brothers and half-sisters, were forbidden in the Mosaic law (Lev. 18:9). However, it is not clear at this stage how far the law was kept. Tamar seemed to think no objections would be raised if Amnon wanted to marry her.

13:13 / **Fool** in this instance, as in Proverbs, refers to somebody who ignores God's ways and wishes and who abandons any sense of morality, integrity, or uprightness.

13:20 / **Tamar** returned to **Absalom's house.** The pattern of life in polygamous marriages seemed to be that the children of different mothers lived in different houses.

13:21 / The reference to **King David** emphasizes David's responsibilities and the fact that he did not exercise them. The LXX adds "he did not trouble the spirit of Amnon his son, because he loved him, for he was his firstborn." The spirit of Tamar his daughter was of little concern to him.

13:23 / Sheepshearing has always been a time of special celebration in farming life. Absalom's party, arranged on his own property, provided a way of getting to Amnon and the opportunity of prearranging an escape route for Absalom. In normal circumstances, Amnon, as heir apparent, would have been accompanied by an entourage, including trained soldiers as a bodyguard. Arranging the killing at the sheepshearing party made it easier to get a drunken Amnon away from them than it would have been on their own territory.

13:39 / This verse is obscure. The verb used here, **"to go forth,"** usually means to go in a hostile way and could mean that David, once the shock of his first grief had worn off, wanted to take action against Absalom. This interpretation fits better with ch. 14 as a whole. However, David had an ability to set the past aside; having lost one son, he perhaps longed for the next one to return, a perspective that 14:1 could reinforce. Perhaps David was incapable of knowing his own mind in relation to his sons.

§37 Absalom—In Geshur and Jerusalem (2 Sam. 14:1–15:9)

14:1 / Although his reason for wanting **Absalom** back in Israel is obscure, **Joab** plays the key role in the account of Absalom's return. Again, the writers' awareness of people, their characters, and their motivations is remarkable. Both Joab and Absalom are portrayed with a great deal of insight. It is possible that Joab had tried before to obtain a pardon for Absalom, as David's comment in verse 19 could indicate. That would then explain the circuitous route that Joab used to get his own way. Later, directly defying David's orders, Joab killed Absalom. However, it seems that at this stage Joab saw Absalom as the best prospect to be David's successor and recognized that would not happen if Absalom remained too long outside of Israel.

14:2–24 / Joab followed Nathan's example in bringing a case study to David. The **wise woman** from **Tekoa** may have been noted for her guile and persuasive skills, or she may have been selected because David did not know her. Certainly Joab's wisdom rather than her own was used in this instance. Apart from the death of one brother at the hands of another, there are few parallels between the story told to David and Absalom's slaying of Amnon. In her story, we have unpremeditated manslaughter rather than a deliberate execution. Also the surviving brother had no children to continue the family name, and that did not apply in Absalom's case at this stage. This means that David, even after he had pronounced judgment in the one case, would not be bound to change his mind in the other. However, the case study was a way of encouraging him to think along different lines. Joab may have felt that he was less likely to persuade David if the king felt as if he had been boxed into a corner.

At Joab's instruction the woman discusses God's perspective, arguing that God **devises ways so that a banished person may not remain estranged** (v. 14), suggesting that Absalom was unfairly being cut off from **the inheritance God gave.** She also flattered David by suggesting that his wisdom was **like** that of **an angel of God,** implying that the only godly way forward was to bring Absalom back. Initially the story was convincing, but once the application to David's own relationship with Absalom began to appear David was no longer deceived. He recognized that the wisdom was from Joab and had little to do with God.

Nevertheless, perhaps David unconsciously responded to the flattery. He could not stand any longer against Joab's constant pressure and agreed to allow Absalom to return. The return was against David's better judgment, as indicated by his insistence that Absalom come back to house imprisonment, isolated from the court. Joab's reaction when David acquiesced to his request (v. 22) reflects the importance that Joab placed on Absalom's return to Israel.

14:25–27 / Certain personal details about Absalom may explain why Joab decided to sponsor him. He had a tremendous reputation, which was enhanced by his physical attractiveness. He had **three sons** as well as **a daughter,** so if he did become king the future of the dynasty was apparently assured.

14:28 / The half forgiveness that allowed Absalom to be physically present in Israel but to have no further role in public life was bound to lead to trouble. Geshur was a small state, but while he was there Absalom could have had some hopes of taking over from his grandfather or at least of working toward that end. His summons to return must have given him the impression that he might take his place as heir to his father's throne. For a man of his character, life under the new conditions must have been intensely irritating and frustrating. It is likely that he resented his father for what he saw as unjust treatment, particularly because Amnon had not been punished. For **two years,** parallel to the two years when his bitterness against Amnon festered (13:22–23), Absalom endured this life, never **seeing the king's face,** but he felt that two years was long enough.

14:29–33 / Once Absalom was back in Israel, Joab kept out of the way, perhaps surprised at how long David had refused to see Absalom and unwilling to provoke him further. But Absalom, after trying unsuccessfully to obtain further help from Joab by more normal methods, "persuaded" him to come and talk by setting **fire** to his **field.** After discussion and maybe being made aware of how determined Absalom was, Joab agreed to intervene once more. Absalom saw himself as innocent and wanted to make a defense that his killing of Amnon should not be regarded as murder (v. 32). If it was judged to be murder then he should be executed; that would have been more endurable to him than the present state of affairs.

David was persuaded and became reconciled to Absalom. For David, this meant that the past was now put behind him, and his acceptance of and love for Absalom was unstinting. But for Absalom, the wounds could not be so quickly healed. The twin desires for revenge and power had eaten away at him and destroyed what chance there might have been for genuine reconciliation. David **kissed Absalom.** We are not told that Absalom kissed David.

15:1–6 / Absalom did not suffer from impetuosity. The first phrase of the chapter—**in the course of time**—reinforces for the reader that time has passed. It is possible that at the beginning Absalom found things to do to fill time. The impression given, however, is that everything he did was part of a conscious, calculated, and clever attempt to win over from his father the affection of the people and his kingly power. It took another four years (v. 7) before he felt secure enough to act. In that time, the public perception of Absalom had changed drastically. He had been the disgraced prince, guilty of fratricide. He became a popular hero.

Absalom had a three-pronged strategy. First the people were going to notice that Absalom was back and be made to think that Absalom was significant. He imitated the custom of surrounding nations with his display of pomp, exploiting his own good looks. The bodyguard of **fifty men** and the showy **chariot** were different from anything known in Israel so far. Jonathan, the ostensible heir in the previous regime, was more often accompanied by one armor-bearer. Obviously Absalom wanted to be seen as a Very Important Person. If his chariot had been intended for speed he would not have insisted on its being preceded by fifty runners. The people were encouraged to look at Absalom as if he were king. Maybe Absalom was exploiting the people's desire for a king "like other nations."

Second, Absalom looked for any vulnerability in David's government, and the weakness he found was in the legal system used for dealing with public and private **complaint**s. We cannot ascertain whether or not any criticisms of David's regime were fair. However, Absalom flattered all those who came seeking judgment, suggesting to each one that the case was obviously **valid and proper.** Yet it might not reach court, and if it did it was unlikely to get the kind of fair treatment that it would if Absalom had been in control. This introduced the thought that perhaps it was time for David to hand over power to one who was more able to handle it.

Third, Absalom, having set himself apart from the people as a great prince, proceeded to treat all who came to pay their respects to him as if they were social equals. In an ironic parallel to 14:33 (where Absalom bowed down before David as king and then received his father's kiss), when the supplicants bowed down, Absalom would reach out **and kiss** them.

This may have been a somewhat cynical manipulation of the people's affections, but it worked. They responded to this "people's defender" approach, and Absalom by his stratagems won many people over to his side.

15:7–9 / David had no inkling of Absalom's real plans, no inkling that it was appropriate to speak of belonging to one side or the other. Perhaps he was encouraged by the way in which his son seemed to be making himself so popular. David had many faults, but he was a straightforward person and knew nothing of the kind of devious scheming that came so easily to Absalom. When Absalom asked leave to go to Hebron in fulfillment of **a vow,** David gave permission. He seems not to have raised any questions as to why, when in **Geshur,** Absalom should have chosen **Hebron** as the site where he would go and **worship the LORD.** With irony, the writers record David's giving his blessing to Absalom as he goes off to start a war against his father: **Go in peace.**

Additional Notes §37

14:1 / Joab's motive for seeking Absalom's return perhaps was not political but arose out of his ongoing concern for what he considered to be David's welfare. The NIV translation has assumed this to be true as it speaks of Joab noting how David's **heart longed for Absalom.** However, went out "to" (Hb. ʿal), translated as "longed for," could equally well be interpreted as went out "against." The latter translation would make more sense of David's reluctance to be persuaded to allow Absalom to return and his refusal to see him for two years after his return home. P. K. McCarter's translation (*II Samuel,* AB 9 [Garden City, N.Y.: Doubleday, 1984], pp. 335–44), "the king's mind was on" Absalom, retains the ambiguity. David was thinking about Absalom, and it was a good time for Joab to act.

14:2 / Many women in OT times were categorized as wise, like the one who dealt with Joab in 20:16–22. They may have built up their own reputations or been part of an identifiable group of recognized counselors or advisers. There seems to have been no problem, theological or otherwise, with accepting advice or teaching from a woman (cf. 2 Kgs. 22:14–20).

In this case, the woman obtained access to David not because she was a **wise woman** but because she came to present a case requiring judgment. Conflict between brothers is a common motif in life as well as in fiction. David would have had no reason to doubt the validity of the woman's story. The dilemma caused by conflict between the need of a **clan** (v. 7) to avenge the death of a kinsman and the importance of maintaining a family line was real in that culture (cf. Ackroyd, *The Second Book of Samuel,* p. 131).

14:20 / The idea that the king was like **an angel of God,** not just in his ability to judge the right thing to do but also in his ability to **know everything that happens in the land,** was introduced to flatter David. However, the concept apparently evolved into the kind of superstitious awe of the king's powers that we see in 18:13.

14:26 / **Two hundred shekels** is a vast weight, far more than could be obtained from weighing one headful of human hair, however luxuriant. It is possible that this reported the exaggerated rumors that abounded about Absalom and, given his later behavior, he probably encouraged them. However, it may be that a different measure was used and that the **royal standard** provided a lesser weight than the sanctuary shekel.

14:27 / 18:18 states that Absalom had no sons at that stage. The mention of the daughter's name in this verse, whereas the sons remain anonymous, may be because all of his sons died in infancy. However, as Tamar was given the same name as her poor, desolate aunt, it may be included to show that in spite of her unmarriageable state, the older Tamar was not forgotten.

14:33 / The parallels between this verse and the story of the lost son in Luke 15:20–24 are noted by Brueggemann (*First and Second Samuel,* p. 298). Absalom comes in and greets David as a servant, but David responds by treating Absalom as a son. The difference is that no insight is given into Absalom's feelings. There are no parallel signs of genuine repentance.

15:2 / As the role of the king developed, the system of open access that had been possible with the less centralized rulers of the judges period may have become unworkable. David may have been too busy to hear all cases, although Absalom owed his return to the fact that he heard some of them (ch. 14). It is also likely that Absalom noticed and worked on the fear that David's judgments were biased against those who came from **one of the tribes of Israel,** as opposed to Judah, which was David's tribe. Hence the significance of Absalom's question as to where the complainants came from.

§38 Absalom's Rebellion Begins
(2 Sam. 15:10–16:14)

Within these chapters there is an interest in the concept of loyalty: loyalty moving from David to Absalom; the loyalty of Ittai, Zadok, and Abiathar to David; Ahithophel's disloyalty and Hushai's apparent disloyalty; Shimei's loyalty to Saul and the ambiguity of Ziba's position. Behind this is the conviction that although human loyalties may be unpredictable and unreliable, God's loyalty can always be trusted.

15:10–12 / Once in **Hebron,** Absalom launched his campaign in earnest. He sought to change those who had done little more than indicate that they thought he would make a good king into full-scale supporters. The **two hundred** who had accompanied him from Jerusalem thinking that this was a religious pilgrimage would have had little choice but to support Absalom. It would have been hard to persuade Joab and his like of their ignorance of Absalom's schemes. As they would be likely to be condemned as traitors anyway, their only hope lay with Absalom's success. David's own counselor, **Ahithophel,** had apparently been aware of Absalom's plans and supported them. Most of the support seems to have been from the northern Israelite tribes, although the choice of Hebron as a base must mean that Absalom was sure of some support from Judah as well. It is possible that he envisaged a bloodless revolution. His confidence in his own abilities may have made him sure that once **trumpets** sounded the whole nation would acknowledge him as the only suitable choice for **king.** If so, he underestimated the extent of support that David had. Not even all those who had acknowledged to Absalom some disaffection would have wanted to see David deposed. But for Absalom there could be no turning back.

15:13–23 / Although David had had no suspicions concerning Absalom's treachery, he grasped the implications of the news immediately. Perhaps the opaque way in which David was informed that the people were no longer behind him helped everything to fall into place. In any case, **the hearts of the men of Israel** were now **with Absalom.** Absalom, even if he established himself as king, would not be able to allow David, or any of those who had been close to him, to live. In Jerusalem they were sitting targets, so David took immediate action and instituted a strategic withdrawal. Most of the royal household accompanied him, leaving only a small group to look after the property. However, Absalom had not won all hearts. It seems as if most of the army remained loyal to David. Certainly the household guard and the crack troops of mighty men with the regiments of non-Israelite troops continued to support David. Any hope that Absalom might have had of a bloodless coup was destroyed from the start. David may have kept himself away from the public in recent times, but the great personal loyalty that he had inspired in those who served him in the past remained firm.

David's offer to **Ittai** that he should **go back** and serve Absalom may indicate that David expected to be in exile, roaming around much as he had done in the latter years of Saul's reign. The **Gittites** were not under threat of death and therefore there was no need for them to be in exile. David had apparently reconciled himself to the inevitability of Absalom's takeover. He was not yet convinced that there was going to be a major battle between the two sides. However, Ittai seems to have little doubt that fighting would be involved and whether that would involve victory or defeat, **life or death,** he and his troops would be fighting on David's side.

The details of the flight are briefly given. The group moves, as quickly as the terrain allows, into the east toward the wilderness area. At this point Absalom's skill in choosing Hebron as a base appears. If David did flee he could not move north, because Absalom's support base was greatest there. To go west meant to enter Philistia, and although the Philistines had been conquered, this would not be a refuge for David. To the south was Absalom and the group with him. Thus the wilderness via the route across the **Kidron Valley** and over the Mount of Olives (v. 30) was the only option. The tears shed by those they passed show that not just the standing army retained some loyalty to David.

15:24–37 / Just as David had retained the hearts of his standing army, so also the current religious hierarchy remained loyal. The senior priests **Zadok** and **Abiathar** put themselves immediately and firmly in David's camp. They brought **the ark of God** with them, and they intended to travel with David and to use the ark as a potent tool to draw support to David's cause. However, David sent them and the ark **back to Jerusalem**. This was a wise strategy but also a clear statement of faith. David recognized that his withdrawal from Jerusalem meant that Absalom would take the city. Perhaps one reason for the withdrawal had been to save Jerusalem, which since he had made it his capital had become precious to David, from siege. Sending Zadok and Abiathar back with the ark was one way of ensuring that information about Absalom's activities and tactics could be gained and passed on to David.

However, David had learned the lesson well that the ark of God was not to be used as a tool to further his own ends (2 Sam. 6; cf. also 1 Sam. 4). He knew that God cannot be manipulated. Sending the ark back was a sign of David's acceptance of God's sovereignty and control, whether that meant David's return to the city or not. He knew that giving Absalom control over the ark made no difference to the truth that God would decide the future. As Hertzberg (*I and II Samuel*, p. 341) succinctly puts it, David "humbly bows himself under the bitter blow and leaves the future to the Lord, without, however, neglecting to take what steps he can."

Sending the ark back into the city brought the awfulness of their situation home to David and his retinue. The start of their withdrawal was far from the triumphant beginning of a campaign that might be expected to result in success. Perhaps David sensed that in this, as in most civil wars, there would only be losers. Any result was going to mean death and distress among his people. Thus David, along with the retreating army, began the journey in ritual mourning (v. 30).

Ahithophel and **Hushai** had both been valued and respected advisers to David. Ahithophel's defection hurt David. He **prayed** that any advice that Ahithophel might give to Absalom might be turned aside. To make this more likely he sends back the loyal Hushai as a spy, or rather as an *agent provocateur*. Zadok, Abiathar, and their sons could then provide a back-up unit. Trusting in God and organizing resistance are not presented as mutually exclusive options. Absalom, secure in his own confidence, had already seen Ahithophel defecting to his side. There was no reason for him to doubt that Hushai had also recognized his superior qualities and done the same. But Hushai remained **David's friend.**

16:1–4 / Ziba, the steward of Mephibosheth, comes back into the picture. Whether or not his support for David is genuine is unclear. As a Saulide, he, like Shimei (vv. 5–8), might have been expected to see this situation as a way of getting revenge on the one who deposed Saul's family. Nevertheless, Ziba gambles on David's success. He brings support, presumably obtained from Mephibosheth's lands. Brueggemann notes (*First and Second Samuel,* p. 305) that Ziba's answer to David's question, **Why have you brought these?** is unhelpful. It must have been clear to David that **the donkeys** were **to ride on** and the food **to eat.**

However, David is distracted by these diversionary tactics. Ziba goes on to inform David that Mephibosheth has betrayed his trust. Ziba's story is unlikely. There was no way in which Mephibosheth could have seen Absalom's rebellion as a means of obtaining his **grandfather's kingdom** for himself, and there had been no previous sign that he had any desire to be king. However, David accepted Ziba's story without question. This is understandable given David's natural distrust of Saul's family, shortly to be confirmed by Shimei's actions. Mephibosheth's relationship with Saul is deliberately stressed, both by David and by Ziba. Also, since David's own son had betrayed him, it was easy to believe that one who had been treated like a son should behave likewise. With characteristic impetuosity David hands over to Ziba all the lands that he had previously cared for on behalf of Mephibosheth.

16:5–14 / David's encounter with **Shimei** is described in vivid terms, probably making use of an eyewitness account. As David's group moved over the rough terrain they met up with Shimei, a relative of **Saul.** Shimei had never been reconciled to David and delighted in his apparent downfall. Shimei's unpredictable aggression and violent hatred must have caused David to recall certain encounters with Saul. Shimei **cursed** David, suggesting that these events were sent by God to punish him for deposing Saul.

David's men, in particular Joab's brother **Abishai,** wanted to take immediate and drastic action against Shimei, but David would not allow this. This **What do you and I have in common?** means "Do not ascribe your feelings to me." David's reaction remains one of faith in God's sovereignty. He was no more super-stitious about the results of a curse than he was about the presence or absence of the ark. If God wished him to be destroyed, then he would be. If God wanted to bless him, then that would happen too. In either case Shimei's ranting was irrelevant and punishing him for opposing David would do no good. However, the constant abuse and stone throwing from **the hillside opposite** must have been irksome to David's forces. When they reached the point where they could feel safe for the moment from any immediate attack by Absalom they were **exhausted.**

Additional Notes §38

15:10 / In addition to its geographic suitability, **Hebron** was perhaps chosen because it was David's previous capital and therefore a recognized place of government. However, it may be that it was far enough away from Jerusalem to avoid being immediately overrun but near enough to use as a base for launching an attack. It was Absalom's birthplace (3:2–3), which may have helped David to make sense of Absalom's request to fulfill his vow to worship God there, but this is unlikely to have influenced Absalom's choice otherwise.

15:12 / **Ahithophel** had served David loyally. If he was Bathsheba's grandfather (see 11:3; 23:34) then his having lost respect for David is understandable, although one might have thought that David's subsequent treatment of Bathsheba would have helped to appease him. In any case, perhaps Absalom was aware of some disaffection in Ahithophel and worked on it.

15:13–29 / In this section the writers constantly speak of David as **the king** to remind readers that the result of this revolution is not a foregone conclusion and the king has not abdicated his position. However unsure David might be about the results of Absalom's campaign, he retreats as king, not as ex–king.

15:16 / The **ten concubines** left behind would have been handed over to another man and probably taken by Absalom himself. This probably reflects unconcern for their welfare on the part of those who left them behind. However, it is unlikely that their lives would have been in danger, and their presence would have decreased the likelihood of damage to the buildings. They were in a real sense taking **care of the palace.** Although the legal texts do not support the keeping of concubines, it was common practice for kings to do so, and the text makes no moral judgment. For this group of women, it probably made very little difference which man's ego they were being employed to boost.

15:18 / The **six hundred Gittites** may be a group who have been with David since his time in **Gath**, but it is more likely that they were natives of Gath who had been exiled, given a welcome by David, and become a loyal part of his army. Ittai's reply to David suggests that he had become a convert to Yahwism.

15:23 / That **the whole countryside wept aloud** may reflect a bitter mourning at the thought of the onset of civil war. However, the impression is that it reflected deep sorrow at what had happened to David.

15:24 / **Abiathar,** who had been with David since his previous days in exile, probably led the Jerusalem priests until he was deposed by Solomon (1 Kgs. 2:27). However, **Zadok** seems to have had special responsibility for the **ark of God** and therefore took the lead in this instance. The two men worked closely together over a long period of time.

The mention of the **covenant** in relation to the ark reinforces David's words concerning God's control over the affairs of king and people.

15:32 / There was apparently a recognized shrine at the top of the Mount of Olives. It was common for such worship centers to be set up at high places, providing panoramic views of surrounding countryside, in this case of the city of Jerusalem. Although such worship centers later became identified with pagan worship and were strongly discouraged, there is no suggestion of that at this point.

The people of **Hushai the Arkite** were originally Canaanites, but their territory became part of Ephraim (1 Chron. 1:15; Josh. 16:2). As an Ephraimite, Hushai might have been expected to follow Absalom and was less likely to create suspicion than if he had been a Judean. That he was **David's friend** implies a personal relationship as well as political support.

16:1–4 / If **Ziba's** support for David was part of a calculated gamble, it was one with the odds stacked in his favor. It was extremely unlikely that if Absalom was successful he would take lands away from Ziba in order to return them to **Mephibosheth.** If Ziba had obtained a land grant from Absalom, David would have taken it from him. The amount of produce that Ziba brought was substantial. Ziba, as a Saulide, probably had been aware of Absalom's plans, and his own plans were well organized by the time of David's flight. Thus many of the provisions could have been prepared in advance. This would add to the suspicions but not provide conclusive proof that his campaign to oust Mephibosheth was also calculated.

16:5–8 / David was not directly responsible for the deaths of Saul, Jonathan, or Ish-Bosheth. If David's whole position was seen as an unlawful usurpation of the rights of Saul's family, then **Shimei's** otherwise irrational statements make some sense. It is also possible that the execution of Saul's seven descendants (21:1–9) had taken place by this time, and that would have added to Shimei's discontent. However, although David had been scrupulously careful not to take action against

Saul, in the matter of Uriah and Bathsheba he was a **man of blood** and a **scoundrel.** This recognition of the accuracy of the charges may have affected his reactions to Shimei.

16:9 / David's men would have had to **go over** to reach Shimei. Presumably he was ranting at them from a ridge, separated from the retreating army by a chasm or ravine and thus safe from immediate retaliation.

The insulting description **dead dog** is used by David of himself in 1 Sam. 24:14 and by Mephibosheth of himself in 2 Sam. 9:8—in both cases indicating that they posed no threat (see additional note on 2 Sam. 3:8).

16:13 / Their destination was presumably "the fords in the desert" (15:28), the crossing point at the Jordan River a little north of the Dead Sea that would provide immediate refreshment and could be fairly easily defended. It was far enough away to be safe from a full-scale attack but near enough to be quickly reached by the spies Jonathan and Ahimaaz.

16:15–19 / **Absalom** duly arrived in **Jerusalem**. **Hushai** presented himself to Absalom and perhaps with a deliberate ambiguity proclaimed **Long live the king!** Absalom showed initial surprise that Hushai should support him rather than David; he had not dared to hope that someone as close to David as Hushai could be on his side. However, Hushai argued that the choice of the Lord and the people overrides personal loyalties and that David was Absalom's **father** and to **serve the son** was a continuation of service of the father. He thus appeared to recognize Absalom's right to rule, by affirmation and by descent. Absalom accepted this without question. He had come to believe his own propaganda.

16:20–17:6 / Now Jerusalem was taken, the stage was set for the next stage of Absalom's campaign. He sought counsel from **Ahithophel,** who advised him to press his advantage by taking action in two areas. First, he should make it clear to all in Jerusalem that David has been deposed, by sleeping with the concubines he had left behind. Ahithophel was noted as a man who knew what he was saying, and Absalom lost no time in acting on his advice. This would make it clear that there could be no neutrality and would make the population of Jerusalem likely to accept that Absalom's kingship was a *fait accompli.*

Second, Ahithophel advised that Absalom should take the force already assembled, **twelve thousand men,** and attack David's forces. To do this before they could organize any resistance but were still **weary and weak** from the shock of Absalom's action was likely to cause panic. If David could be quickly killed without further bloodshed, opposition to Absalom would disappear overnight, and there would be no ongoing resentment from those who had lost families in a protracted campaign. Ahithophel's reference to David as **the king** (v. 2) was only a slip of the tongue, but in the overall narrative it has added significance.

Absalom could not be king until David was dead. Ahithophel's plan was good and Absalom recognized it as such. However, Absalom wanted to get **Hushai**'s opinion as well.

17:7–14 / Hushai also recognized Ahithophel's advice as good and therefore cleverly counseled differently. David had a great reputation as a strategist and a warrior that had given the people an almost superstitious respect for his abilities. Hushai played on this reputation. He also raised doubts about the ability of Absalom's troops to find David—he does not state that Saul had never been able to, but he nevertheless introduces the thought. If David cannot be quickly killed, then Ahithophel's plan will not work. It would be better therefore to gather the full army first from all the tribes. Hushai's advice was based on the rather idealistic assumption that the whole country was behind Absalom, but nobody in Absalom's court was going to admit that this was not so. What he said about David's reputation was true, and his approach made sense to the people. There is also a surreptitious appeal to Absalom's pride. When all the forces you can muster are assembled, then the fight can begin **with you yourself leading them into battle.** The implication is that with such a leader defeat is unthinkable. The great victory envisaged by Hushai appeals to Absalom even more than the possibility of the quick but quiet success Ahithophel presented. Ahithophel's advice was therefore rejected and Hushai's plan accepted. The immediate possibility of David's defeat was deflected.

Even from this position of strength, once Hushai's advice was accepted, the writing was on the wall for Absalom. The Lord, whom the writers present as being in ultimate control, had answered David's prayer to thwart **the good advice of Ahithophel.** Only **disaster** awaited Absalom's amassed forces.

17:15–22 / This episode, telling of the success of David's spy network, reads like an eyewitness account that was perhaps told and retold to young soldiers around the campfire. Hushai sent **a message** to David explaining the situation and advising him to take advantage of the pause in activities, presumably before Absalom realized the flaws in the arguments that Hushai had presented. The priests' sons **Jonathan and Ahimaaz,** who had been staying outside the town, carried the message to David.

The message could not have got through without the help of two women: the **servant girl** who carried the initial message and the quick-thinking farmer's wife at **Bahurim.** They remain anonymous, but the loyalty of these two women was considered significant enough to mention. The success of David's intelligence system depended on the capabilities of the two women and on society's assumption that women were incapable of subterfuge. Thus, as so often in the OT narratives, we are presented with an awareness and a critique of the culture's assumptions.

The text portrays the tension as Absalom's soldiers **searched** while the young spies lay hidden in the disguised **well**. Perhaps there is also a sense of gloating with victor's hindsight as the story is told. Surely better trained soldiers, such as those who had remained loyal to David, would have discovered the hiding place. In any event, the message was delivered before the end of the day. There had not been too much delay. David reacted immediately and by working all night was able to move all his forces across **the Jordan** before **daybreak**. Ahithophel's plan was no longer possible.

17:23 / **Ahithophel**, when **his advice** was ignored, gave up all hope of Absalom's success. He knew that there was no return for him to a kingdom where David reigned, so he went back to his own **hometown**, put all his affairs **in order**, and **hanged himself**. The story is told with no assessment of Ahithophel's motivation, indeed, with no editorial comment. But there is a hint of sympathy in recording that he **was buried in his father's tomb**. However much his final acts betrayed David, they were preceded by a lifetime of service to his God, his country, and his king. The story of his death forms a sad prelude to that of Absalom's defeat.

17:24–29 / By the time Absalom and his army **crossed the Jordan**, David had moved on to **Mahanaim**, Ish-Bosheth's old capital (2:8) and a good defensive center. The stage was set for battle to take place. The account reads more like the court page of a newspaper than an official military history. It is not concerned with technical military details, only with the personal story. The leadership structure of Absalom's troops is unclear. Verse 26 could imply that Absalom had taken Hushai's advice (v. 11) and led the army himself. However, he also appointed **Amasa** as commander. The detailed description of Amasa's background brings out the way in which civil war divides families as well as communities. Amasa was cousin to David and Joab.

David had received support and a whole range of necessary supplies from a number of wealthy allies. **Makir**, Mephibosheth's patron, possibly backed David because of the latter's previous generosity to Mephibosheth. **Shobi** was the son of David's old ally **Nahash** and had probably been made governor of Ammon after the defeat of his brother Hanun. The old man **Barzillai** is thus far unknown, although we hear more of him later (ch. 19).

Additional Notes §39

16:21 / Taking his **father's concubines** was more than an act of defiance. It was an unforgivable insult to David. Absalom's challenge to David's authority could end only with the death of one party or the other. Ahithophel reasoned that this act would convince the people that there could be no possibility of reconciliation between Absalom and his father. Thus Absalom's supporters would lose the fear of a future betrayal that would leave them to take responsibility and would also know that to lose would probably mean their own death. Thus they would have a much greater motivation to fight to win. Their **hands** would indeed be **strengthened.** It may also be that those who had not yet taken sides would be less likely to gamble against one who was so sure of his own victory.

16:23 / **Ahithophel's** reputation was legendary. Although he was not a prophet, his awareness of human nature was such that he could predict how people would react and therefore how situations would turn out. The **advice** he gave was based on that knowledge. He had proved so successful in the past that he had proved as reliable as a prophet or an interpreter of the Urim and Thummim (Exod. 28:30; Num. 27:21), in other words, his advice was as good as **that of one who inquires of God.**

17:1 / Again, the **twelve thousand** may refer to twelve troop units or battalions, which would have had fewer than a thousand men in each one.

17:16 / To take David's whole group across **the fords** of the Jordan, even with the limited supplies they would have managed to gather in the short time available, would have been a mammoth task. Hushai, knowing the kind of chaotic traffic jam that would build up and aware of the temptation to take a rest before moving over, pushed David to move with as much haste as he could muster.

17:17 / It is not clear why, if Zadok and Abiathar were able to stay safely in the city without suspicion, **Jonathan and Ahimaaz** were not. It may be that if they had entered the city they would have had no choice but to join with Absalom's forces and then could not deliver a message to David. So they stayed in hiding at **En Rogel,** which was a short distance from Jerusalem where the Kidron and the Hinnom valleys meet. Their presence in or departure from there was considered suspicious, because the young man who spotted them went to Absalom, and they were pursued.

17:18 / **Bahurim** was somewhat further away from the town on the route toward the river. Presumably the loyalty of the family there had already been ascertained. Any civil war brings conflict within small as well as large communities. Bahurim was the town from which Shimei came, so it was not a whole village devoted to, or opposed to, David.

17:23 / **Ahithophel** is often compared with Judas in terms of the betrayal and the taking of his own life. A. F. Kirkpatrick (*The Second Book of Samuel* [Cambridge: Cambridge University Press, 1886]) sees his suicide as "prompted by mortification at the rejection of his counsel; by the chagrin of baffled ambition; by the conviction that now the rebellion would inevitably fail and that he would live only to suffer a traitor's death." However, it is possible to see the writers' and David's approach to Ahithophel as sad rather than angry. Perhaps he genuinely believed that David had forfeited the right to rule and that Absalom was the right man to maintain the security of the nation. Whatever his motivation, however, he could not live with the consequences of his action. His burial in the family tomb indicates that suicide was not seen as a matter for disgrace.

17:25 / There is a tradition followed by some manuscripts that **Amasa**'s father was an Ishmaelite (1 Chron. 2:17). If so, this would explain the need to be clear about his mother's Israelite credentials. It is possible that Abigail and Zeruiah were full sisters but that they were only half sisters to David. 1 Chron. 2:16 gives no indication that they were not Jesse's daughters, so that would mean that **Nahash** was their mother, but Nahash is not a woman's name. It has been suggested that as another Nahash is mentioned in v. 27, what we have here is a copyist's error that has been incorporated into the main text.

Joab still controlled those troops who had remained loyal to David, which appears to have been a good proportion of the standing army. However, Absalom presumably had control of large numbers of Israelites who were pressed into military service only at times of emergency. In his capacity of managing these troops, Amasa was **in place of Joab.**

§40 Absalom's Defeat (2 Sam. 18:1–19:8a)

18:1–5 / David's forces may have been more limited than he had been used to in recent times, but he and Joab were skilled in making the most of limited resources and in fighting battles where they were outnumbered. The description of his army's structure leaves the impression that these are well-organized professional forces, as opposed to Absalom's perhaps more haphazard arrangements. We are given only an outline, but the campaign appears to have been well-organized. David intended to lead his troops in person, but his men were able to dissuade him from this. There is recognition, perhaps responding to Ahithophel's counsel of Absalom, that David's personal safety was vital. If he was killed, then, as Ahithophel had recognized, Absalom would be king.

Although David is not to take part in the fighting, he is fully involved in what is going on. His standing **beside the gate,** watching each soldier as they **marched out,** would have given focus to their action and a great boost to their morale. David had been angry with Absalom and presumably was angered by his present actions. However, neither this nor his underlying conviction that it was not time to hand over the throne that God had entrusted to him alter the fact that Absalom is his son. He is concerned for Absalom's welfare, and everybody knows it. Although it is hard to see how they could ensure anybody's safety in battle, each divisional commander is given specific instructions that Absalom is not to be treated harshly. David the king remains David the father.

David's enthusiasm here contrasts with his lethargy in 11:1. It seems that David preferred battling against the odds; once he reached a position of strength he lost interest in the fight. This characteristic helps to explain why the presentation of David before he gained control of the kingdom is so much more positive than that of David in power.

18:6–8 / The fighting took place over a wide area of countryside, in a mixture of trees and tangled undergrowth in craggy terrain. There was little to sustain life if supplies were cut off and plenty of pitfalls to trap the unwary. It was not a matter of two forces meeting head on but of smaller groups battling in separated situations. In this context the trained men would have a tremendous advantage. The **army of Israel**, that is, the tribal forces assembled at Absalom's call, **was defeated**. There were mass **casualties**. Many were killed in the fighting, but a greater number died because they were ill-equipped to survive in that kind of terrain. Absalom's ambitions to bring glory to the land and solve all the people's problems (15:4) had brought only conflict and death.

18:9–15 / The defeat of Absalom's forces came about through the skill of David's loyal troops, but Absalom's capture was the result of an accident. Again we have a vivid picture, maybe even as it was reported by the soldier who found him. There is a tradition (cf. Josephus *Ant.* 7.239) that Absalom's long hair, which had been part of his pride and reputation (14:26), became his downfall. He was left, helpless and humiliated, **hanging** in a tree as his transport disappeared from beneath him. Everyone was aware of David's wishes about Absalom's safety, and because of this, no one would take the responsibility of killing him. Joab, with harsh realism, believed that Absalom had to die. He understood that the young prince, whom he had previously encouraged and supported, was too dangerous to be allowed to live. He took the initiative, and his personal bodyguard finished the job.

18:16–18 / Any threat from Absalom's forces was over as soon as he died. There was no cause for them to fight for; only his charisma had brought them together. There may have been some disenchantment with David's government, but not enough to lead to open rebellion for its own sake. Joab recognized that Ahithophel's comments concerning David (17:2) applied equally to Absalom. Any further killing was unnecessary and was likely to prove counterproductive. Therefore Joab called an immediate cease-fire. Verse 18 describes the **pillar** that Absalom had set up as his own memorial. Apart from a heap of stones piled in the forest, this **monument** was all that remained to mark Absalom's potential.

18:19–33 / Another vivid account tells how the news of Absalom's death reached David. **Joab** shows again how well he understood David's character, how well he could predict David's reactions, and how skillfully he could manipulate the presentation of news to further his own ends. **Ahimaaz** wanted to take the news of victory to David. Joab knew that however glad David was of victory, the messenger who thought to gain credit for being the first to proclaim victory was likely to bear the brunt of David's distress at Absalom's death. Joab wanted to protect the young and gifted Ahimaaz, perhaps seeing him as a potential future leader. Therefore a **Cushite,** probably a slave, was sent instead. Ahimaaz was an intelligent man, and he picked up immediately the significance of Joab's qualms but asked to be allowed to run anyway.

David **was sitting between the inner and outer gates** (v. 24). This meant that he could be in touch with the **watchman** on the top of the wall by the gate but could also watch. He remained keenly interested to hear what was going on at the front. With a greater knowledge of the territory, Ahimaaz was able to outrun the Cushite and, just as Joab had predicted, he found that David's first concern was for Absalom. He therefore gained what credit might be found by announcing the victory but left the Cushite to bring the news of Absalom's death. David's almost pathological approach to his sons prevented him from recognizing the necessity of Absalom's death as a moral judgment as much as, or as well as, a political necessity. He immediately went into deep mourning, his grief inconsolable. Verse 33 could indicate that David recognized his own guilt in the affair.

Given the interest of the writers in the question of power and control, in this section the reader may be deliberately faced with the question as to whether the search for power or the retention of power brings joy or fulfillment to the powerful. Neither Absalom's ambition nor David's victory brought happiness to either. The impression is that the struggle for power and holding power can corrupt and are likely to lead to grief.

19:1–8a / The boost to morale provided by David's presence in the gateway as the men marched out to war was not repeated as they returned. Instead, David's deep mourning at Absalom's death left a sour taste in the mouths of the troops. In effect, as Joab pointed out, his behavior became a humiliating insult to the people who had served him so loyally, who had **saved**

. . . **the lives** of all David's other children. He was making them feel guilty as if they, rather than Absalom, had betrayed him. In addition, while David remained in Mahanaim, Israel remained without a government, and further rebellion or serious attack from outside remained real possibilities. Joab eventually managed to persuade David of the effects of his behavior, and David's return to **the gateway** (still in the city of Mahanaim) indicated that he was again available to the people, interested in their needs and concerns. The gateway was where court sessions and public meetings took place. David's presence there was evidence that he had returned to public life and perhaps that he had taken note of the complaints about lack of access that Absalom had been able to exploit. The writers are well aware of the negative effects of David's behavior, and his reactions are not praised, but they are understood. The whole episode becomes part of the ongoing tragedy that was the hallmark of David's family life.

Additional Notes §40

18:1 / **Thousand** and **hundred** are used as technical terms for army units rather than as actual numbers.

18:9 / A **mule** was probably not the best way of getting around that kind of forest, but only very senior figures would have mules to ride during a battle. It is possible that Absalom did not want to lose his dignity by dismounting from his mule and walking as the ordinary soldiers would have had to do. If this was so, then his vanity was the cause of his downfall through more than just his luxuriant hairstyle.

18:12–13 / Joab may have been a brilliant general, but his troops were aware of his reputation for manipulation. This soldier did not trust Joab enough to believe that he would protect him from David's wrath. His loyalty to David or his fear of disobeying David was greater than his fear of Joab's displeasure.

The soldier's statement, **nothing is hidden from the king,** may indicate his fear that some informant would let the king know but more probably indicates a popular superstitious view of David as having access to supernatural knowledge (cf. chs. 19–20).

18:14 / The significance of the **three javelins** ("darts" is probably a better translation), is not clear. It may be a symbolic action, perhaps deliberately organized in such a way that there was no individual executioner—the whole corps was involved.

18:18 / At a time when any consciousness of life after death was limited, the importance of children, specifically sons, to give meaning to existence and to carry one's memory into the future was inestimable. Not only had Absalom apparently lost his sons (cf. additional note on 14:27), but in spite of his relative youth he had given up hope that other sons would be born. Thus building a personal memorial pillar could be seen as a sign of arrogant ostentation, but it could also mean that the desecration of his sister and the death of his children had left him with a sense of deep insecurity. Or he may have had a premonition that he would not live long enough to have more sons. Absalom remains a fallen hero rather than a straightforward villain.

18:21 / Cush was south of Egypt, in parts of Sudan and Ethiopia. It is possible that this **Cushite** was a resident alien who had allied himself with David in the same way as Ittai the Gittite. However, it is more probable that he was a slave.

18:28–29 / Brueggemann (*First and Second Samuel*, p. 322) views Ahimaaz as "blurting out" the news of victory and then exhibiting cowardice as he fails to give David the news of Absalom's death. However, it is equally likely that the young man exhibits diplomatic skills, imitating Joab's wiliness.

18:33 / David's desire to have **died instead of** his son may be an expression of parental grief but seems likely to portray his own sense of responsibility. However, it is not clear whether he saw his original actions with Bathsheba and Uriah, or his handling of Absalom before and after Amnon's death, as the key factor. Perhaps the two cannot be separated.

§41 Return to Jerusalem (2 Sam. 19:8b–43)

19:8b–15 / After any civil war feelings and tensions take time to settle. Bitter enemies do not become friends in a moment. Even if they had been stirred up more than was necessary, Absalom's followers had felt genuine grievances against David. Nevertheless, after Absalom's death people recognized that there had been many good times under David and felt a growing desire to restore the old regime (vv. 9–10). David, with a glimmer of his old diplomatic skills, used the rivalry between north and south to stimulate action in his own tribe of **Judah** (vv. 11–12). This may have had negative effects on a long-term basis by encouraging the rivalry to simmer. But David's master stroke for reuniting the kingdom was to appoint **Amasa**, Absalom's commander, as **commander** of the whole Israelite **army**. This made a statement that David recognized that support for Absalom might have come from a genuine desire to benefit the country and therefore was not to be seen as unforgivable betrayal. Amasa's appointment also served as a rebuke to Joab, though whether this was for his part in Absalom's death or because of a growing resentment at the extent of Joab's power over David is not clear. In either case, the picture of Joab's character would lead any reader to expect further trouble. Joab was not going to take his effectual demotion lying down, particularly as Amasa had far less military experience.

By his actions David **won over the hearts of all the men of Judah** (v. 14). Judah, at least, was no longer a tribe of divided loyalties; they were **as . . . one man.** The northern Israelite tribes had spoken widely of David's return, but Judah sent an official invitation. David and his entourage therefore left Mahanaim and came back as far as **the Jordan,** where he was met by a Judean delegation that escorted them **across.** These regional tribal groupings that had all accepted David's rule now reemerge as separate entities, showing the rather fragile nature of the national unity within Israel.

19:16–23 / The rest of this chapter presents the next stage in the relationships with various individuals. The writers' interest in national politics does not override their interest in the lives of individual characters.

The first character to be reintroduced is **Shimei.** Presumably in an attempt to avoid a war trial and fearing summary execution, he came to show his support for David. He brought with him **a thousand Benjamites** to play their part in taking **the king's household over.** **Ziba** was also part of this delegation. Shimei was well aware that the only way he could avoid the consequences of his previous action was to throw himself on David's mercy. He made no attempt to hide the severity of his offense but asked for forgiveness. Not surprisingly, **Abishai,** who had wanted to kill Shimei in the first place, balked at the thought of a pardon being offered now. He pointed out that by all the usual measures, Shimei deserved execution. But Shimei's timing had been perfect. David knew that he would win far more support by mercy than by judgment, and support from the nearby tribe of Benjamin was crucial to ongoing stability. He also sensed that there had been enough killing, and amnesty would bring more political advantage than further violence. His presenting a free pardon to Shimei was an act of strength from a confident king, not the act of weakness that Abishai implied.

19:24–30 / The next character to appear is **Mephibosheth.** The writers tell us, as opposed to presenting Mephibosheth's words as they did with Ziba in 16:3, that Mephibosheth had been in mourning from the time David left to **the day he returned.** As mourning customs in those days were so visible, this information would have been easily checked to confirm or refute Ziba's original accusation. Mephibosheth's claim that he has been **slandered** and that Ziba used his lameness to prevent him from following David is backed up by evidence as well as argument. His ongoing loyalty is emphasized by the way he addresses David, five times calling him **my lord the king.** David makes an immediate pronouncement that Ziba and Mephibosheth are to share Saul's property. This decision may have been a wise and considered move by David, recognizing that Ziba had brought him real help and wanting to reward them both. It could also be a petulant emotional reaction, showing an unwillingness to admit he has made a mistake and wanting to deal with the matter as quickly as possible. The writers present Mephibosheth as a positive character, although his statement in verse 30 is formal politeness. The ambiguity in their presentation of David's reaction may be the writers' deliberate indication that the situation is not as clear cut as it might seem.

19:31–40 / The ancient **Barzillai the Gileadite** had been of great help to David, and he should be honored and rewarded. He had provided for David's forces, and David now offered to **provide for** him. He was offered a position in the king's household, but he did not need the financial reward and was too old to appreciate the status. He preferred to stay at home. But his son **Kimham,** presumably a younger son who would not be responsible for managing the family estates, would be delighted to take up David's offer. Providing Kimham with a significant position in David's court kept good relations with the surrounding tribes and confirmed David's reputation as a worthy ally to have.

19:41–43 / The whole of Israel, north and south, wanted David back as king. However, there is no question yet of a happy ending. The bitter rivalry between the tribes continued even as they sought to reassert loyalty to David, and angry words were exchanged. Judah's having taken the leading role in the ceremonies at the Jordan was a matter for particular resentment. Creating conflict between different groups even within one nation is simpler than resolving such conflict. The split portrayed prepares the way for Sheba's rebellion (ch. 20) and provides background to the later, more permanent split that arose after Solomon's death (1 Kgs. 12).

Additional Notes §41

19:9 / It was probably not until after the division of the kingdom at the time of Rehoboam and Jeroboam (1 Kgs. 12–14) that the name **Israel** was used to mean just the northern tribes. The usage here is likely an anachronism the writers used to help later readers understand what was going on.

19:17 / **Ziba** is part of the group of **Benjamites** who accompany Shimei. In spite of his protestations of loyalty (16:1–4), he had not accompanied David across the Jordan. It seems likely that he had hedged his bets by affirming support for David and yet remaining closely associated with those Saulides who had particularly opposed

David. It was important that he gave a further affirmation of loyalty to David before the inevitable exposure of his lies concerning Mephibosheth.

19:18a / Bringing David back across the Jordan would involve providing safe conduct as well as physical help in transporting people and property over the fords, just north of the Dead Sea, where it was possible to get across the river. The fords were situated in Benjamite territory, and thus it might be expected that they would take responsibility for the crossing.

19:18b–20 / The calmly persuasive Shimei seen here is very different from the ranting, maniacal stone thrower of ch. 16. It seems unbelievable that, however great the danger, he could have lowered himself to be **prostrate** before David. Perhaps the severe mood swings and the periods of great hatred resulting in uncontrolled violence were part of a genetically inherited condition shared by Shimei and Saul.

19:21–22 / **Abishai,** Joab's brother, is again described as a **son of Zeruiah.** The women in Joab's family seem to have been of particular significance (cf. 17:25), although the stress on Zeruiah may be because she was a sister or half-sister of David. Abishai is presented as opposing David. It is not just that he was an adversary, acting against David's interests, but that he was setting himself up as a "satan" or public accuser, acting as if he and not David had the right to make this kind of judgment (cf. additional note on 24:1).

David's grant of pardon to Shimei was an act of political expediency and not a heartfelt expression of mercy, as is made clear in 1 Kgs. 2:8–9, where David charges Solomon to do what he can to get around David's pardon and kill Shimei.

19:30 / David had **arrived home safely,** which implies that the encounter with Mephibosheth took place later, at or near Jerusalem, and was perhaps fitted in here to follow on from the reference to Ziba.

19:37–38 / There is a nice example in these verses of the way in which formal negotiations took place. Barzillai asks David to do for Kimham **whatever pleases you.** David replies that he will do **whatever pleases** Barzillai.

§42 Sheba's Rebellion (2 Sam. 20:1–26)

20:1–2 / In many ways this incident is presented as an appendix to Absalom's rebellion rather than as a separate story. **Sheba, a Benjamite** described as a **troublemaker,** perhaps thought he could take up where Absalom left off. This incident could have occurred toward the end of David's reign, although **happened to be there** may indicate that it happened at the rather bad-tempered meeting between representatives of the northern and southern tribes relating to David's return after Absalom's rebellion (19:41–43).

Sheba, whether as an intentional encouragement to full-scale rebellion or as an assertion of independence against what might be seen as Judean arrogance, called the Israelites to boycott the procession and return to their own homes—which they did. The Judeans were left to accompany David, who was **their king,** that is, belonging to their tribe, **all the way from the Jordan to Jerusalem.** Sheba's statement, **we have no share in David,** implies that he intended this to be a rebellion against David's kingship over Israel. However, there is no indication that any fighting took place in this rebellion, and it may be that most of the **men of Israel** who **deserted David to follow Sheba** only accompanied him as he moved away from David's camp and went home.

20:3 / When **David returned to his palace in Jerusalem** it was necessary to reorganize his household. There is no question of any second withdrawal from the capital, thus showing the minimal impact envisaged from Sheba's call. A hint of the human tragedy so often found among the women in David's life is the mention of the **ten concubines** who, like Tamar, are **kept in confinement** for life. Absalom's defilement of these women meant that they could no longer form part of David's court, but neither were they eligible for normal marriage. It is not clear whether the guard was for their own protection or to prevent them forming any relationship with another man that might have been seen as a further insult to David. Any public appearance would be likely to bring to mind David's vulnerability, and therefore they were kept safely locked away. The care taken to describe their position suggests that the writers were aware of what this must have meant for the women. For Absalom his conduct was a political move, an attack on David but not meant as a personal offense against the women. For David their later confinement was a political necessity—sad, perhaps, but inevitable—and the women were well cared for. For the women the original offense was rape, and the follow up a dehumanizing tragedy. The interest in their fate indicates that the writers, and God, do not see such nameless and victimized people as insignificant.

20:4–13 / Whether the threat was extensive or minor, David planned to eliminate Sheba quickly, maybe following Ahithophel's advice to Absalom (17:2). There was no doubting the loyalty of any of the forces of Judah, and **Amasa**, the new commander, was given **three days** to gather the troops. This **took longer** than expected. Many of the men had just returned home, and perhaps Amasa did not have the influence with them to organize such a speedy muster. David decided therefore to send **Abishai** with an advance party of the crack troops of the household guard. It seems as if David was determined to replace Joab, but Joab had other ideas and decided to accompany his brother. It fits with what we know of Joab that he would not tolerate Amasa, relative or not, as captain of David's forces.

Amasa could not have been too far delayed as he was able to meet up with Abishai's party at the **great rock in Gibeon.** The vivid, if gruesome, account of what happened next again suggests an eyewitness report. Amasa approached Joab without fear, assuming himself to be in the presence of allies if not friends. Joab murdered him and headed off to complete the military objective. The strange reference to Joab's **dagger** dropping out (v. 8) may imply that the dagger slipped into Joab's hand by accident and the killing was thus unpremeditated opportunism. This possibly reflects the way the story was later told to David, but the writers convey explicitly the deliberate nature of Joab's actions. Amasa's body was left where it fell; his dying agonies ignored. The body was eventually moved and covered—not as a mark of respect but only when a resourceful member of Joab's company recognized that its presence hindered the task at hand.

20:14–22 / **Sheba's** rebellion was no real threat to David; although Sheba passed through **all the tribes of Israel**, only the **Berites** could be persuaded to follow him. He and this group were cornered in the town of **Abel Beth Maacah**, which was put under full siege with the intention not of starving Sheba out but of destroying the town. The siege was probably more a demonstration of Joab's power and a deterrent to other rebel towns than a necessary way of dealing with this incident.

However, a **wise woman** from the town intervened. She argued that destruction of a town was likely to inflame passions against David rather than demonstrate strength. She persuaded **Joab** and her fellow citizens to give up Sheba and save the rest, including seemingly any of the Berites who had accompanied Sheba. In spite of his violent nature, Joab recognized that the best military tactic was to accept the woman's advice: the rebellion would end quickly, no one would lose face, and problems with Israel would not increase. It is also possible that he knew that the woman's theologizing arguments would appeal to David and that his own position with David would be irretrievable if he ignored such arguments. Abishai was technically commander of the army after Amasa's death, but no one would question that Joab was back in charge.

20:23–26 / **Joab's** determined, fierce loyalty forced David, at least for the moment, to give up the struggle to replace him. This list of the major official positions in David's government updates that found in 8:15–17. Life in Israel was getting back to normal, and this list provides an appropriate end to the section.

Additional Notes §42

20:1 / **Sheba** is repeatedly called the **son of Bicri,** who is unknown outside of this chapter. Beker was a son of Benjamin (Gen. 46:21) and Becorath an ancestor of Saul (1 Sam. 9:1). There is no reference to Saul, but it it has been suggested that links with Saul are being deliberately if subtly emphasized. Sounding **the trumpet** could be a call to arms, but it could equally sound the retreat to tell the men to go home, as it is in v. 22.

20:10 / Joab had been involved in Uriah's death at David's request (ch. 11). His killing of Abner could be understood as part of a blood feud after his own brother's death (ch. 3). His involvement in Absalom's death could be interpreted as a political necessity (ch. 18). But the writers emphasize that there can be no excuse for Amasa's death. It was gratuitous violence prompted by jealousy.

20:14 / The text of this verse is confused, and the name of the town is probably Abel (cf. v. 18), with the other part of the full name providing further description of the area. The site cannot be identified with certainty, but it was in the northern regions of Israel, probably within reach of Aram. The **Berites** are unknown outside of this verse, and many manuscripts have Bicrites here, implying that only members of his own clan followed Sheba.

20:16 / There are some parallels with the **wise woman** of ch. 14. These references are sometimes seen as providing evidence of the writers' links with the so-called wisdom schools. However, the presence of these women could be further evidence of the writers' interest in the significant part played by women in David's fortunes. Few women had leadership roles within Israel, but those who did (e.g., Deborah, Judg. 4–5; Huldah, 2 Kgs. 22:14) were accepted without question. This woman had no problem in speaking on behalf of the town or in persuading the townspeople to act on her advice.

20:18 / The town of **Abel** seems to have had a reputation in terms of settling disputes and relaxing tensions. To destroy a town with such a reputation could only add to Joab's reputation for unnecessary violence. The strong awareness of community reflects Deuteronomic thinking regarding the importance of the covenant community and the need to maintain and strengthen national links. The idea is that the whole nation would be diminished by the destruction of one of its member towns in this way.

20:22 / The irregular levied troops were dismissed immediately after they completed the action to which they were called. They had no need to return to a base in Jerusalem before going home. This perhaps explains why it took time to recall the Judean troops (v. 4), even though David had just returned to Jerusalem.

20:23–26 / The differences between this list and that in ch. 8 are interesting. David's sons are not mentioned as royal advisers, but David's personal chaplain **Ira** is introduced.

Sheva is **secretary** in place of Seraiah, although these may be variations of the same name.

A new department of **forced labor** has been formed, indicating the large number of those from captured nations who had become slaves of the state of Israel. In Solomon's time, native Israelites were also conscripted into service because of the vast demands of Solomon's building program (1 Kgs. 5:13–18). However, this seems not to have been a normal procedure, for the forced enslavement of fellow Israelites could have been seen as a violation of covenant principles (Lev. 25:39, 42; Deut. 24:7).

Additional Information (2 Sam. 21:1–24:25)

Chapters 21–24 form an appendix to 2 Samuel. They are distinct from the preceding narrative, which continues in 1 Kings chapter 1. They contain six independent sections only marginally related to each other. Each section includes information and incidents relating to David that the writers thought was helpful or important for their readers to be aware of but that did not fit in with the natural flow of the main narratives.

A. F. Kirkpatrick (*The Second Book of Samuel*, p. 21) identifies a structure to this appendix to 2 Samuel, describing it as "a general supplement to the history of David's reign illustrating a) God's providential discipline of Israel, by two national punishments, b) David's character, by two of his own writings and c) the heroic spirit of the age, by the catalogue of his mighty men and examples of their valorous exploits." However, it remains debatable as to whether any structure was intentional.

§43 The Famine, Its Cause, and Its Remedy (2 Sam. 21:1–14)

21:1–2 / At some stage during David's reign a serious **famine** took place. For **three successive years**, the harvest was lost. This would have a devastating effect on any agriculturally based society. The timing of this extensive famine is uncertain, but, given the references to Saul's family, it probably took place early in David's reign. Disasters of this nature were often, if not always, interpreted as sent from God, usually as a judgment for a specific offense. Therefore it was necessary to search for the reason for such a judgment. How the search for God's answer was conducted and how that answer was given are not made explicit. It may have involved the use of the ephod (cf. 1 Sam. 23:9) or some other priestly oracle that could give a more precise answer than choosing between two alternatives.

By whatever means, the reason for the famine was identified as the treatment of **the Gibeonites** during Saul's reign. A number of Gibeonites had been killed to clear the land of non-Israelite tribes. Saul's motivation is presented as positive, misguided but well-meaning, **in his zeal for Israel and Judah.** However, this bloodshed was in clear defiance of a peace treaty Joshua had made with the Gibeonites (Josh. 9).

21:3–8 / To violate a covenant of this kind was viewed seriously throughout the OT—whoever was involved (cf. Amos 1:9). Throughout the ancient Near East such action would have been seen as instituting a bloodguilt in which the whole nation could be involved. As is still common in some Middle Eastern countries, the victims were asked for their views on how the offense could be atoned for or what should be done to those who might be held responsible (vv. 3–4). The Gibeonites are initially wary of offending David and aware of their own subservient position within the nation. They had no more right to call for a death sentence than did the Jews under the Roman occupation. Their eventual request may be seen as remarkably self-restrained. They ask only that **seven** of Saul's **descendants** be **killed** as reparation for their own dead. David agrees and identifies two of Saul's sons and five of his grandsons for execution, sparing Jonathan's son **Mephibosheth**. Seven may have been chosen as a symbol to signify completeness. After the reburial of these seven with Saul and Jonathan the incident was considered closed, at least by the Gibeonites and by David, if not by members of Saul's clan such as Shimei (16:8).

21:9–14 / There are many ambiguities in this story. For instance, the kind of representative human sacrifice described is seen elsewhere in the OT as unacceptable (cf. Ezek. 18). **Rizpah** protected **the bodies,** including those of her own sons, from the elements. Her grief moved David and challenged him into taking the action Rizpah would not have had the authority to do—giving the bodies a proper burial. Whether this was done from kindness, from a sense of duty (as in the case of the sparing of Mephibosheth), or from a desire to close the episode and make the existence of the bodies less likely to inspire a Saulide revolt is not made explicit.

The episode ends with the statement that **God answered prayer in behalf of the land.** That is, presumably, the famine ended, perhaps as a result of the **rain** that fell on the crops as well as on the exposed bodies. This answer to prayer could be seen as a further endorsement of David's lack of responsibility for these events. It was all a demonstration of God's sovereignty, expressed first in judgment and now in grace.

Additional Notes §43

Shimei's cursing of David (ch. 16) presupposes the death of Saul's family, although his words are too general for certainty on that point. There is debate as to whether the searching out of Mephibosheth (ch. 9) comes before or after these events. 2 Sam. 21:1–14 assumes that David knows Mephibosheth, whereas ch. 9 presupposes no prior knowledge—indicating that ch. 9 must come first. But if Saul had so many descendants at that time it seems strange that David would not know of them and would have to set up the kind of search that is described in ch. 9. The interpretation of either incident is not greatly affected by which came first.

21:1 / The text does not explain why the **famine** was allowed to go on for three years before anyone attempted to identify a cause of God's judgment. Perhaps a shorter famine was considered to be a normal hazard of life. Num. 35:33 makes it clear that the kind of bloodshed that might be seen as unexpiated murder "pollutes the land" and that such defilement can be removed only by the death of those involved.

21:2 / 1 Kgs. 3:4 speaks of an important high place at Gibeon where Solomon offered sacrifices, and Josh. 9:27 tells us that the Gibeonites were appointed as temple servants. It has been suggested that Saul's zeal was related to a belief that it was inappropriate to allow non-Israelites to serve at such a shrine. If such service had been prevented by Saul, this would make sense of David's call for the Gibeonites to restart their blessing of the LORD's inheritance.

21:5–6 / The Gibeonites' request for the death of only a limited number of Saul's descendants was an astute move. The choice of Saul's family as representatives of the nation would be seen as fair because Saul had been in charge when the original offense was committed. It was enough to make the Israelites feel satisfied that their own guilt was dealt with and thus that the famine was likely to end. However, it was not enough to rouse further animosity against the Gibeonites by Saulide dissidents. Furthermore, the Gibeonites must have been aware that this request would make it easier for David to strengthen his grip on the kingdom. It seems that they hoped this would strengthen their own position within the community. Unlike other such groups, they had never become absorbed into the mainstream of Israelite society. The text avoids any hint of blame falling on David for the death of Saul's family. David may have benefited from the Gibeonites' decision, but there is never any question that he manipulated or influenced the decision. His sparing of Mephibosheth and eventual burial of the bodies indicates his positive personal attitude to Saul's family.

21:10 / The story may be enigmatic, but there is little to support Hertzberg's suggestion that Rizpah's protection of the bodies of her sons involved "rain-magic" (*I and II Samuel*, p. 385). Rizpah may have hoped that the sacrifice of her sons would be given meaning by the coming of rain, but the account presents us only with her grief. Given that it was often the bodies of criminals that were exposed in this way (cf. additional note on 4:12), Rizpah's grief may have been exacerbated by the thought that her sons were being treated as criminals.

§44 War Stories (2 Sam. 21:15–22)

21:15–17 / Four separate incidents tell of spectacular victories over Philistine giants. The stereotyped format probably indicates that the accounts are selected from a larger document, perhaps a military archive. The first story involves David himself. At the end of a particular battle he **became exhausted.** It is possible that this event took place in the early stages of David's reign or before he came to the throne and that David was overtired or had temporarily lost his enthusiasm for fighting. However, it seems likely that it took place later in his reign and that his age had caught up with him. In any event, he was no longer able to cope with the huge Philistines, and his nephew **Abishai** had to come to his **rescue** to get rid of **Ishbi-Benob.** It may be that David had become more of a hindrance than a help to his troops in battle, but the diplomatic statement that he was too valuable to lose and therefore should no longer join in the fighting was also true. The **lamp of Israel** must not be extinguished. It is possible that this incident introduces the reader to the idea of David's increasing weakness in anticipation of his frailty and incapacity described in 1 Kings 1.

21:18–22 / The other three incidents are recorded to demonstrate that the army was not dependent on David or on the sons of Zeruiah as army commanders. Others were equally capable of valiant deeds. This section provides evidence that David's mighty men, many of whose names are recorded in chapter 23, deserved their reputation as great warriors. Questions have been raised about the description of **Elhanan** killing **Goliath the Gittite.** First Chronicles 20:5 speaks of Elhanan killing Lahmi the brother of Goliath. It is possible that 1 Chronicles was the original and that the text of 2 Samuel has lost a couple of words. It is also possible that Goliath had become a common name for this group of massive Gittites. Those who brought the different texts together were aware of the tradition that Goliath was killed by

David, and this is not placed here as a correction of that fact. Early Jewish tradition solved the problem by suggesting that Elhanan was an alternative name for David.

Additional Notes §44

Possibly a defective gene among a group of Philistines caused giantism, a likelihood increased by the further genetic problem of extra digits mentioned in v. 20. If these Philistines suffered from this kind of genetic problem, it is probable that neither their strength nor their agility matched their looks. In this case their regular destruction by Israelite warriors is more likely to be record rather than legend.

21:17 / The title "lamp of Israel" emphasizes the value that David had for the nation. In spite of his problems he inspired loyalty and service from his own people, and his reputation for being a good ally and a fierce enemy also gave them greater security against outside attack. "Lamp" is used elsewhere as a symbol for life (Job 21:17; Prov. 20:20), and the symbol of the lamp continuously burning in the temple may be in mind here (cf. Anderson, *2 Samuel*, p. 255). This would emphasize the continuity David was seen to provide.

21:18–21 / The site of **Gob** cannot be identified precisely, but it, like **Gath,** is part of the hill country west of Judah.

There are minor problems of identification with each of the three named Israelite soldiers. **Elhanan** from Bethlehem is identified in 23:24 as one of the Thirty, David's top army corps. However, there his father's name is Dodo, not **Jaare-Oregim.** It is possible that Dodo is a nickname or a family name. 1 Chron. 20:5 uses an alternative form, Jair, for the father's name.

Sibbecai the Hushathite is named as one of the Thirty in 1 Chron. 11:29, but in 2 Sam. 23 Mebunnai the Hushathite's name comes at the same spot in the list.

The link between Jonathan the son of Shimeah and **Jonathan the son of Shammah** (the same name as Shimeah) **the Hararite** who is mentioned in 2 Sam. 23:33 and who in 1 Chron. 11:24 becomes Jonathan son of Shagee the Hararite (cf. 2 Sam. 23:11) is not clear. We know that David's brother Shimeah did have a son Jonadab who played a major role at the time of Amnon's crime against Tamar and after Absalom killed him. Thus it is possible that a case of mistaken identity has taken place here. It is of course also possible that Shimeah had another son named Jonathan or that as with the previous two warriors we have alternative names for the same people.

§45 A Psalm of Thanksgiving (2 Sam. 22:1–51)

22:1 / David was a noted poet and musician, and it was important to include an example of his artistic skills in any record of his life. There are, as Gordon points out (*1 and 2 Samuel: A Commentary*, p. 309), marked similarities in theme between this psalm and Hannah's song (1 Sam. 2). One reason for including this psalm may be to provide a parallel to that song and to draw the reader's attention to the strength and the care of God at both ends of this part of the history.

There is no reason to doubt that David composed as well as sang this psalm, which with minor variations is recorded as Psalm 18. It may be that this was an earlier version, a first draft that was then formalized for use in corporate worship. The pattern or form of the psalm as we have it here is of a **song** (v. 1) of thanksgiving from an individual. The dating of the psalm is uncertain, although it is likely to have been written after David was settled into the kingdom and before the episode with Bathsheba and Uriah. The heading speaks of deliverance from Saul and from all of David's enemies, implying that it was not written as a response to any individual incident. It sums up and explains all of the king's military career and also gives an overriding impression of a personal relationship with God. The psalm includes a significant number of military metaphors; at this point David views himself as primarily a soldier and speaks with a soldier's vocabulary. The focus moves between David's situation and the reality of God and his intervention in David's life. It begins and ends with a meditation on God as David's **rock**, using the same imagery that Hannah had introduced in her psalm (1 Sam. 2).

The focus in these two psalms on God, and in particular on his power, form an *inclusio* around the stories of human power struggles that fill 1 and 2 Samuel. It puts the history into perspective and turns the spotlight away from human aspirations and back to God. Just as Hannah's song formed an appropriate introduction to the history of the monarchy, this psalm forms an ap-

propriate conclusion to the history of the early monarchy found
in 1 and 2 Samuel.

22:2–4 / Verses 2–4 speak of God's worthiness to receive David's **praise**. The major reason given is the security that
God provides. David's LORD was for him a safe place and an active **savior**. Passively he was a **rock, fortress,** a **refuge,** and a
stronghold—all providing a hiding place and a barrier to protect
against enemy weapons. Actively he was the **deliverer** who dealt
with **violent men** of all kinds.

22:5–7 / These verses tell of the awful desperation with
which David at times viewed his situation. Death felt as close as a
rope **coiled around** him. Even **in** his **distress** in the midst of that
awfulness he was able to reach out to God with confidence that
he would at least be **heard**.

22:8–16 / Here the discussion focuses on God's greatness, this time without any direct reference to David, although it
could be interpreted as explaining what it was like when God intervened on his behalf. The imagery uses the fiercest and most
compelling images drawn from nature. The power of God is
compared with that of great earthquakes and storms. God is
capable of anger and of judgment as well as of providing comfort
and strength. He is not a God to be taken lightly or for granted.

22:17–20 / These verses explain how this great, omnipo-
tent God has intervened on David's behalf. At this point David
reflects on his experience of what God has done rather than anticipates or requests any action from God in the future. He recalls
the times when he has felt that he had been brought out from the
deep waters that threatened to crush and overwhelm him into
the freedom of **a spacious place**.

22:21–25 / In this section the authors assume that the
reason God has blessed David in this way is that David has lived
a **blameless** life, trusting in God and keeping **his laws**. There is a
youthful arrogance that is missing in later writings like Psalm 32
or Psalm 51. In those psalms David is aware of his own weaknesses, of his own need for forgiveness, and of God as a God of
mercy and grace who in spite of his righteousness can still relate
to sinners. Here David knows the greatness of God who rewards
the righteous with blessing and brings help to the deserving in
times of great need. He has not yet learned the greatness of the

God who relates to human beings in times of moral as well as physical weakness. The tone and content of this section strongly indicate that the psalm was written before the incident with Uriah and Bathsheba that so overshadowed his later life.

22:26–46 / These verses provide an extended meditation on the nature of God and his work in the world. The God that David has encountered responds to human beings. He shows different elements of his character depending on the human beings in question. He will make mincemeat of the wily and cut the arrogant down to size, but for those who trust him and recognize his sovereignty he brings encouragement and direction, enabling them to continue in their life and service. With God's help even overwhelming odds can be overcome (v. 30). David speaks eloquently if generally of the examples he has seen of the ways that God has dealt with himself and with his enemies.

22:47–51 / Verses 47–51 present a final burst of praise to the God who provides security and salvation, victory and blessing. Because God does all these things David is bound to give him praise **among the nations,** and he does so with gladness. Throughout the psalm God is portrayed in universal terms. He is God of the whole world, not just David's personal deity.

Additional Notes §45

All Hebrew poetry makes full use of parallelism, in which the same thought is expressed two or more times in succeeding lines. This psalm (2 Sam. 22:1–51) is no exception. Verses 14, 15, and 26 are examples of synthetic or synonymous parallelism where the same thought is conveyed using different words. Verses 27 and 40 illustrate antithetic parallelism where the same idea is approached from an opposite perspective.

22:1 / Anderson (2 *Samuel,* p. 261) argues against Davidic authorship largely on the grounds that there are no specific references to identifiable elements within David's reign. However, there is no real reason to suppose that David was less capable than any other poet of composing a psalm that was generally rather than specifically relevant to his circumstances. There was no occasion when David remained without enemies, but his reign did reach a point of security that was realistic to describe in those terms (cf. 7:1).

22:4 / The tense used indicates that David's salvation was not a single occasion. He kept being **saved from** his **enemies.**

22:7 / There was no temple as such during David's reign. The term used could refer either to God's heavenly sanctuary or to the main Jerusalem worship center, which was gaining in importance since the bringing of the ark to Jerusalem.

22:29 / David has been described as the "lamp of Israel" (21:17). He is aware that the one who brings true life and light is **the** LORD.

22:35 / The **bow of bronze** could have been one decorated with bronze but was probably an ordinary bow strengthened by bronze plating, difficult to draw but effective when used.

§46 A Final Statement (2 Sam. 23:1–7)

23:1–7 / David's **last words** are presented as a formal **oracle**. Although there is little reason to doubt that David wrote this oracle, it is unlikely to reflect his actual last words; rather, it is his last major pronouncement, comparable to a last will and testament. Jacob, Moses, and Joshua make similar speeches (in Gen. 49; Deut. 32–34; Josh. 23–34, respectively). Such a pronouncement would be given tremendous significance as a dying wish. This document would have been difficult to place within the court narratives but nevertheless would have been of vital interest to readers from the time of later kings. This interest would be partly curiosity, much as similar royal pronouncements receive wide media coverage today because of wide public interest. But David's reputation as a poet and a man who was close to God would also generate interest in this oracle. He might have something to say that would affect God's treatment of the whole people. This speech therefore fits well within this appendix, and it is particularly well placed after David's psalm (ch. 22). The description of God as Israel's **Rock** (22:47; 23:3) directly links the two passages.

David, through this oracle, is presented as a prophet as well as a poet. He desperately wanted his descendants to be aware of the lessons he had worked so hard at learning, and verse 2 emphasizes that he viewed what he was about to say as coming directly from God. Nevertheless the significance of these words as a prophecy was perhaps drawn out only after his death. He presents, focusing primarily on the future of his own descendants and addressing them, a prophetic summary of what kingship could and should entail. It is, as Hertzberg points out (*I and II Samuel*, p. 399), "a theological program for the future of the dynasty." It anticipates the story that will unfold throughout the two books of Kings. It establishes David as the paradigm of the good king, a standard often invoked in 1 and 2 Kings. It provides a better final impression of a great man than the rather more vengeful charge to Solomon recorded in 1 Kings 2.

The oracle consists of three points. Statements pointing out the effects of righteous and unrighteous rule enclose an expression of David's hope for the future. The one who **rules ... in righteousness,** that is, justly and in line with God's pattern, will bring tremendous benefit to the people. The images of verse 4 are evocative for every generation. Who has not marveled at the beauty brought by the sun as it glistens on the moisture left by a refreshing shower of rain? The Davidic covenant could bring and should bring this kind of blessing to Israel.

However, **evil men,** those who ignore God's pattern, bring no more benefit than a thorn bush and will be cast aside for burning in much the same way (vv. 6–7). Verse 5, although it is phrased in questions that appear to expect a positive answer, is an expression of hope rather than of certainty. David longs that his desire for a posterity that lives in the service of **God** will be granted. But verse 6 makes it clear that he knows such a desire could be thwarted by his descendants; hence the sense of urgency within the whole prophecy. However, it may be that the promises made to him in the covenant described in 2 Samuel 7 had given him the confidence to speak in this way. God had promised much more for and from his descendants than he had yet seen in his sons.

Chapter 22 is in the form of a psalm of thanksgiving and 23:1–7 forms a charge to David's descendants, but both describe the way in which David envisages relationship with God. His conviction that righteous service brings blessing and that God stands by those who are in covenant with him reminds readers of the teaching of Deuteronomy. Chapter 22 concentrates on God and what he can and will do for his people. Chapter 23:1–7 reflects more on the king and what could be done through him. Together these passages emphasize the writers' conviction that what counts in life is relationship with God. Whatever the interests and lessons found in the human history recorded in these chapters, the point is for the reader to understand who God is and what it means for both kings and people to live in covenant relationship with him.

Additional Notes §46

This passage forms a parallel to the last words of Jacob (Gen. 49) and Moses (Deut. 33). However, in this case we have a prophetic oracle rather than the formal blessing seen previously. It is likely that v. 1 is an editorial formulation rather than part of David's oracle. David is not elsewhere in Samuel portrayed as having prophetic gifts or calling, and it is unlikely that he thought he might be presented as a prophet as well as a poet. However, it is possible that the writers intended this placement of this oracle to emphasize the variety and extent of David's gifts. Acts 2:30 refers to David as a prophet in the context of looking at what David says about his descendants.

This oracle takes for granted the concept of sacral kingship, that is, the king had a religious role as well as a secular function. Kingship is a gift and a task given by God. There are parallels between this passage and Ps. 72, which also explores the nature of righteous kingship.

Oracles like this one, that envisaged righteous descendants for David, often formed the basis for the development of a messianic hope. As more and more of David's descendants did fail, the hope that the next king would fit the envisaged pattern grew weaker. It eventually became transferred to an eschatological or end-time hope that God would intervene directly and send a descendant for David who would change things forever.

23:2 / Verse 1 takes it for granted that God is with the king, he has been exalted and anointed by . . . God. The evidence that **the Spirit of the LORD** was with Saul was provided by his joining a group of ecstatic prophets and behaving in a way that was unintelligible to watchers. David evinces the Spirit of God by speaking the words of God with clarity.

23:6–7 / Gordon (*1 and 2 Samuel: A Commentary*, p. 311) assumes that the godless men described in these verses are "enemies of the Davidic dynasty," but the concept of disobedient rulers fits better with the context, particularly if David had been meditating on God's words recorded in 2 Sam. 7.

§47 The Honors List (2 Sam. 23:8–39)

Given the extent to which David's fortunes were influenced by his supportive soldiers, it was appropriate to include a military honors list. It is possible that the information about these names came from the same kind of military records as did 21:15–22. The list appears to come largely from the first part of David's reign; a more extensive list in 1 Chronicles 11 and 12 probably covers a wider time period. "The Thirty" seems to have been the name of the finest troop of David's soldiers, indicating its fixed number of members. It is possible that the Israelite army was following an Egyptian model. When a member of the Thirty died or retired, he would have been replaced. This explains why there are more than thirty names on the list in this chapter and a further sixteen names added to the list in Chronicles. It seems likely that this list was up-to-date at the time when Uriah died, and the list in Chronicles includes the names of all those who belonged to the Thirty during the whole of David's reign. Joab would have been the undisputed commander of the army at the time these lists were drawn up, but his name is mentioned only as the brother of Abishai and Asahel.

23:8–12 / **The Three** appear to have been first-class heroes, although whether they were a separate group from the Thirty or simply a noted group within the Thirty is not clear. None of the leaders mentioned in the first part of the section are named among the Thirty. That may have been because their names had already been given, or perhaps because these were the equivalent of officers and the Thirty were the top group of noncommissioned men.

The famous three, **Josheb-Basshebeth, Eleazar,** and **Shammah,** in spite of their significant exploits in the campaign against **the Philistines,** are unknown elsewhere, although Shammah's son Jonathan was apparently one of the Thirty (cf. additional note on 21:18–21). Perhaps these three were singled out because the war against the Philistines was considered to be a holy war in a way that many later campaigns were not. This idea picks up on the repeated comment, **the LORD brought about a great victory** (vv. 10, 12). It also explains why later heroes, like Abishai and Benaiah, were not placed in the same category.

23:13–17 / There is no indication as to whether the **three** heroes of verses 13–17 are those already mentioned or a different group. One suggestion is that it was Joab and his two brothers. Reckless courage fits with what we know of the sons of Zeruiah, but such an identification is only speculative. In one sense, this is a minor incident; the writers give it no symbolic significance. It serves as an additional example of the loyalty and devotion that David inspired in his men and a further insight into David's character. David's somewhat whimsical desire for a **drink of water** from the **Bethlehem well** was picked up by the three men. In spite of the fact that the well was behind **Philistine lines,** they obtained some water and brought it to him. Water that had been acquired at the risk of life was too precious to drink, so David **poured it out before the LORD.** This pouring out was in effect a ritual sacrifice that would have emphasized the specialness of their gift. Their offering was seen as worthy to be offered to God.

23:18–23 / Verses 18–23 specify **Abishai** and **Benaiah** as noted warriors. Unlike the three from verses 8–12, these two are well known within the main narrative. The episode in which Benaiah killed **a lion** on **a snowy day** was probably remembered because snow was unusual.

23:24–39 / The names of many of the men detailed as members of the Thirty are not recorded elsewhere. Those of special significance are Joab's brother **Asahel,** later killed by Abner attempting another brave though foolhardy escapade; **Eliam,** possibly Bathsheba's father (11:3) and the son of David's noted counselor **Ahithophel;** and **Uriah.** Closing the list with Uriah's name is probably deliberate, an implicit reminder of David's failings and an indication that all heroes, even these mighty men, have clay feet.

Additional Notes §47

There are a number of minor textual problems within 23:8–39, as indicated by the number of footnotes in some versions of the NIV. However, although this means that it is difficult to be sure of the precise form of some names, it does not cause significant difficulties as to the meaning of the text.

23:8 / The **mighty men** have been identified as the chief members of the standing army. 1 Chron. 27 gives more details of the way in which the army was organized into divisions. Including lists like this in the national records served several purposes. First, it made it clear that the king did not stand alone, that the fortunes of Israel were in the hands of more than one man, and that the contributions of all were significant in the sight of God and the nation. Second, honoring crack troops by creating and recording lists like these would have motivated soldiers who could aspire to join their ranks. Third, it would provide a focus for contemporary and later members of the families who could search out the lists for members of their own tribes and families, adding to a sense of national identity.

Certain LXX manuscripts have "Ish-Bosheth" instead of **Josheb-Basshebeth.**

23:13 / The incident described in vv. 13–17 is not phrased in the same way as the other lists and probably comes from a different source. The incident occurred while David was fleeing from Saul but continuing the fight against the Philistines. The three men are identified as belonging to David's thirty chief men, but whether this was as formalized a group as it became during David's kingship is not clear.

23:18–23 / That Abishai and Beniah were so significant and yet not **included among** the three supports the view that the earlier fighting but not the later was considered to be part of a holy war. As Hertzberg put it (*I and II Samuel*, p. 406), "These were daring deeds but not 'saving' deeds." Benaiah replaced Joab as commander of the army after having been involved in his execution (1 Kgs. 2:35).

The point of mentioning the **snow** (v. 20) is probably its rarity in those parts, but it may be because it made the tracks visible. The Moabite *ʾariēl* of the early part of the verse are correctly translated as **best men.** Although the term is often used metaphorically for heroes, literally it means "lions of God." Similarly, the lion (*ʾᵃrî*) in the pit is almost certainly a mountain **lion** but could refer to another Moabite hero.

23:30 / Benaiah the Pirathonite is to be distinguished from Benaiah son of Jehoiada (vv. 20–23).

23:39 / It is hard to be precise about the exact numbers of mighty men. One of the places where the text is obscure is in v. 32, but if **the sons of Jashen** is the correct text, then we cannot be sure how many such sons there were. However, as there are only thirty names in the list apart from those sons, it is likely that the **thirty-seven** is intended to include Abishai, Benaiah, and the Three. Gordon (*1 and 2 Samuel: A Commentary*, p. 316) suggests that the number also includes Joab, who is not mentioned only because his inclusion is taken for granted.

§48 The Census and Its Aftermath (2 Sam. 24:1-25)

This is not an easy passage for a number of reasons. The equivalent passage in 1 Chronicles 21 has a number of differences, not the least being the inspiration of David's action, presented as the Lord in 2 Samuel and as Satan in 1 Chronicles. In the context of 2 Samuel, in particular the appendix, this passage has a parallel in 21:1-14, where Saul's sin brought tragedy to the nation. The writers may intend to make it clear that the actions of any ruler, not just the disgraced Saul, have consequences that go far beyond the action. In both instances the accounts end with God again answering prayer in behalf of the land (21:14; 24:25). In this instance there is a looking forward to Solomon's reign. The details given concerning the threshing floor of Araunah are explained by the fact that this was where the temple was to be built. Thus this account forms an appropriate end to 2 Samuel and a link with 1 Kings.

24:1-3 / The picture in verse 1 of God **incit**[ing] **David** because of his **anger . . . against Israel** is difficult to comprehend, particularly in the light of the parallel in Chronicles, where Satan incites David. Are we to understand that God causes David to take action that is against God's will and for which David and the nation will be punished? If so, then God is to be viewed as the tempter, something that James 1:13 suggests is not possible. One way of reconciling this is to see God as allowing and overruling while Satan tempts. Another approach is to see David as God's tool used to punish Israel. This would explain why David's action was **against them,** but it does not clarify why the action received the punishment.

It is difficult at first to see what the problem was in David's action. Conducting **a census** is not a great sin. The numbering itself was not wrong, but the motivation behind it was. If a census is undertaken as a means to take pride in achievement and to glory in human success, then it becomes a problem. All Israel was involved (v. 1), and this makes sense if the census, although instigated by David, reflected the pride of the nation and their forgetfulness of the God who lay behind their success.

A second possibility is that the census was taken as a means of changing the method of forming the army by calling up troops from different tribes. Then, as Hertzberg states (*I and II Samuel*, p. 412), "this represents a direct inroad into the sacral sphere, the replacement of a charismatic institution by the measures of human organization. It is a challenge to God himself." In this instance rules that had been set up by God were being set aside, which means that David would have been usurping a function that did not belong to him—an action that would deserve condemnation. If the census was concerned with army formations, this would make sense of the involvement of **Joab.** Joab was not renowned for spiritual insight or for great concern with righteousness or the will of God, but in this instance he was clear that David's action was inappropriate. Kirkpatrick *(The Second Book of Samuel)* suggests that Joab's motivation was "fear of exciting disaffection among the people by a scheme to increase the burdens of military service." This view makes sense, although it is possible that theological understanding played some part in Joab's disquiet.

24:4–10 / For once, Joab was **overruled.** Maybe David's determination was strengthened by Joab's opposition and his desire to get the better of Joab overrode his ability to listen to advice. David's offense against Uriah, when he put himself into Joab's power, appears to have been the beginning of the mistrust between the two and thus had ongoing serious consequences, just as Nathan had suggested. Such a census was a major undertaking. This one took almost ten months to complete, and not until it was over did David begin to realize the significance of what he had done and come to the point of repentance. In fact, it is possible that carrying out the census eventually revealed to David and the people the pride in their own achievements that had developed and that therefore led to repentance for this attitude. If this is so, it would make sense of the idea that because of his anger at the people's pride, God tempted David to conduct the census that would stimulate him to realize the folly of depending on numbers rather than on God.

24:11–17 / On this occasion, unlike Nathan in 2 Samuel 12, the prophet came to David only after he had admitted and regretted his sin. His old companion **Gad** brought David a terrible choice. Death and destruction for the people was inevitable. Should it be through **three years of famine, three months** of war, or **three days of plague?** Each of these choices would lead to national devastation. The shorter the time the more serious the effects, but each option would lessen the numbers of which David had been so proud. He rejected war because of the way it would make the fate of the nation dependent on others, specifically on the human revenge of David's enemies. David's experience had convinced him of God's mercy. He was convinced that the punishment that God would bring would be no more than they deserved, causing as little hurt as was possible for the satisfaction of justice. Even in his **deep distress,** David retained awareness of God's nature.

The phrase **your enemies** in verse 13, along with David's **do not let me fall** in verse 14, could imply that this would be a personal pursuit, affecting David more seriously than the whole of Israel. However, there is no further comment on this implication and it seems not to be the point of the text. Eventually a **plague** is sent, and **seventy thousand** people from throughout the whole nation die as a result. The writers clearly present the limitation of the effects of the plague and in particular the preservation of Jerusalem as an exercise of the mercy of God in which David had put his trust. In verse 17, David, with characteristic passion, wants to take on himself the blame for what has occurred. The writers make no further comment on this, but the implication that the people have shared his proud attitude remains.

24:18–25 / Verse 25 could be seen as portraying the sacrifice, made at **the threshing floor of Araunah,** as the means of reconciliation and therefore possibly as the reason for stopping the plague. However, in the earlier verses (16–18) the sacrifice is presented as a response to, not as the cause of, the plague's end. The site is chosen because it was the place where the plague stopped, presumably the point where the final victim died. The mention of the **angel of the LORD** (v. 16) emphasizes the writers' conviction that God was responsible for the plague and God chose the site for the sacrifice. The portrayal of the negotiations with Araunah over the purchase of the land provides an insight into bargaining techniques. The story forms a parallel to that of Abraham's purchase of a burial site in Genesis 23. In both instances the proposal to provide freely what was requested is part of the bargaining procedure rather than a serious offer.

The repeated phraseology from 21:14 as well as the "again" from verse 1 indicates a deliberate link between 21:1–14 and 24:1–25. The reader is intended to think about the links between Saul's action with its consequences and David's action with its consequences. Saul's tortured bitterness had prevented God from working out his purposes through him, but David's repentant trust provided a context in which God could answer prayer. The final mention of David in this book is his fair treatment of Araunah and his desire to pay whatever cost is needed for proper service of God—and the final sentence focuses on the God who answers prayer.

The collection of largely unconnected narratives that make up these final chapters of 2 Samuel could seem an anticlimax after the exciting stories of the earlier court narratives. However, the psalm of chapter 22 and the oracle of 23:1–7 leave the reader with a strong sense of the character and purposes of the God of Israel. In addition, this final story reemphasizes the nature of human perfidy and God's faithfulness and mercy. It also provides a context for the continuing story as recorded in 1 and 2 Kings. God still has a purpose for Israel, God still desires worship and service, God still acts on Israel's behalf. The site is purchased, the sacrifice is made, the plague is over, life in the land continues under the blessing of God. The temple site is ready. This part of the narrative is complete, and the readers are prepared for the introduction of the temple builder.

Additional Notes §48

24:1 / As in Job 1–2, the use of the term śāṭān in 1 Chron. 21:1 does not have all the trappings that are associated with the word by NT times. In OT times, the term could refer to the Accuser, a kind of public prosecutor who could, as in Job or Chronicles, be an Accusing Angel or a human accuser acting as Abishai did (2 Sam. 19:21). Both Samuel and Chronicles use the same source material, but it is not possible to determine which is the original at this point. It could be that the Chronicler wanted to avoid describing God as tempter and therefore introduced the concept of Satan. It is equally possible that the writers of Samuel wanted to emphasize God's sovereignty and that all things are under God's control, so all supernatural actions were automatically ascribed to God. Thus the writers could be aware of the role of a satan but choose to concentrate rather on the overruling providence of God.

24:8 / The timing of this census cannot be determined precisely, but it must have taken place during a time of settled peace. Thus it must have been after the major wars were completed and was probably in the latter part of David's reign.

24:9 / The numbers vary somewhat from those given in Chronicles. 1 Chron. 27:24 suggests that no official records were kept, in which case these numbers could have been preserved only through an oral tradition, which may have varied. As elsewhere in Samuel it is possible that a **thousand** was a military formation of a now indeterminable size rather than a literal number.

24:11 / The prophet Gad had been with David since his days fleeing from Saul (1 Sam. 22:5). He appears to have had a parallel ministry to that of Nathan. Both of them are spoken of as record keepers as well as prophets (1 Chron. 29:29).

24:14 / The text as it stands leaves famine and plague as equal options, although the LXX adds "and David chose the plague." Perhaps famine would have made the nation dependent on others, in this case the grain merchants.

24:16–17 / It is not clear whether God decided that the plague should be stopped at the end of the three days or earlier than that. It is also unclear whether the **angel** was a visible supernatural messenger or a metaphorical way of describing the progress of the plague. Verse 17 could point to the former, although David's prayer seems to indicate that he was unaware that the events of v. 16 had taken place—which is strange if he had seen the angel for himself. The prayer provides evidence of David's attitude, but its further significance is not discussed. The stopping of the plague is presented as resulting from God's sovereign mercy, not as a direct response to David's actions either in prayer or in sacrifice.

In the Hebrew text of Chronicles **Araunah** is given the alternative name of Ornan. Araunah was a **Jebusite,** one of the original inhabitants of Jerusalem. That his land was purchased and not requisitioned shows the way in which those inhabitants appear to have been absorbed into, rather than enslaved by, the conquering Israelite community. However, it could be that the writers have chosen to include these negotiations to make it clear that the temple site had been fairly purchased and could not be seen as being provided by non-Israelites who might be seen as unclean.

24:24 / The account in Chronicles speaks of six hundred shekels of gold being paid for the site as opposed to the mere **fifty shekels of silver** described here. It is possible that the lesser amount was paid for the site of the altar and the greater for the whole temple area.

For Further Reading

Commentaries

Ackroyd, P. R. *The First Book of Samuel.* Cambridge: Cambridge University Press, 1971.

_____. *The Second Book of Samuel.* Cambridge: Cambridge University Press, 1977.

Anderson, A. A. *2 Samuel.* WBC. Waco: Word, 1989.

Baldwin, J. *1 and 2 Samuel: An Introduction and Commentary.* TOTC. Downers Grove: InterVarsity, 1988.

Brueggemann, W. *First and Second Samuel.* Interpretation. Louisville, Ky.: John Knox, 1990.

Eaton, M. A. *1 Samuel: Preaching Through the Bible.* Tonbridge: Sovereign World, 1996.

_____. *2 Samuel: Preaching Through the Bible.* Tonbridge: Sovereign World, 1996.

Gordon, R. P. *1 and 2 Samuel: A Commentary.* Exeter: Paternoster, 1986.

Hertzberg, H. W. *I and II Samuel.* Translated by J. Bowden. OTL. London: SCM, 1964.

Jensen, I. L. *First and Second Samuel.* Chicago: Moody, 1995.

Kirkpatrick, A. F. *The First Book of Samuel.* Cambridge: Cambridge University Press, 1888.

_____. *The Second Book of Samuel.* Cambridge: Cambridge University Press, 1886.

Klein, R. W. *1 Samuel.* WBC. Waco: Word, 1983.

Laney, J. C. *First and Second Samuel,* Chicago: Moody, 1995.

Mauchline, J. *1 and 2 Samuel.* NCB. London: Oliphants, 1971.

McCarter, P. K. *I Samuel.* AB 8. Garden City, N.Y.: Doubleday, 1980.

_____. *II Samuel.* AB 9. Garden City, N.Y.: Doubleday, 1984.

Provan, I. W. *1 and 2 Kings.* NIBCOT. Peabody: Hendrickson, 1995.

1 and 2 Samuel

Other Studies

Ackerman, J. S. "Knowing Good and Evil: A Literary Analysis of the Court History in 2 Samuel 9–20 and 1 Kings 1–2." *JBL* 109 (1990), pp. 41–60.

Arnold, B. T. "The Amalekite Report of Saul's Death." *JETS* 32 (1989), pp. 289–98.

Bailey, R. C. *David in Love and War: The Pursuit of Power in 2 Samuel 10–12.* JSOTSup 75. Sheffield: JSOT Press, 1990.

Barrick, W. B. "Saul's Demise, David's Lament and Custer's Last Stand." *JSOT* 73 (1997), pp. 25–41.

Ben-Nahum, Y., "What Ailed the Son of Kish?" *JBQ* 19 (1990–91), pp. 244–49.

Beuken, W. A. M. "1 Samuel 28: The Prophet as 'A Hammer of Witches.' " *JSOT* 6 (1978), pp. 3–17.

Brueggemann, W. "The Trusted Creature." *CBQ* 31 (1969), pp. 487–98.

_____. "Kingship and Chaos." *CBQ* 33 (1971), pp. 317–32.

_____. "On Trust and Freedom: A Study of Faith in the Succession Narrative." *Int* 26 (1972), pp. 3–19.

_____. "On Coping with Curse: A Study of 2 Samuel 16:5–14." *CBQ* 36 (1974), pp. 175–92.

_____. "2 Samuel 21–24: An Appendix of Deconstruction." *CBQ* 50 (1988), pp. 383–97.

_____. "Narrative Intentionality in 1 Samuel 29." *JSOT* 43 (1989), pp. 21–35.

_____. "The Abuse of Command: Exploiting Power for Sexual Gratification." *Sojourners* 26 (1997), pp. 22–25.

Caird, G. B. "The First and Second Books of Samuel: Introduction and Exegesis." Pages 855–1176 in vol. 2 of *The Interpreter's Bible.* Edited by G. A. Buttrick et al. 12 vols. Nashville: Abingdon, 1953.

Campbell, A. F. *The Ark Narrative, 1 Sam 4–6, 2 Sam 6: A Form-Critical and Traditio-Historical Study.* SBLDS 16. Missoula, Mont.: Society of Biblical Literature, 1975.

Childs, B. S. *Introduction to the Old Testament as Scripture.* Philadelphia: Fortress, 1979.

Clines, D. J. A., and T. C. Eskenazi, eds. *Telling Queen Michal's Story: An Experiment in Comparative Interpretation.* JSOTSup 119. Sheffield: JSOT Press, 1991.

Coats, G. W. "2 Samuel 12:1–7a." *Int* 40 (1986), pp. 170–73.

Cook, A. " 'Fiction' and History in Samuel and Kings." *JSOT* 36 (1986), pp. 27–48.

Deboys, D. G. "1 Samuel 29:6." *VT* 39 (1989), pp. 214–19.

Del Olomo Lete, G. "David's Farewell Oracle (2 Samuel 23:1–7): A Literary Analysis." *VT* 34 (1984), pp. 414–37.

Dumbrell, W. J. "The Content and Significance of the Books of Samuel: Their Place and Purpose Within the Former Prophets." *JETS* 33 (1990), pp. 49–62.

Edelman, D. V. *King Saul in the Historiography of Judah.* JSOTSup 121. Sheffield: Sheffield Academic Press, 1991.

Evans, M. J. " 'A Plague on Both Your Houses': Cursing and Blessing Reviewed." *VE* 24 (1994), pp. 77–89.

Exum, J. C. *Tragedy and Biblical Narrative.* Cambridge: Cambridge University Press, 1992.

_____. *The Historical Books: A Sheffield Reader.* Sheffield: Sheffield Academic Press, 1997.

Exum, J. C., and J. W. Whedbee. "Isaac, Samson, and Saul: Reflections on the Comic and Tragic Visions." *Semeia* 32 (1985), pp. 5–41.

Flanagan, J. W. " 'Court History or Succession Document': A Study of 2 Samuel 9–20, 1 Kings 1–2." *JBL* 91 (1972), pp. 172–81.

Fontaine, C. "The Bearing of Wisdom on the Shape of 2 Samuel 11–12 & 1 Kings 3." *JSOT* 34 (1986), pp. 61–67.

Frisch. A. " 'For I Feared the People and I Yielded to Them.' 1 Samuel 15:24. Is Saul's Guilt Attenuated or Intensified?" *ZAW* 108, no. 1 (1996), pp. 98–104.

Gordon, R. P. "David's Rise and Saul's Demise: Narrative Analogy in 1 Samuel 24–26." *TynBul* 31 (1980), pp. 37–67.

_____. *1 and 2 Samuel.* Old Testament Guides. Sheffield: JSOT Press, 1987.

_____. "Word Play and Verse Order in 1 Samuel 24:5–8." *VT* 40 (1990), pp. 139–44.

Gros Louis, K. R. R. "The Difficulty of Ruling Well: King David of Israel." *Semeia* 8 (1977), pp. 15–33.

Gunn, D. "David and the Gift of the Kingdom (2 Samuel 2–4, 9–20, 1 Kings 1–2)." *Semeia* 3 (1975), pp. 14–45.

_____. *The Fate of King Saul: An Analysis of a Biblical Story.* JSOTSup 14. Sheffield: Sheffield Academic Press, 1980.

_____. *The Story of King David: Genre and Interpretation.* JSOTSup 6. Sheffield: University of Sheffield, 1982.

Hagan, H. "Deception as Motif and Theme in 2 Samuel 9–20, 1 Kings 1–2." *Bib* 60 (1979), pp. 301–26.

Howard, D. M. "The Transfer of Power from Saul to David in 1 Samuel 16:13–14." *JETS* 32 (1989), pp. 473–83.

Humphreys, W. L. "The Tragedy of King Saul: A Study of the Structure of 1 Samuel 9–31." *JSOT* 6 (1978), pp. 18–27.

Jones, G. H. *The Nathan Narratives*. JSOTSup 80. Sheffield: Sheffield Academic Press, 1990.

Kleven, T. "Hebrew Style in 2 Samuel 6." *JETS* 35 (1992), pp. 299–314.

———. "Up the Waterspout: How David's General Joab Got Inside Jerusalem." *BAR* 20, no. 4 (1994), pp. 34–35.

Lawton, R. B. "1 Samuel 18: David, Merob and Michal." *CBQ* 51 (1989), pp. 423–25.

Mays, J. L., D. L. Petersen, and K. H. Richards, eds. *Old Testament Interpretation: Past, Present and Future*. Edinburgh: T&T Clark, 1995.

McCarter, P. K. "The Apology of David." *JBL* 99 (1980), pp. 489–504.

———. "The Historical David." *Int* 40 (1986), pp. 117–29.

Miller, P. D., and J. J. M. Roberts. *The Hand of the Lord: A Reassessment of the "Ark Narrative" of 1 Samuel*. Baltimore: Johns Hopkins University Press, 1977.

Moberley, R. W. L. "To Hear the Master's Voice: Revelation and Spiritual Discernment in the Call of Samuel." *SJT* 48, no. 4 (1995), pp. 443–68.

Nicol, G. C. "Bathsheba: A Clever Woman." *ExpTim* 99 (1988), pp. 360–63.

———. "The Alleged Rape of Bathsheba: Some Observations on Ambiguity in Biblical Narrative." *JSOT* 73 (1997), pp. 43–54.

Payne, D. F. "Apologetic Motifs in the Books of Samuel." *VE* 23 (1993), pp. 57–66.

Peckham, B. "The Deuteronomistic History of Saul and David." *ZAW* 97 (1985), pp. 190–209.

———. *History and Prophecy: The Development of Late Judean Literary Traditions*. Garden City, N.Y.: Doubleday, 1993.

Perdue, L. G. " 'Is There Anyone Left of the House of Saul . . . ?' Ambiguity and Characterization of David in the Succession Narrative." *JSOT* 30 (1984), pp. 67–84.

Peterson, D. L. "Portraits of David: Canonical and Otherwise." *Int* 40 (1986), pp. 130–42.

_____. "Why Did Uzzah Die? Why Did David Dance?" *Crux* 31 (1995), pp. 3–5, 7–8.

Pleins, J. D. "Son-Slayers and Their Sons." *CBQ* 54 (1992), pp. 29–38.

Polak, F. H. "David's Kingship—A Precarious Equilibrium." Pages 119–47 in *Politics and Theopolitics in the Bible and Postbiblical Literature.* Edited by H. Graf Reventlow et al. JSOTSup 171. Sheffield: JSOT Press, 1994.

Prouser, O. H. "Suited to the Throne: The Symbolic Use of Clothing in the David and Saul Narratives." *JSOT* 71 (1996), pp. 22–37.

Powis Smith, J. M. "The Character of King David." *JBL* 52 (1933), pp. 10–11.

Reis, P. T. "Collusion at Nob: A New Reading of 1 Samuel 21–22." *JSOT* 61 (1994), pp. 59–73.

_____. "Eating the Blood: Saul and the Witch of Endor." *JSOT* 73 (1997), pp. 3–23.

Richardson, H. N. "The Last Words of David: Some Notes on 2 Samuel 23:1–9." *JBL* 90 (1971), pp. 329–30.

Rosenberg, J. "The Intentional Matrix of Treachery in 2 Samuel 11." *Semeia* 46 (1989), pp. 103–16.

Smith, J. "The Discourse Structure of the Rape of Tamar: 2 Samuel 13:1–21." *VE* 20 (1990), pp. 21–42.

Spina, F. A. "Eli's Seat: The Transition from Priest to Prophet in 1 Samuel 1–4." *JSOT* 62 (1994), pp. 67–75.

Van Seters, J. *In Search of History.* New Haven, Conn.: Yale University Press, 1983.

Weisman, Z. "Anointing as a Motif in the Making of the Charismatic King." *Bib* 57 (1976), pp. 378–98.

Wesselius, J. W. "Joab's Death and the Central Theme of the Succession Narrative." *VT* 40 (1990), pp. 336–51.

Wong, G. C. I. "Who Loved Whom? A Note on 1 Samuel 16:21." *VT* 47 (1997), pp. 554–56.

Yee, G. A. "Fraught with Background: Literary Ambiguity in 2 Samuel 11." *Int* 42 (1988), pp. 240–53.

Subject Index

Aaron, 25, 56
Aaronic priesthood, 25
Abiathar, 78, 99, 103, 105, 175, 202, 204, 207, 212
Abigail, 112–16, 213
Abinadab, 136, 165
Abishai, 117–19, 120, 154, 179, 205, 220, 222, 224, 225, 232, 241, 242, 243, 244, 248
Abner, 6, 71, 84, 95, 117–18, 121, 146, 150–55, 157, 226, 242
Abraham, 170, 247
Absalom, 3, 12, 77, 95, 148, 182, 189, 192–94, 196–99, 199–201, 202–7, 209–12, 212, 214–17, 219, 223, 224, 226
Achish, 97, 122–24, 127, 128
Ackermann, J. S., 13, 194
Ackroyd, P. R., 139, 169, 200
Adonijah, 78, 148, 189
Adullam, 98, 101, 109
Adultery, 182, 185, 186, 187
Ahijah, 65–67, 69, 99, 100
Ahimaaz, 208, 216, 218
Ahimelech, 97, 99, 100, 101, 175
Ahimelech the Hittite, 120
Ahinoam, 116, 192
Ahithophel, 6, 182, 202, 204, 206, 209–12, 212, 213, 214, 215, 224, 242
Alien(ation), 103, 139–40
Altar, 70, 71, 249
Amalekite(s), 73–76, 77, 99, 127, 130–32, 135, 138–41, 152, 153
Amasa, 211, 213, 219, 224, 225
Ammon, 180, 183, 187
Ammonites, 51, 53, 59, 65, 135, 178–79, 180, 186, 191
Amnon, 95, 116, 148, 189, 192–95, 197, 233
Amorites, 38, 144
Anderson, A. A., 149, 160, 236
Anoint(ed), 53, 73, 78, 107, 108, 110, 113, 119, 120–21, 134, 139, 157, 182, 240

Anointing, 46, 107; of David, 79–80, 83, 145, 148, 159; of Saul, 44–48, 52
Aphek, 35, 125, 128
Aram, 180, 226
Aramean(s), 172, 175, 179, 180, 194
Araunah, 245, 247, 248, 249
Archers, 134
Ark, 28, 29–30, 31–37, 50, 62, 63, 66, 68, 135, 161–64, 170, 183, 204, 206, 207, 237
Ark Narrative, 3, 12, 31–37, 161–64
Armor, 83–84, 86, 134
Armor-bearer(s), 66, 67, 81, 134, 198
Army, armies, 61, 69, 70, 73–74, 83, 87, 102, 126, 129, 133–34, 138, 142, 144, 145, 179, 183, 187, 188, 210, 211, 214, 215, 217, 219, 243
Arnold, B. T., 141
Asahel, 120, 147, 152, 153, 155, 242
Ashtoreths, 39, 136
Atoned, atonement, 118, 229
Authority, 9, 23, 41

Baal Perazim, 160
Baalah, 161, 165
Baals, 39
Baanah, 153–54, 155, 156
Bahurim, 210, 213
Baldwin, J., 3, 11, 13, 26, 32, 39, 73, 96, 116, 120, 176, 189
Barak, 57, 59
Barren(ness), 15, 21, 164
Barzillai, 212, 221, 222
Bathsheba, 149, 160, 178, 182–87, 188, 206, 208, 218, 234, 236, 242
Battalions, 107
Battle(s), 67, 114, 120, 138, 153, 203, 210, 214
Battlefield, 31, 182
Beersheba, 30, 39
Benaiah, 175, 242, 243, 244
Benjamin, 98, 147, 155, 158, 220
Benjamite(s), 46, 146, 147, 151, 220, 221, 222, 223
Berites, 225, 226

Beth Aven, 63, 67
Beth Shemesh, 34, 37, 39
Bethel, 63, 170
Bethlehem, 79, 84, 86, 93, 101, 242
Betrayal, 182, 219
Blaspheme, 186
Blessing, 16, 23, 34, 63, 66, 72, 94, 95, 119, 146, 162, 170, 231, 235, 239, 240
Blood, 23, 70, 120, 208, 226, 229
Bloodguilt, 120, 128, 229
Book of Jashar, 142, 144
Bowman, R. G., 91, 165
Bride price, 88–89
Brother(s), 83, 132, 143
Brotherhood, 44, 133
Brueggemann, W., 3, 7, 9, 12, 13, 14, 18, 22, 120, 128, 200, 205, 218
Burnt offering, 38, 70

Caird, G. B., 18, 27, 29, 39, 58, 86, 91, 120, 128
Campbell, A. F., 12
Canaan, 39, 48
Canaanite, 35, 101, 136, 155, 207
Celebration, 20, 45
Census, 245–48
Ceremonial, 52, 161
Ceremony, ceremonies, 38, 46, 51, 55, 221
Chariot(s), 61, 139, 175, 180, 198
Charisma(tic), 5, 50, 69, 81, 246
Cherubim, 165
Child, 29, 183, 186
Childlessness, 9, 16, 164
Childs, B. S., 13–14
Civil war, 209–12, 219
Clairvoyant, 44, 50, 125
Clines, D. J. A., 91, 149, 154
Coats, G. W., 190
Community, 1, 35, 181, 226, 231
Concubines, 189, 206, 209, 212, 223
Confirmation, 157–59
Consecrated, consecration, 80, 82, 97, 100, 167
Conspiracy, 98, 113
Cook, A., 144
Coronation, 61, 151; of Saul, 49
Covenant, 3, 8, 35, 38, 44, 57, 85, 93–95, 98, 119, 124, 132, 133, 143, 159, 164, 167–70, 171, 183, 207, 226, 227, 229, 239
Cremation, 136–37

Curse(d), 69–71, 114, 118, 206
Cursing, 72, 155, 230

Dagon, 33, 136
Daughters, 159, 200
David(ic), 167, 169, 239, 240; lament of, 142–43, 144; sons of, 95, 175, 177, 189, 205
Dead Sea, 105, 106, 208, 222
Death sentence, 70, 190, 139–40, 154, 229
Deborah, 57, 226
Deception, 7, 13
Deliverance, deliverer, 20, 235
Depression, depressive, 81, 87
Deuteronomic, Deuteronomist, 57, 71, 77, 78, 158, 190, 226
Deuteronomistic History, 2, 10–11, 55, 170
Disobedience, 74–75, 81
Divination, 77
Divorce, 187
Doeg, 97, 99, 100, 101
Donkeys, 44, 45, 49, 205
Dreams, 124, 128
Drunk, 183, 195
Dumbrell, W. J., 13
Dynasty, 62, 167–69, 184, 240

Ebenezer, 35, 38, 39
Ecstatic, 87, 90, 91, 92, 163
Edelman, D. V., 77, 110
Egypt, 36, 56, 73, 112
Egyptian, 131, 241
Elders, 28, 41
Eleazar, 35, 165, 241
Elhanan, 86, 232–33
Eli, 6, 17, 21, 23–25, 28–30, 32, 42, 56, 69, 74, 95, 100; sons of, 23–24, 32, 41, 95
Eliab, 80, 82
Elkanah, 15–18, 21, 45, 79
Empower(ment), 28, 63, 80
En Gedi, 105, 107, 110
Enthronement, 78, 157
Ephod, 26, 53, 65, 68, 77, 100, 103, 105, 124, 127, 131, 159, 229
Ephraim(ite), 15, 148, 207
Eskenazi, T. C., 91, 149, 154
Evil spirit, 81, 87
Execution(er), 194, 196, 217, 220, 230, 243
Exile, 3, 8, 98, 203
Exum, J. C., 86, 110, 113, 163

False prophet, 168
Famine, 229–30, 231
Fasting, 69, 152
Father, 109, 110, 214
Fear, 87–91
Feast(s), 45, 46, 47, 94, 135
Fellowship offering, 16, 23, 45, 52
Flanagan, J. W., 5, 12
Foreskin(s), 88, 91
Forgiveness, 24, 75, 189, 235
Fortune teller, 44
Fouts, D. M., 37
Friendship, 85, 86, 95

Gad, 100, 101, 144, 247
Gath, 85, 39, 98, 1Geba 63, 68
Geshur, 194, 197, 199
Geshurites, 127
Giant, 84
Gibeah, 48, 51, 63, 65, 67, 90, 127n101, 122, 126, 127, 130
Gibeon, 146, 224, 231
Gibeonites, 176, 229, 230, 231
Gideon, 57, 179, 189
Gift(s), 4, 5, 17, 86, 114
Gilboa, 124–26, 128, 142
Gilgal, 47, 52, 54, 60–62, 66, 71, 74
Gittite, 83, 85–86, 126, 165, 203, 207, 218
Giving, 7, 13
Goliath, 82, 83–84, 85–86, 98, 154, 232
Gordon, R. P., 12, 27, 33, 39, 47, 92, 113, 120, 136, 165, 234, 240, 244
Grasping, 7, 13
Gros Louis, K. R. R., 7, 13, 110
Gunn, D., 12, 13, 76

Hagan, H., 13
Hagar, 16
Hannah, 3, 15–18, 23; song of, 20–22, 234
Hanun, 53, 178–79, 212
Hebrew(s), 1, 3, 11–12, 36, 37, 59, 60, 63, 66, 68, 126, 129, 141, 144, 155, 162, 170, 176, 189, 190, 199, 236
Hebron, 106, 145, 147, 150, 151, 154, 157, 199, 202, 206
Heir, 6, 164
Herem, 73, 77, 99, 127, 191
Hertzberg, H. W., 18, 149, 179, 194, 204, 231, 238, 243, 246
History of David's Rise, 4, 164
Hittite(s), 120, 188, 189

Holy, holiness, 21, 34, 161, 162
Hophni, 23, 25, 26, 31
Horn, 20–21, 22, 81
Howard, D. M., 82
Huldah, 226
Humphreys, W. L., 47
Hushai, 202, 204, 207, 209, 210, 212

Idol, 90, 91, 136, 160
Idolatry, 32, 75
Immorality, 33, 186
Institution(al), 5, 167, 246
Integrity, 56, 155, 183, 195
Ish-Bosheth, 6, 125, 145, 146, 148, 150–55, 157, 207, 211, 243
Israel, 8, 9, 10, 20, 24, 30, 31, 38, 42, 45, 46, 48, 50, 72, 78, 88, 89, 96, 103–4, 109, 115, 119, 127, 139, 142–43, 145, 150, 153, 155, 158, 159, 168, 170, 197, 201, 215, 219, 221, 225, 229, 245
Israelites, 5, 31–35, 38, 39, 43, 48, 51, 53, 55, 65–67, 68, 73, 77, 83, 96, 99, 102, 129, 133, 136, 138, 139, 147, 149, 150, 157, 159, 188, 202, 219, 223, 229, 231, 241

Jabesh Gilead, 51, 53, 135, 146, 147, 148
Jacob, 238, 240
Janzen, J. G., 30
Jebusite(s), 86, 157, 158, 159, 190, 249
Jephthah, 57, 70
Jerusalem, 26, 39, 86, 149, 157, 158, 159, 161–64, 179, 182, 204, 206, 209, 223, 226, 237
Jesse, 79–81, 84, 85, 101
Jesus Christ, 2, 25, 28, 160, 170
Jezreel, 125, 128, 146, 148, 192
Joab, 3, 6, 9, 117, 120, 147, 152, 153, 154, 155, 159, 175, 179, 181, 182, 183, 184, 187, 188, 196–97, 199, 202, 211, 213, 214–17, 217, 219, 224, 225, 226, 241, 243, 244, 246
Jonadab, 192, 194
Jonathan, 10, 61, 65–67, 84–85, 88, 89, 92, 93–95, 98–99, 103–4, 133, 135, 136, 139, 140, 142–43, 174, 176, 207, 230
Jones, G. H., 190
Jordan, 51, 61, 208, 211, 219, 221, 223
Joshua, 34, 55, 115, 238

Judah, 5, 74, 83, 88, 98, 103, 105, 109, 127, 133, 144, 145, 146, 147, 149, 150, 159, 201, 202, 219, 221, 224, 229
Judean, 98, 102, 142, 223, 226
Judge, 39, 108
Judgment, 21, 23, 29, 76, 109, 120, 167, 168, 186, 199, 201, 206, 222, 229, 230, 231, 235

King, 5, 18, 42, 45, 47, 48, 49, 50, 55, 57, 75, 77, 81, 87, 88, 101, 104, 109, 110, 119, 133, 138, 143, 145, 146, 148, 151, 154, 159, 175, 183, 188, 190, 194, 195, 197, 200, 202, 206, 209, 211, 217, 220, 238, 243
Kingdom(s), 1–2, 5, 95, 109, 205, 211, 214, 231
Kingship, 21, 38, 41–42, 43, 49, 53, 58, 60, 62, 78, 80, 105, 120, 138, 151, 152, 155, 158, 159, 172, 187, 209, 238, 240, 243
Kiriath Jearim (Baalah), 35, 38, 68
Kirkpatrick, A. F., 213, 228, 246
Kish, 47, 79
Klein, R. W., 39, 43, 59, 77, 82, 119, 120, 136
Kleven, T., 160
Knight, D. A., 10

Lament, 142, 152
Law, 41, 99, 161, 183, 188, 189, 190
Lawton, R. B., 91
Leader(s), 7, 46, 48, 55, 78, 151, 210
Leadership, 4, 5, 13, 31, 39, 41, 50, 57, 102, 153, 211
Leah, 16, 91
Levites, 27, 34, 162
Linen ephod, 26, 163
Long, V. P., 77
Lots, lottery, 50, 53, 70, 71, 172
Loyalty, 6, 85, 93, 126, 143, 146, 176, 178, 193, 202–6, 211, 217, 220, 221, 233

Mahanaim, 146, 147, 149, 211, 217
Makir, 173, 174, 211
Manasseh, 128, 136
Marriage, 115, 223
Mauchline, J., 11, 139
Mays, J. L., 10
McCarter, P. K., 10, 12, 191, 200
Medium, 124, 128
Melchizedek, 166

Mephibosheth, 96, 148–49, 153, 155, 173, 176–77, 178, 205, 207, 208, 220, 222, 230, 231
Mercy, 190, 247
Messianic, 168–69
Michal, 71, 88–90, 91, 110, 115, 116, 144, 151, 154, 163–66
Military, 6, 7, 39, 48, 51, 69, 83, 86, 88, 105, 122, 153, 157, 164, 172, 184, 188, 211, 213, 232, 234, 241, 249
Miller, P. D., 12
Ministry, 25, 168
Mizpah, 38, 39, 47, 49, 52, 59
Moab, 57, 98, 101, 172
Monarchy, 5, 8, 42, 43, 53, 77, 78, 184, 189, 234, 235
Moses, 55, 56, 79, 189, 238, 240
Mourning, 184, 186–87, 190, 216
Murder, 182, 184–85, 190, 198
Music(ian), 80–81, 87, 162, 234

Nabal, 6, 113–16, 119, 120, 128, 148, 155
Nahash, 53, 57, 59, 178, 180, 212, 213
Nathan, 78, 144, 160, 167–69, 170, 184–85, 189, 190, 196, 246, 249
Nation(s), 25, 31, 41, 43, 50, 100, 124, 198, 221, 236, 246
Necromancy, 76, 128
New Moon festival, 93–95, 96
Nob, 86, 97, 98, 99, 100, 103
Noth, M., 10

Oath, 69–71, 89, 94, 127, 190
Obed-Edom, 162, 165
Obedience, 21, 42, 75–76
Occult, 124
Offering(s), 16, 23, 32, 36, 39, 48, 70, 118, 242
Oracle(s), 75, 77, 104, 107, 229, 238, 240

Paltiel, 90, 116, 151, 154, 166
Payne, D. F., 12, 78
Peckham, B., 10
Peninnah, 15–16
Perdue, L. G., 176
Petersen, D. L., 10
Philistine(s), 5, 31–35, 38–39, 45, 48, 56, 61, 63, 65–67, 69, 70, 83–84, 88, 89, 97, 99, 102–4, 110, 127, 129, 133–35, 139, 142, 148, 151, 152, 153, 158, 159, 160, 161, 173, 232, 241
Phinehas, 23, 25, 26, 31

Pleins, J. D., 110
Poet(ry), 142, 234, 238, 240
Polak, F. H., 12, 189
Politics, political, 3–6, 7, 220
Power(s), 5, 7, 8–10, 15, 17, 20–21, 23,
  28, 31, 38, 41–43, 46, 50, 56, 57, 64,
  67, 74, 78–79, 84, 89, 107, 112, 125,
  139, 145, 148, 152, 155, 158, 161,
  162, 178, 183, 185, 192, 193, 199,
  200, 214, 216, 219, 235
Powerful, 51, 216
Powerless, 9, 15, 20, 28, 33
Prayer, 16, 171
Priest(s), 23, 24, 25, 26, 27, 28, 32, 35,
  39, 62, 65, 68, 71, 78, 92, 98, 100, 175,
  210
Priestly, 41, 55, 67, 97, 163, 166, 229
Prophecy, 49, 56, 92, 105, 238, 239
Prophet(s), 1, 4, 26, 29, 30, 44–45, 48,
  78, 92, 100, 101, 124, 157, 167, 185,
  238, 249
Prophetic, 1–2, 11, 26, 28, 29, 55, 65,
  87, 90, 95, 98, 163, 170, 240
Prostitutes, religious, 26
Provan, I. W., 3, 10
Purification, 82

Rabbah, 182, 184, 186, 187
Rachel, 15, 90, 91
Ramah, 17, 38, 45, 80, 90, 93, 95, 110
Rape, 182, 193, 224
Rebellion, 108, 182, 186, 223, 225
Recab, 153–54, 155, 156
Rehoboam, 179, 221
Reign(s), 1, 71, 78, 179, 232 , 236, 237,
  241, 249,
Reis, P. T., 101
Rejection, 74–76, 79, 85, 109
Repentance, 24, 38, 119, 186, 189, 200,
  246, 248
Richards, K. H., 10
Righteousness, 235, 239
Ritual, 1, 62, 69, 75, 100, 163, 190
Rizpah, 150, 230
Roberts, J. J. M., 12
Rock, 234, 235, 238
Rost, Leonhard, 5
Ruth, 101

Sacred(al), 31, 34, 48, 240, 246
Sacrifice(s)(d), 17, 18, 23–24, 34, 45,
  47, 61, 62, 70, 71, 72, 75, 79, 82,

93–94, 96, 136, 163, 230, 231, 242,
  247, 248
Samuel's calling, 28–30
Samuel's sons, 41–42, 55, 95
Saul's son(s), 113, 133, 136, 230
Seer, 10, 44, 45
Servant, service, 23–24, 168, 210
Sex(uality), 24, 95, 97, 186, 193, 194
Sheba, 221, 223–25
Shepherd, 84, 103, 157
Shiloh, 3, 5, 16, 17, 21, 26, 32, 35, 39,
  100, 170
Shimei, 205, 207, 208, 213, 220, 221,
  222, 230, 230
Shrine(s), 5, 18, 26, 36, 48, 49, 50, 121,
  173
Sin(s), sinfulness, 23–24, 34, 64, 70–71,
  77, 125, 182, 183, 185, 186, 189, 192,
  193, 235, 247
Sisera, 57, 59
Smith, H. P., 120
Solomon, 5–6, 12, 20, 25, 78, 95, 149,
  160, 168, 179, 186, 189, 190, 221,
  226, 231, 239
Son(s), 1, 6, 7, 15, 17, 22, 41, 66, 70, 95,
  109, 110, 113, 118, 119, 120, 149,
  153, 192, 194, 197, 200, 209, 218,
  222, 230
Song(s), 20, 87, 126
Son-in-law, 86, 88, 110
Sovereignty, 9, 13, 34, 204, 206, 230,
  236, 248
Spear, 87, 89, 101, 118, 119, 120, 147
Spina, F. A., 36
Succession Narrative, 3, 12
Sword, 97, 134, 186, 189
Syncretism, 91, 127

Tabernacle, 163
Tamar, 159, 192–94, 194, 195, 223, 233
Tekoa, 185, 196
Temple, 5, 18, 20, 26, 28, 29, 45, 71,
  167–69, 170–71, 173, 231, 233, 237,
  245, 248, 249
Throne, 5, 6, 7, 94, 109, 110, 122, 161,
  214, 232
Thummin, 53, 212
Tribe(s), 4–5, 24, 44, 46, 50, 150, 151,
  159, 178, 201, 221, 223, 246
Troop(s), 51, 66, 69, 70, 74, 87, 107,
  140, 158, 203, 210, 211, 212, 213,
  214, 215, 226, 243

Unity, 5, 219
Uriah, 7, 91, 97, 120, 178, 180, 183–84, 188–90, 208, 218, 226, 234, 236, 241, 242, 246
Urim, 53, 124, 127, 212
Uzzah, 34, 162, 165

Vow, 17, 199

Warrior, 21, 210
Weak(ness), 9, 21, 33
Weapons, 66, 97, 120, 134, 142

Worship, 5, 17, 20, 38, 41, 45, 47, 49, 76, 199, 234

Yahweh, Yahwism, 13, 26, 31, 32, 34, 36, 56, 73, 78, 121, 129, 156, 171, 188, 207

Zadok, 25, 27, 28, 78, 165, 175, 176, 202, 204, 207, 212
Zeruiah, 120, 213, 222, 232
Ziba, 173, 176, 202, 205, 207, 221, 222
Ziklag, 123, 126, 127, 130–32, 135, 140, 154

Scripture Index

OLD TESTAMENT

Genesis **8:1**, 16; **16**, 16; **18**, 170; **19:29**, 17; **21:2**, 19; **22:4**, 237; **29:30**, 16; **31:19**, 90; **46:21**, 225; **49**, 238, 240; **49:24**, 157

Exodus **2:24**, 17; **3:4**, 79; **12:48**, 139; **15:18–21**, 159; **17:8**, 73; **22:21**, 139; 23, 247; **23:9**, 139; **25:22**, 165; **27:20–21**, 29; **28:30**, 53, 212; **29:9**, 25; **38:8**, 26

Leviticus **3:17**, 70; **5:14–6:7**, 36; **7:1–10**, 36; **7:11–18**, 16; **15:18**, 188; **18:9**, 195; **19:31**, 124; **20:27**, 128; **24:5–9**, 100; **28–36**, 23; **35:29–30**, 227

Numbers **1:51**, 35; **3:2**, 35; **6**, 18; **8:24–26**, 26; **10:10**, 96; **13:30**, 115; **14:43**, 73; **23:9–11**, 188; **23:19**, 76; **25:13**, 25; **27:21**, 212; **28:14**, 96; **35:30**, 99; **35:33**, 231

Deuteronomy **12:5–7**, 1; **12:10–11**, 167; **12:17–18**, 1; **16:18–19**, 1; **17**, 43; **17:6**, 99; **17:14–20**, 1, 53, 159; **17:16**, 175; **17:17**, 158; **18:9–14**, 124; **18:11**, 128; **19:4–10**, 1; **20:1–4**, 1; **23:10–15**, 183; **24:4**, 155; **24:7**, 227; **24:16**, 99; **25:17**, 77; **25:17–18**, 73; **32–34**, 238; **32:9**, 1; **33**, 240

Joshua **2:16**, 207; **3–4**, 34; **4:19**, 61; **7:14–18**, 53; **9:27**, 231; **10:12–13**, 144; **11:6**, 175; **11:9**, 175; **12:15**, 101; **14:6–15**, 115; **21:16**, 34; **23**, 55

Judges **3:8**, 59; **3:9**, 59; **4–5**, 226; **4:2**, 59; **4:3**, 59; **4:5**, 67; **7:1**, 125; **7:15–18**, 179; **9**, 189, 229; **10:7**, 59; **10:10**, 59; **11**, 71; **13**, 18, 71; **13:24**, 19; **16:24**, 135; **17:5**, 53; **20**, 51; **20:1**, 52; **21:1**, 52; **21:5**, 52; **21:8**, 52; **23–34**, 238

Ruth **4:15**, 22

1 Samuel **1**, 2; **1–3**, 35; **1–7**, 4; **1–15**, 4; **1:1**, 18, 44; **1:1–2**, 15; **1:1–11**, 18; **1:1–28**, 15–17; **1:2**, 18; **1:3**, 18; **1:3–4**, 1; **1:3–8**, 16; **1:4–5**, 18; **1:9**, 26, 36, 170; **1:9–16**, 16; **1:11**, 18; **1:11–12**, 139; **1:17–20**, 17; **1:19**, 18; **1:20**, 19; **1:20–23**, 19; **1:21–28**, 17; **1:23**, 19; **2**, 8, 234; **2:1**, 22; **2:1–2**, 20; **2:1–8**, 22; **2:1–11**, 20–21; **2:3–5**, 21; **2:5**, 22; **2:6**, 22; 101; **2:6–10**, 21, 33; **2:8**, 22; **2:11**, 13, 18, 21; **2:12–36**, 23; **2:17**, 24; **2:18**, 26; **2:18–21**, 23, 24; **2:18–26**, 26; **2:18–30**, 26; **2:18–36**, 24; **2:21**, 22; **2:22**, 26; **2:22–26**, 24; **2:25**, 26; **2:27**, 26; **2:27–36**, 24, 25; **2:29**, 32; **2:30**, 26; **2:30–33**, 65; **2:35**, 27; **2:35–36**, 27; **2:36**, 27; **3**, 24; **3:1**, 28, 29; **3:1–4:1a**, 28–29; **3:2–18**, 28; **3:2–4:1a**, 29; **3:3**, 26, 29; **3:3–20**, 30; **3:10**, 30; **3:14**, 26; **3:15**, 30, 170; **3:19**, 30; **3:19–4:1a**, 29; **3:20**, 30; **3:21**, 29; **4**, 53, 204; **4–6**, 4, 12, 35, 135; **4:1**, 35; **4:1–11**, 31, 39; **4:1a**, 40; **4:1b–5:12**, 32; **4:1b–7:1**, 31–35, 164; **4:3–6:6**, 36; **4:6**, 36; **4:8**, 36, 56; **4:9**, 36; **4:10**, 36, 161; **4:12–22**, 32; **4:13**, 36; **4:15**, 25; **4:18**, 36; **5:1–12**, 32; **5:1–6:12**, 33; **5:5**, 36; **5:6**, 36; **5:11**, 36; **6**, 39, 161; **6:1–12**, 33; **6:1–7:1**, 34; **6:3–4**, 36; **6:6**, 36, 56; **6:13–7:1**, 34, 35; **6:19**, 37; **7**, 8, 13, 38, 42, 59; **7:1**, 165; **7:2**, 35, 39; **7:2–13a**, 38; **7:2–17**, 38, 39; **7:4**, 40; **7:4–16**, 40; **7:5**, 52; **7:6**, 40; **7:10**, 40; **7:12**, 35, 40; **7:13**, 40; **7:13b–17**, 39; **7:16**, 40; **8–15**, 4; **8:1**, 1; **8:1–5**, 41; **8:1–22**, 41, 42; **8:3**, 41; **8:4–5**, 55; **8:4–18**, 43; **8:4–22**, 43; **8:5**, 1; **8:6–20**, 42; **8:11**, 1; **8:11–18**, 43, 56; **8:20**, 42; **8:21–22**, 42; **8:22**, 79; **9–31**, 47; **9:1**, 53, 72, 225; **9:1–2**, 47; **9:1–10**, 44; **9:1–27**, 45; **9:1–10:8**, 44; **9:2**, 44, 80, 86; **9:5**, 18; **9:6**, 30; **9:11–13**, 45; **9:13**, 47; **9:14–17**, 45; **9:16**, 48, 134;

9:18–27, 45; **9:18–10:8**, 46; **9:20**, 62; **9:21**, 44, 46; **9:25**, 46, 80; **9:27**, 46, 47, 80; **10**, 60; **10:1**, 48, 49; **10:1–6**, 48; **10:1–8**, 46, 47; **10:3–4**, 48; **10:5–6**, 48, 52; **10:6**, 46; **10:7**, 62; **10:8**, 54, 60, 61; **10:9–16**, 49; **10:9–11:15**, 49; **10:10**, 52, 87; **10:14**, 46; **10:16**, 49; **10:17**, 52; **10:17–25**, 47, 49; **10:17–27**, 50; **10:17–11:15**, 53; **10:18**, 50; **10:19**, 42, 50, 53; **10:20–21**, 49, 53; **10:23**, 86; **10:25**, 53; **10:26**, 48; **10:26–27**, 50; **10:26–11:11**, 51; **10:27**, 50, 53; **11**, 59, 60, 61; **11:1–2**, 53; **11:1–11**, 51; **11:1–15**, 52; **11:8**, 53; **11:11**, 51; **11:12–13**, 52, 53; **11:14–15**, 52, 53, 54; **12**, 8, 13, 78, 115; **12:1**, 60; **12:1–2**, 55; **12:1–25**, 55–58; **12:2**, 58; **12:3–5**, 55; **12:3–11**, 56; **12:6**, 58; **12:6–8**, 58; **12:6–11**, 56; **12:6–12**, 59; **12:6–19**, 57; **12:8**, 56; **12:9**, 56, 59; **12:9–10**, 59; **12:10**, 56; **12:11**, 59; **12:12**, 59; **12:12–15**, 57; **12:16–19**, 57; **12:16–25**, 58; **12:17**, 42; **12:20–25**, 58; **13**, 60, 65, 70, 76, 166; **13–15**, 77; **13–16**, 139; **13:1**, 60; **13:1–2**, 47; **13:1–7a**, 60; **13:1–22**, 60; **13:2**, 61; **13:2–4**, 60; **13:2–7**, 61; **13:3**, 63, 68, 101, 129; **13:5**, 61; **13:5–7**, 61, 63; **13:7–15**, 54; **13:8**, 60; **13:8–12**, 62; **13:8–22**, 62; **13:11–12**, 186; **13:13**, 71; **13:13–14**, 62, 63, 64, 76, 169; **13:14**, 13, 65, 75, 85; **13:15–22**, 62, 63; **13:16–18**, 63; **13:23–14:1**, 65; **13:23–14:23**, 65; **14**, 61, 63, 75, 114; **14:1**, 67; **14:2**, 67; **14:2–3**, 68; **14:2–5**, 65; **14:2–19**, 66; **14:2–22**, 68; **14:3**, 32, 69, 100; **14:6–14**, 66; **14:12**, 66; **14:15–19**, 66; **14:15–23**, 67; **14:16**, 67; **14:17**, 68; **14:18**, 65, 68; **14:20–23**, 67; **14:21–22**, 68; **14:21**, 129; **14:23**, 40; **14:24–30**, 69; **14:24–52**, 69–71; **14:31–35**, 69; **14:31–46**, 70; **14:35**, 70, 71; **14:36–46**, 70; **14:36–52**, 71; **14:37**, 72; **14:38–42**, 53; **14:40–42**, 71; **14:45**, 72; **14:46**, 69; **14:47–52**, 69, 71; **14:49**, 136; **14:50**, 84, 146; **14:50–51**, 72; **14:51**, 47; **15**, 60, 76, 79, 136, 138, 141; **15:1**, 12; **15:1–3**, 73; **15:1–35**, 73; **15:2**, 77; **15:2–35**, 77; **15:3**, 77, 99, 127, 130; **15:4–6**, 73; **15:5**, 77; **15:7–9**, 73; **15:7–15**, 74; **15:7–26**, 127; **15:10**, 76, 77; **15:10–11**, 74; **15:12**, 77; **15:12–15**, 74;

15:12–33, 5; **15:13–21**, 186; **15:16–23**, 75; **15:19**, 191; **15:22**, 77; **15:23**, 77; **15:24**, 75, 77; **15:24–35**, 76; **15:26**, 85; **15:28**, 87; **15:30**, 79; **15:32**, 77; **15:33**, 75; **15:34–35**, 76, 77; **16**, 53, 84, 167; **16:1**, 12; **16:1–3**, 79, 81; **16:1–13**, 78; **16:1–23**, 78, 82; **16:2**, 93; **16:4–13**, 79; **16:4–23**, 80; **16:5**, 82; **16:6–7**, 82; **16:7**, 80; **16:11**, 157; **16:11–12**, 82; **16:13**, 158; **16:13–14**, 82; **16:14**, 12; **16:14–23**, 80, 81, 82, 87; **16:16–18**, 80; **16:21**, 84; **17**, 80; **17:1**, 85; **17:1–58**, 83; **17:1–18:5**, 83, 84; **17:4–7**, 85; **17:4–18:5**, 86; **17:12**, 86; **17:32**, 1; **17:43**, 154; **17:54**, 86; **17:55–58**, 86; **18**, 91; **18:1–5**, 84, 85; **18:3**, 93; **18:3–4**, 86; **18:5**, 86; **18:6–9**, 87; **18:6–19:24**, 87–91; **18:10**, 91, 144; **18:10–11**, 89; **18:10–16**, 87; **18:10–29**, 88; **18:16–17**, 91; **18:17–27**, 91; **18:17–29**, 88; **18:17–19:10**, 89; **18:22**, 89; **18:23**, 88; **18:25**, 91; **18:29**, 89; **18:30**, 89; **19:1–7**, 89; **19:1–17**, 91; **19:1–24**, 92; **19:3**, 92; **19:6**, 93; **19:8–10**, 89; **19:8–24**, 90; **19:9**, 144; **19:11–17**, 90; **19:13**, 91; **19:17**, 90; **19:18–24**, 90, 91; **19:20**, 48, 92; **19:24**, 92; **20**, 85, 91, 92; **20:1**, 90, 95; **20:1–4**, 93; **20:1–42**, 93–95; **20:3**, 93; **20:4**, 93; **20:5**, 95; **20:5–7**, 93; **20:7**, 95; **20:8**, 93; **20:8–17**, 93; **20:8–42**, 94; **20:14–15**, 95; **20:14–16**, 173; **20:14–42**, 96; **20:15**, 177; **20:17**, 94; **20:18–34**, 94; **20:19**, 40, 41; **20:24–27**, 95, 96; **20:25**, 96; **20:30**, 96; **20:35–42**, 94, 95; **20:41–42**, 96; **21–22**, 101; **21:1**, 100; **21:1–22:23**, 97–100; **21:4**, 100; **21:5**, 183; **21:7**, 100; **21:7–22:2**, 101; **21:9**, 86, 97; **21:10–15**, 97, 122; **21:10–22:10**, 98; **21:11**, 101; **22:1**, 98; **22:1–5**, 98, 101; **22:5**, 170, 248; **22:6–10**, 98; **22:6–23**, 99; **22:8**, 98; **22:9**, 100; **22:9–10**, 100; **22:11–23**, 99, 100; **22:13**, 114; **22:14–15**, 97; **22:18**, 26; **22:18–19**, 98, 100; **22:20**, 175; **22:22**, 97, 101; **23:1–6**, 102; **23:1–29**, 102–5, 103; **23:3**, 105; **23:4**, 105; **23:6**, 100, 105, 124; **23:7–14**, 103; **23:9**, 53, 68, 229; **23:9–12**, 104; **23:13**, 105; **23:14**, 103; **23:15–29**, 103, 104, 105; **23:17**, 105; **23:19**, 106, 117; **23:19–25**, 106; **23:19–24:22**, 119; **23:24–25**, 106; **23:25**, 40; **24**,

118; **24–26**, 47, 128; **24:1**, 110; **24:1–7**, 107; **24:1–15**, 108; **24:1–16**, 110; **24:1–22**, 107–9; **24:2**, 114; **24:3**, 117; **24:4**, 107, 118; **24:6**, 110; **24:8**, 108, 110; **24:8–13**, 110; **24:8–15**, 108; **24:8–22**, 109; **24:10**, 110; **24:11**, 109, 122; **24:13–14**, 109; **24:14**, 154, 174, 208; **24:16**, 110; **24:16–21**, 110, 111; **24:16–22**, 109; **24:17**, 119; **24:21**, 111, 115; **25:1–44**, 112–15; **25:1a**, 112; **25:1b–3**, 112; **25:1b–13**, 113; **25:2**, 113; **25:3**, 115; **25:8**, 113; **25:4–9**, 113; **25:10–13**, 113; **25:10–31**, 114; **25:14–21**, 114; **25:14–44**, 115; **25:18–19**, 116; **25:18–44**, 116; **25:25**, 155; **25:32–44**, 115; **25:37–38**, 115, 120; **25:41**, 116; **25:42–44**, 116; **26**, 124; **26:1–3**, 117; **26:1–25**, 117–19; **26:2**, 117; **26:4–12**, 117; **26:4–20**, 118; **26:5**, 117; **26:6**, 120; **26:6–11**, 120; **26:8**, 118; **26:9–10**, 118; **26:10**, 120; **26:11**, 120; **26:11–19**, 121; **26:13–16**, 118; **26:17**, 1, 118; **26:17–25**, 119; **26:19**, 121; **26:20**, 118; **26:21–25**, 119; **27**, 85; **27–29**, 122–27; **27:1**, 119, 122; **27:2**, 127; **27:2–7**, 122; **27:2–28:2**, 123; **27:3**, 127; **27:4**, 122; **27:6**, 127; **27:8**, 127, 130; **27:8–11**, 123; **27:8–12**, 123; **28**, 76, 128, 133; **28:1**, 126; **28:1–2**, 123; **28:1–10**, 124; **28:4**, 125, 128; **28:4–29:11**, 128; **28:6**, 53; **28:6–7**, 128; **28:8–10**, 124; **28:11**, 128; **28:11–20**, 125; **28:11–29:1**, 125; **28:15–16**, 128; **28:21**, 128; **28:21–25**, 125; **29**, 128; **29:1**, 123, 125, 128; **29:1–11**, 126, 128, 129; **29:2–3**, 129; **29:2–5**, 126; **29:3–5**, 127; **29:6**, 129; **29:6–11**, 126, 127; **30**, 127; **30:1–5**, 130; **30:1–31:13**, 130; **30:3**, 140; **30:4**, 131; **30:6**, 130, 131, 132, 135; **30:6–10**, 130; **30:6–15**, 131; **30:7**, 68, 124; **30:9**, 135; **30:10**, 77; **30:11**, 140; **30:11–15**, 131; **30:11–25**, 132; **30:14**, 135; **30:16**, 132; **30:16–20**, 132; **30:20–31:12**, 136; **30:21–31**, 136; **30:26**, 123; **30:26–31**, 133; **30:27–31**, 136; **31**, 140, 141, 145; **31:1–3**, 133; **31:1–10**, 134; **31:2**, 136; **31:4–5**, 134; **31:6–7**, 134; **31:7**, 136; **31:8–10**, 134; **31:8–13**, 135; **31:9–10**, 136; **31:11–13**, 135; **31:12**, 136

2 Samuel **1**, 128, 141; **1–4**, 78; **1:1–3**, 138; **1:1–16**, 138; **1:3**, 141; **1:4–10**, 138; **1:9–10**, 141; **1:9–13**, 141; **1:13**, 141; **1:13–16**, 140; **1:14–16**, 139; **1:15**, 152; **1:17–18**, 142; **1:17–27**, 11, 142, 143; **1:18**, 144; **1:19–22**, 142; **1:20**, 144; **1:21**, 144; **1:23–24**, 142; **1:23–27**, 142; **1:24**, 144; **1:25–26**, 143; **1:26**, 144; **1:27**, 143; **2**, 53, 83; **2–4**, 12, 13; **2:1–4**, 145; **2:1–30**, 118; **2:1–3:5**, 145–49; **2:2**, 148; **2:4**, 136, 148, 159; **2:4–7**, 145, 148; **2:8**, 136, 148, 155, 211; **2:8–11**, 146; **2:10–11**, 149; **2:12–32**, 146; **2:23**, 153; **2:28**, 147; **3**, 226; **3:1–5**, 147; **3:2–3**, 116, 206; **3:2–5**, 149; **3:6–12**, 150; **3:6–4:12**, 150–56; **3:8**, 154, 208; **3:8–17**, 150; **3:12**, 90; **3:12–21**, 150; **3:13–14**, 90; **3:16**, 116; **3:17–18**, 155; **3:21**, 157; **3:21–23**, 155; **3:22–30**, 184; **3:22–39**, 152; **3:29**, 155; **3:30**, 155; **3:33**, 155; **4:1–12**, 153; **4:2**, 155; **4:4**, 155, 173; **4:6–7**, 11, 156; **4:8–9**, 156; **4:12**, 152, 156; **5**, 164; **5:1**, 145, 149; **5:1–3**, 159; **5:1–25**, 157–60; **5:3**, 149, 167, 171; **5:4–5**, 159; **5:5**, 159; **5:6**, 159; **5:6–8**, 157; **5:7**, 157; **5:8**, 160; **5:9–16**, 158; **5:10**, 12; **5:11**, 160; **5:12**, 54; **5:14–16**, 160; **5:17–25**, 158, 160; **5:20**, 160, 165; **5:21**, 160; **5:25**, 12; **6**, 4, 12, 34, 63, 164, 170, 204; **6:1**, 165; **6:1–5**, 161; **6:1–23**, 161–66; **6:2**, 35, 171; **6:3**, 165; **6:6–11**, 162; **6:8**, 165; **6:10**, 165; **6:12–15**, 162, 165; **6:14**, 26; **6:16**, 90, 163, 165; **6:17–19**, 163; **6:18**, 166; **6:20**, 166; **6:20–23**, 163; **7**, 8, 12, 13, 54, 164, 170, 184, 185, 239, 240; **7:1**, 170, 172, 236; **7:1–4**, 167; **7:1–7**, 167; **7:1–29**, 167–71; **7:2**, 170; **7:5–7**, 168; **7:6**, 170; **7:8**, 171; **7:8–11**, 168; **7:8–29**, 167; **7:11**, 171; **7:12–16**, 168; **7:13**, 171; **7:14–15**, 171; **7:15**, 189; **7:17**, 212; **7:17–29**, 169; **7:18**, 171, 213; **8**, 164, 165, 170, 180, 226; **8:1**, 175; **8:1–14**, 172; **8:1–18**, 172; **8:1–9:13**, 172–77; **8:3**, 175; **8:3–6**, 178; **8:4**, 175; **8:9**, 175; **8:12**, 178; **8:16–17**, 175; **8:17**, 165; **8:18**, 135, 166, 175; **9**, 96, 164, 180, 230; **9–20**, 4, 13, 173; **9:1**, 176; **9:1–5**, 71; **9:1–13**, 173; **9:2**, 176; **9:6**, 176; **9:8**, 154, 208; **9:11**, 177; **10**, 53, 180; **10:1**, 180; **10:1–19**, 178–80; **10:2**, 53, 180; **10:4**, 180, 187; **10:6**, 180; **10:11**, 90; **10:12**, 181; **11**, 97, 173, 178, 180, 185;

11:1, 178, 182, 187; **11:1–12:31,** 182–91; **11:2–5,** 182, 187; **11:3,** 206, 242; **11:6–13,** 183; **11:8,** 188; **11:9,** 188; **11:13,** 120; **11:14–17,** 183; **11:14–25,** 188; **11:18–22,** 152; **11:18–27,** 184; **11:21,** 189; **12,** 173, 246; **12:1,** 189; **12:1–6,** 184; **12:1–7,** 189; **12:7–9,** 185; **12:8,** 189; **12:9,** 189; **12:10–12,** 189; **12:10–14,** 186; **12:13,** 182, 190; **12:14,** 190; **12:15–25,** 186; **12:18,** 190; **12:25,** 190; **12:26–31,** 182, 187; **12:27–28,** 152, 182; **12:30,** 190; **12:31,** 191; **13,** 95, 192–95; **13:1–11,** 192; **13:3,** 194; **13:7,** 194; **13:11–13,** 194; **13:12–19,** 192; **13:13,** 195; **13:20,** 195; **13:20–29,** 193; **13:21,** 195; **13:22–23,** 197; **13:23,** 195; **13:30–39,** 194; **13:38,** 127; **13:39,** 195; **14,** 185, 195, 201; **14:1,** 196, 199; **14:1–3,** 152; **14:1–15:19,** 196–201; **14:2,** 200; **14:2–24,** 196; **14:11–16,** 1; **14:18–19,** 200; **14:19,** 196; **14:25–27,** 197; **14:26,** 200, 215; **14:27,** 200, 218; **14:28,** 197; **14:29–33,** 197; **14:33,** 199, 200; **15,** 95; **15:1–6,** 198; **15:2,** 201; **15:4,** 215; **15:7,** 198; **15:7–9,** 199; **15:10,** 206; **15:10–12,** 203; **15:10–16:14,** 203–8; **15:12,** 182, 206; **15:13–23,** 203; **15:13–29,** 206; **15:16,** 206; **15:18,** 207; **15:23,** 207; **15:24,** 207; **15:24–29,** 165; **15:24–37,** 203–4; **15:28,** 208; **15:32,** 207; **16,** 4, 6, 222, 230; **16:1–4,** 71, 174, 205, 207, 221; **16:3,** 220; **16:5–8,** 204, 207; **16:5–14,** 204; **16:8,** 230; **16:9,** 154, 207; **16:13,** 208; **16:15–19,** 209; **16:15–17:29,** 209–13; **16:20–17:6,** 209; **16:21,** 212; **16:21–22,** 189; **16:23,** 212; **17:1,** 30, 212; **17:2,** 224; **17:3,** 215; **17:7–14,** 210; **17:15–22,** 210; **17:16,** 212; **17:23,** 211, 213; **17:24–29,** 211; **17:25,** 213, 222; **17:27,** 174; **17:27–29,** 71; **18:1,** 217; **18:1–5,** 214; **18:1–19:8a,** 214–18; **18:6–8,** 215; **18:9,** 217; **18:9–15,** 215; **18:12–13,** 217; **18:13,** 200; **18:14,** 217; **18:16–18,** 219; **18:18,** 200, 218; **18:19–33,** 216, 218; **18:21,** 218; **18:28–29,** 218; **18:33,** 218; **19,** 212; **19–20,** 217; **19:1–8,** 216; **19:8b–15,** 219; **19:8b–43,** 219–22; **19:9,** 221; **19:16–23,** 220; **19:17,** 221; **19:18,** 222; **19:19–20,** 220; **19:21,** 248; **19:21–22,** 222; **19:30,** 222; **19:31–40,**

221; **19:37–38,** 222; **19:41–43,** 221, 222; **20,** 1, 221; **20:1,** 225; **20:1–2,** 223; **20:1–26,** 223–27; **20:3,** 223; **20:4–13,** 224; **20:8,** 40; **20:10,** 226; **20:14,** 226; **20:14–22,** 225; **20:16,** 226; **20:16–22,** 200; **20:18,** 226; **20:22,** 226; **20:23–36,** 225, 226; **21–24,** 164, 228–49; **21:1,** 231; **21:1–2,** 229; **21:1–9,** 207; **21:1–14,** 176, 229–31, 245, 248; **21:2,** 231; **21:3–8,** 229; **21:5–6,** 231; **21:9–14,** 230; **21:10,** 40, 231; **21:14,** 245, 248; **21:15–17,** 232; **21:15–22,** 85, 232–33, 241; **21:17,** 233, 237; **21:18–22,** 232, 233, 241; **21:19,** 86; **22,** 8, 14, 238, 239, 248; **22:1,** 236; **22:1–51,** 234–37, 236; **22:2–4,** 235; **22:4,** 237; **22:7,** 237; **22:8–16,** 235; **22:17–20,** 235; **22:21–25,** 235; **22:26–46,** 236; **22:29,** 237; **22:35,** 237; **22:47,** 238; **22:47–51,** 236; **23,** 232, 233; **23:1–7,** 238–40, 248; **23:2,** 240; **23:3,** 238; **23:5,** 171; **23:6–7,** 240; **23:8,** 243; **23:8–12,** 241, 242; **23:8–39,** 120, 241–44; **23:11,** 233; **23:13,** 243; **23:13–17,** 242; **23:18–23,** 242, 243; **23:20,** 243; **23:23,** 233; **23:24–39,** 242; **23:30,** 243; **23:34,** 182, 206; **23:39,** 182, 244; **24,** 1, 245–49; **24:1,** 222; **24:1–3,** 245; **24:4–10,** 246; **24:8,** 249; **24:9,** 249; **24:11,** 249; **24:11–17,** 245; **24:14,** 249; **24:16–17,** 249; **24:16–18,** 247; **24:18–25,** 247; **24:24,** 249; **24:25,** 245

1 Kings 1, 9, 185, 190, 232; **1–2,** 1, 4, 13, 148; **1:39,** 148; **2:8–9,** 222; **2:27,** 207; **2:35,** 25, 243; **3:4,** 231; **5:3,** 171; **5:13–18,** 227; **6:17–19,** 163; **8:16,** 60; **8:27–30,** 163; **11,** 95; **12,** 179, 221; **12–14,** 221; **14:23,** 47; **19,** 84; **22:10,** 67

2 Kings 2, 239; **3,** 85; **4:23,** 96; **8:13,** 154; **9:1–13,** 47; **11:12,** 148; **11:17,** 171; **17:32,** 47; **21:6,** 128; **22:14,** 226; **23:5,** 47; **23:8,** 47; **25,** 2

1 Chronicles 1:15, 207; **2,** 82; **2:16,** 213; **2:17,** 213; **3:1,** 116; **3:1–5,** 147; **3:3,** 148; **3:5–9,** 160; **4:4,** 86; **6:33–47,** 18; **8:33,** 136, 148; **8:34,** 149; **9:36,** 47, 72, 136, 148; **9:39,** 47, 72, 136, 148; **9:40,** 149; **10,** 147; **11,** 145, 241;

11:1–9, 159; **11:29**, 233; **11:34**, 233; **12**, 241; **13**, 161; **13:14**, 162; **14:4–7**, 160; **14:17**, 160; **15:2**, 162; **17**, 169; **18:10**, 175; **19**, 180; **20:5**, 232, 233; **21**, 245; **21:1**, 248; **22:8**, 171; **22:14–20**, 200; **27**, 243; **27:24**, 249; **28:2**, 171; **29:29**, 10, 144, 249

2 Chronicles **9:29**, 144; **12:15**, 144; **26:16–21**, 166

Nehemiah **10:33**, 96

Job **1–2**, 24; **2:8**, 22; **3**, 2; **21:17**, 233

Psalm **2**, 170; **18**, 234; **32**, 189, 235; **34**, 101; **42:7**, 160; **51**, 189, 235; **72**, 169, 240; **89**, 171; **100**, 170; **110:4**, 166; **113**, 20; **132:12**, 171

Proverbs **20:20**, 233; **21:3**, 77

Isaiah **1:14**, 96; **9:1–7**, 170; **11:1–16**, 170; **14**, 22

Jeremiah **7:4**, 170; **7:12–15**, 32; **7:20**, 170; **7:24**, 170; **23:25–28**, 128; **28**, 168; **33:14**, 169

Ezekiel **6:36**, 33; **11:23**, 171; **18**, 230; **43:1**, 171; **44:4**, 171

Hosea **3:4**, 53; **5:7**, 96; **6:6**, 77

Amos **1:9**, 229; **2:1**, 136; **6:10**, 136

Jonah **4:2**, 26

Micah **1:10**, 144; **1:15**, 76; **5:1–5**, 170

NEW TESTAMENT

Matthew **12:3–4**, 100

Luke **3:23–37**, 170; **3:31**, 160; **15:20–24**, 200

Acts **1:26**, 53; **2:40**, 240; **13:22**, 7, 13

2 Corinthians **12:9**, 9

Philippians **2:6**, 10

James **1:13**, 245